The Last Sex
feminism and outlaw bodies

CultureTexts

Arthur and Marilouise Kroker   *General Editors*

CultureTexts is a series of creative explorations of the theory, politics and culture of postmodern society. Thematically focussed around key theoretical debates in areas ranging from feminism and technology to social and political thought, *CultureTexts* books represent the forward breaking-edge of contemporary theory and practice.

Titles

THE LAST SEX
feminism and outlaw bodies

Edited with an introduction by
Arthur and Marilouise Kroker

First published 1993 by
THE MACMILLAN PRESS LTD
Houndmills, Basingstoke, Hampshire RG21 2XS
and London
Companies and representatives throughout the world

ISBN 0-333-60519-5
a catalogue record for this book is available from the British Library.

Printed in Canada.

Dedicated to resisters against the will to purity, the current manifestation of cultural fascism

Acknowledgements

The artist Elsbeth Rodger's work is reproduced with the permission of the Diane Farris Gallery, Vancouver.

Against Ordinary Language: The Language of the Body by Kathy Acker is reprinted by permission of the William Morris Agency, on behalf of the author © 1992 by Kathy Acker. All Rights Reserved.

Losing It by Shar Rednour. An earlier version appeared in *On Our Backs*, San Francisco.

Disappearing by Dianne Rothleder was first published in *Philosophy Today*.

The Excess by Sue Golding will also be published in the UK by *New Formations*.

Personal Needs by Linda Dawn Hammond. All photographs © Linda Dawn Hammond. All Rights Reserved. The quotation from *Coldness and Cruelty* reprinted by permission of Zone Books.

Wedding Woes by Gwen Bartleman was first published in *XTRA*, Toronto.

CONTENTS

I
PREFACE

II

III
PERFORMING (FEMINIST) THEORY

IV
SEXUAL DOUBLINGS

V
ORGANS WITHOUT BODIES

SCENES FROM THE LAST SEX
Feminism and Outlaw Bodies

Arthur and Marilouise Kroker

Forensic Feminism

Elsbeth Rodger is the painter of the history of women as the last sex. The artist, that is, of women as remainder, their bodies a site of cancellation and loss, of what's left over from a great subtraction forced by the enclosures within which they are confined. In Rodger's artistic productions, the warmth and suppleness of women's bodies are always framed by hard-line enclosures: sometimes a cloister, a curiosity chest, a sea-equivalent of an autopsy table, a persian rug, a suitcase, an elevator, a trunk. Here, there is no sense of motion, only women's bodies in melancholic waiting poses. Whether they are dead or alive doesn't make much difference, since Rodger's paintings intimate a terrible equivalency between being framed and being dead (both negate identity), and even death is revealed to have its own fetishistic attractions. In all of her painterly productions, women are presented as desperately trying to fit into categories that do not work for women. The result: the fatal silence of absence where the hyper-realism of the bodily imagery only heightens the reduction of women to a metonymic gesture in the accompanying frame. In her artistic imagination, women are always framed, literally and aesthetically.

What makes Rodger's work so fascinating is that she has painted the visual topography of a new mode of feminism: forensic feminism. Stripped of romanticism and without the moral relief of the nostalgic gesture, Rodger's paintings show women's bodies at a point of maximal vulnerability. Indeed, if she can paint women's bodies with such faithful attention to the most minute forensic detail, it is only to emphasize the absence within: the absence of life *(Water Line, Sea Trail, Secret Disorder)*, the absence of identity *(Pattern Imposed, Flying Carpet)*, the absence of freedom from the panoptic gaze *(Cloister, Stand Clear of the Gate)*, and the absence of identity *(Fetish Doll, Glass Bead Eye)*. In her work, women's bodies are reduced to that fatal remainder left over when the power of the imposed pattern has been subtracted from the governing calculus. Here, we suddenly stumble upon catastrophe scenes that always have about them a doubled sense of melancholic menace: the death scenes themselves, whether real or aesthetically configured, and the invisible power on behalf of which this detritus of bodily remainders is splayed out across the arc of Rodger's paintings and about which nothing is said, or perhaps can be said.

Which is the way it must be because Rodger's forensic feminism is really a detailed study of the pathology of sacrificial power. Of power, that is, in its last disaccumulative phase where it speaks the language of sacrifice (always women's bodies), imposes itself by an aesthetics of absence (the framing of the bodies in bathtubs, chests, cloisters), and functions best reducing its victims to silence (Rodger's paintings are about cancelled identities, that point where the fleshly history of the face is covered by entangling hair, turned away from our gaze as it drowns in the bathtub, or looks the other way into the dead-end space of the cloister or the elevator). Forensic feminism is a pathology lab where the silenced remainders of the excluded are finally recorded in their last spasmodic poses. From *Fetish Doll* to *Sea Trails,* Rodger's work is a dream-like history of women's deaths at the hands of an invisible power, a death-scape which serves as a reminder of the shared complicity of all members of the last sex in a common language of suffocation and inertness.

Consider the terminal aesthetics of *Error in Judgement.* Here, the woman's body is found curled up in the suffocatingly tight space of the trunk. The trunk is open, but its lines form a second frame. In addition, the trunk is framed within the painting. An "error in judgement," then, because not only is this a death scene, but also a scene of an almost invisible aesthetic cancellation: a three-dimensional frame with the woman's body as a reminder of the death of identity. In this forensic report, a double death takes place: one biological, the other aesthetic; one a killing-field for woman's bodies, the other a cancellation of the defining woman's identity. As to which is the real death, Rodger is perfectly ambivalent.

Double Bind, for instance, speaks the double language of framing and death. Might it be possible that Rodger has done that which is most difficult: stripped death of its fatal sovereignty as the last of all the referential illusions, bringing sacrificial violence against women under the sign of a more enduring aesthetic? In this case, we would have to speak about forensic feminism in the language of the aesthetics of apperception. To say, that is, that what is at stake in Rodger's paintings, what is struggled with and against in each of her painterly gestures is the cancellation of the reality of death, and its substitution by a death of a thousand aesthetic cuts. The close-cropped frames maximize anxiety, and the frames within frames maximize the labyrinthine sense of confinement of the body within the dream-like reversals between the implied violence of the death scenes and the visceral dream-like state of the final body positions. This is not really a painting about death at all, but about sub-death: a permanent, terminal state of cancellation, sometimes biological but always aesthetic, that hard-frames woman's identities, and on account of which dreams of escape (*Sacred Banquet, Flying Carpet, Secret Disorder*) are always played out against the background text of an inhabiting violence. Sub-death, therefore, is that indeterminate space, between aesthetic cancellation and sacrificial violence, that forms the ruling bodily architecture of the last sex.

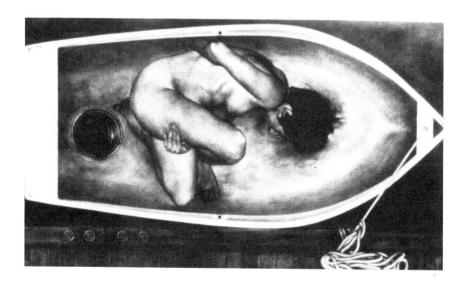

Elsbeth Rodger
Sea Trail, 1990
Diane Farris Gallery

Elsbeth Rodger
Pattern Imposed, 1990
Diane Farris Gallery

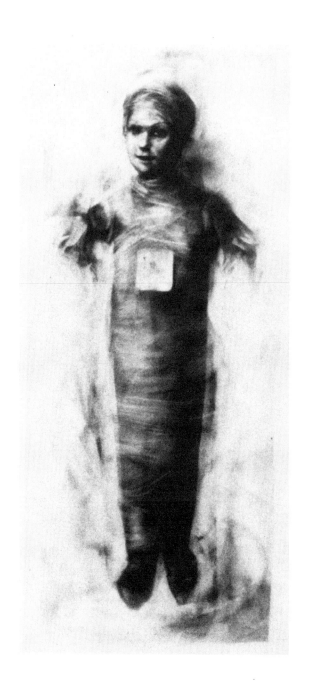

Elsbeth Rodger
Fetish Doll, 1991
Diane Farris Gallery

Elsbeth Rodger
Cloister, 1987
Diane Farris Gallery

Elsbeth Rodger
Error in Judgement, 1985
Diane Farris Gallery

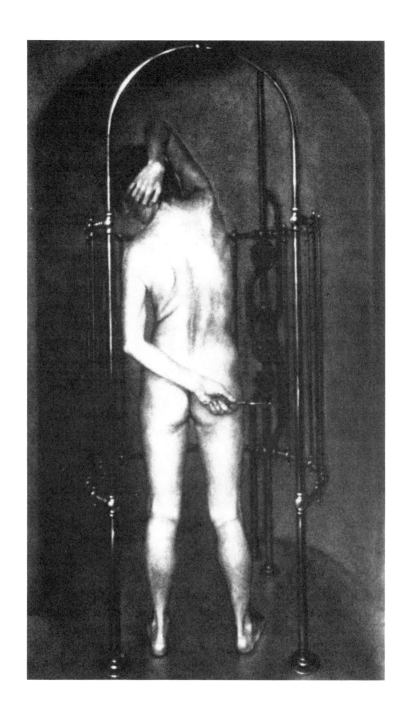

Elsbeth Rodger
Probe, 1988
Diane Farris Gallery

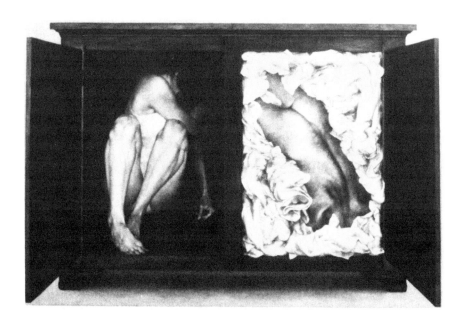

Elsbeth Rodger
Double Bind, 1990
Diane Farris Gallery

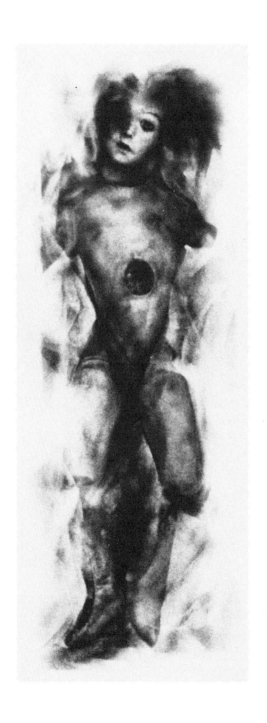

Elsbeth Rodger
Glass Bead Eye, 1991
Diane Farris Gallery

The Will to Purity

We began *The Last Sex* thinking about our mothers, and specifically about the problem of aging when women slide suddenly from being sexually harassed to bodily invisibility. Like all women before them, our mothers have been framed by the fiction of age as though they are one of the incarcerated subjects in Rodger's paintings, and suffer the same penalty for this sequestration: cancelled identities and suffocating isolation. A pre-set category was imposed on them, and against this power of the referential illusion of aging they were victimized. Maybe, in fact, women are not the last sex after all, but the first sex: the first to be sexually abused and certainly the first to be disappeared at the merest intimation of a facial wrinkle. For women, the history (of her face) has always meant the negation of identity, and the certainty of a life's journey from harassment to invisibility.

But if the negation of human identity is posed in terms of the aesthetics of framing as Rodger's artistic optic intimates, then there are many more members who belong to the last sex. Certainly women who suffer all the violence generated by the collapsing star of the hysterical male, as well as gays and lesbians whose refusal of the hegemonic heterosexual club, whose 'No' to the aesthetics of heterosexual framing, renders them sacrificial victims in the dark days of splatter culture. The population of the last sex swells daily: men who are feminists, women who would meet violence with violence, clit club activists, transgendered bodies, abused women who cure themselves, and us, by gathering to tell their stories of disappearance, and fiction writers who make of words exploding viral infections that contaminate the antiseptically closed world of binary gender signs. What all members of the last sex have in common are three things: a courageous refusal of all pre-set categories (whether sexual or intellectual), a daring insistence on an engaged politics (but one that also privileges ambivalence, irony and paradox), and a common rejection of emotional investment, spurning, that is, any single position or referent as a fixed point of stoppage. Members of the last sex experience the vicissitudes of a floating reality with magnificent intensity, and just when it seems that they might colonize difference as a new referential illusion, they move right on through, simply refusing to be cancelled out by assenting to the perspectival politics of framing. Floating sex is the

antithesis of instrumental signification. That's what makes it so dangerous, and probably accounts for the current violent intensity of the will to
purity.

The will to purity? That's the politics of the 1990s: sexual cleansing,
ethnic cleansing, bodily cleansing, intellectual cleansing, racial cleansing.
The politics of an entirely fictional search for a purity that never existed,
and never will. The violent spasms of pure sex (witness gay and lesbian
bashing); pure bodily fluids (the so-called "war on drugs" with African-
Americans as scapegoats or as NWA raps: "...thinking every nigger is
selling narcotics"); the sacrificial victims of the fictionally pure and united
family (the sexual abuse of children and domestic violence against women
all under the sign of restoring 'good family values'); intellectual cleansing
(the hysterical backlash in the popular press and of many in academia
against feminism and for the "renaturalization" of gender); and cultural
cleansing (the dogmatic exterminism of difference in art, writing, and the
imagination by defenders of a decomposing culture that seeks to stabilize
itself by cancelling the floating Other).

If there can be such a hysterical turn to the will to purity today, that is
because we are living now in the time of crash sex and splatter culture. We
are living in times of violent event-scenes, where none of the fictional
unities can be put together again because we have finally recognized that
they never existed, that all the big referents, from the family and gender
to sexual identity, were always purely perspectival products, policed
frames, produced by a power that would be hegemonic. The will to purity
is everywhere, and it's getting uglier all the time because of its impossibility. The great code of the West cannot continue because we no longer live
in a time of the restless, dynamic will, but in the detritus of the recline of
western civilization. If there can be such violence on behalf of all the
referential illusions today, it is because of the hysterical energies contained
in the repression of denial. The referents have disappeared. Everyone
knows it. The violence of denying this knowledge is what we call the will
to purity. The metaphysics of the hangman.

The will to purity is about drawing lines, about imposing fictional
frames around other people's lives and, of course, about injecting the
hegemonic signification of those lines into one's own subjectivity. What
makes the politics of the will to purity so particularly vicious is that no one
really believes anymore in the myth of framing. The will to purity finally

stands exposed for what it has always been: a cynical attempt to will something, even nothingness, rather than not will at all. That is why we are living in the recline of western civilization. The will to purity has always been about nothingness, about the violent defense of decomposition and decline. People who are exposed for what they really are, the last defenders of pure fiction, react on the psychological basis of sacrificial violence. They search out victims, particularly powerless ones, on whom they can mete out, and really beat out, compensation for their own lack. Not sacrificial violence in the classical sense of renunciation for the restoration of a sustaining myth, but sacrificial violence in the age of crash culture, that point where sacrifice splits from mimesis, exploding outwards in a vengeance-seeking search for scapegoats on whom expiation can be found for the absence at the centre of society. Maybe this is why the 1990s looms ahead of us as such a spectral scene of mean violence in the form of pure cynicism, the growing awareness of the lack within, which stacks up innocent victims on its table of values. The formula: sacrificial violence increases in direct relation to the implosion of all the referential illusions into wavering crash event-scenes.

A double mechanism is at work in the will to purity: libidinally driven pleasure in inflicting pain, humiliation and death on accidental victims; and a panic fear of viral contamination by swirling impurities: exchanges of bodily fluids, transgressionary thoughts, women rebelling against the sovereignty of lines, quick reversals in the sexual register, and dirty toilet seats. The will to purity, therefore, as a new form of cultural fascism, with its nostalgic defense of pure referents that never existed and its panic fear about a dirty world. And, of course, dirty is what the last sex is all about.

Recombinant Sex

In the beginning was the mouse.

In the laboratories of Ohio University a DNA microinjection was recently developed to allow for the mutation of a virus free mouse. A transgenic mouse.

So why could we not have a transgenic gender, a virus free gender? Should gender be our most fundamental distinction? Or is gender just another cult as described by Kate Bornstein in this volume, or, something even more insidious? Is gender a deadly virus? A malignant infection injected into babies from birth, that point where the culture war between the sexes fuses with the molecular process of cellular division, becoming hard-wired into our identity as girls and boys, then women and men? Gender, then, as a nano-virus that takes possession of the body at inception, setting itself into the molecular ganglia of bio-social identity.

That's why we are interested in the creation of a virus free gender, a transgenic gender. That's why we think that the only good sex today is recombinant sex. Sex without origin, localizing gender, or referential signifier. Beyond predatory sex then, a transgendered sex for an age of transsexuality where sex, most of all, has fled its roots in the consaguinity of nature, refused its imprisonment in the phallocentric orbit of gender, abandoned the metaphorical sublimations of discursive sexuality, finally finding its home in a virtual sex. The last sexual economy consists of doubled pleasure and pain which occupies an indeterminate zone of the in-between, a sex that, like the language of recombinant technology of which it is a brilliant aesthetic expression, can speak of aliasing, displacement, sexual stretching, and sexual compression (not sexual repression). A floating world of sexual software that can be massaged, mirrored, uplinked and downloaded into a body that always knew it didn't have to be content with the obsolete carcerals of nature, discourse, and ideology. In the galaxy of sexual software, morphing is the only rule: the quick mutation of all the binary signs into their opposites.

Recombinant sex is the next sex, the last sex. If there can be such an explosion today of sexual aesthetics, it is because we now live in the age of genetic engineering, a time of radical experimentation where all the old gender signs have been deleted and replaced by sex without secretions. Recombinant sex is an *art of sex* that keeps pace with evolutionary shifts in the *scientia sexualis*, translating the language of the bio-apparatus— cloning, sequencing, transcription—into an aesthetics of sexual play, into an ecstasy of sexual perversion. A time of flash-meetings between the cold seduction of cyberspace and the primitive libido of trash sex. That's the way it is: genetic surgery on the human biological code finds its outlaw riders in those occupants of a previously forbidden sex who have long spoken the double language of an accidental sexual economy. The result: a floating sex for the electronic body where fetishes can be transcribed into the cold language of data, and the digital libido made to send out its sex scent as part of the coded games of electronic sex. But then, we have been this way before: we, the children of the digital age born in the white heat of the atomic blast, have always known the electronic body as our shadowy other. For us, Heisenberg's uncertainty principle has been less a principle of quantum mechanics than a commentary on the exchanges of sexual fluids of the electronic body, that point where machine sex becomes the real world of sexual pleasure. Some outlaw bodies have been known to swim for centuries in a sea of electronic fetishes and watery exchanges of sexual codes.

Or maybe it is the reverse. Not simply sex without blood in the age of recombinant technology, but sex without secretions for the age of body invaders. All that plastic and all those leathers, then, as lines of flight tracing a great fear of viral contamination. In this case, the art of sex is pushed on by the fear of bodily fluids. Recombinant sex, then, as a direct expression of our bodily immersion in the culture of Draculaland. When the penis becomes a parasite/predator, then sexual pleasure immediately reverts to the cool aesthetics of SM.

It's all perfectly post-Marxist for the age of post-capitalism. Transgender is the new relation of sexual production that corresponds to a new force of technological production. Outlaw bodies are the insurgent sexual class who have an objective alliance with the ascendancy of recombinant culture. Rebelling against the "cult of gender" they exhibit at the level of sexual aesthetics what recombinant technology exhibits economically at the level of technology. That's why there is such a delightfully perverse entanglement between techno-fetishists and outlaw bodies: they both spin around in an indefinite chiaroscuro in the dreamland of future sex.

Intersex States

In genetics "intersex states" is the name given to a dozen conditions in which there is a mixing of male and female traits (*Discover*, June 1992). Among the most common is "androgen insensitivity." In androgen insensitivity, the genetic makeup of the subject is that of the male (XY chromosomes) but the physical appearance is that of a female. The result: genetic men with the outward appearance of women. Not surprisingly, many androgen insensitive males have become female fashion models.

When we first began thinking about the implications of androgen insensitivity for sexual politics, we immediately concluded that this was another instance of male appropriation of the female body. In this case, the very traits that are ascribed to female fashion models as the "feminine ideal" were, in fact, the working-out of the male genetic code. The entire fashion apparatus, therefore, from the promotional culture of female models to the runway "hangers" with their long legs, achingly thin bodies, and perfectly fashion physiques were nothing more than a narcissistic *trompe l'oeil*: men lusting, really unself-consciously, after their own genetic code in the outward guise of women's bodies.

That was last year, when we were still members in good standing of the "cult of gender," still holding to the feminist ideal of critiquing any male appropriations of the female body. Now we have changed. Maybe it was the cumulative psychological weight of the violent backlash against women, heterosexuals, and lesbians, and most certainly against gays that caused this change. Perhaps it was the growing realization that this deeply fascist backlash against radical sexual politics couldn't be contested any longer within the old feminist terrain that struggles to maintain the sovereignty of the binary genetic codes. If feminism couldn't see its way to recombinant sex in the age of transgenders, then it was in serious danger of allying itself with the most vicious of neo-conservative forces. We had no desire to truck with neo-conservatives, and no intention of allying ourselves to maintain the referential illusion of gender. And so, on the issue of intersex states we arrived at a radically different conclusion than before.

Now we hold that what we desperately require are more intersex states, and less predatory ones. Perhaps intersex should be the last sex. No longer intersex states as a governing model for "abnormality" in the order of genetics, but the return of intersex to that point from whence it has originated and on behalf of which it speaks so eloquently. The return of intersex to the realm of recombinant culture as the governing model of a new sexual politics.

Indeed, we do daily exercises to heighten our own androgen insensitivity, to cut, blur, disturb, crash and tear the great binary divisions marking the territorial codes of the gender cult. Not really to be male on the outside and female on the inside or the reverse (that would simply mimic the transgressionary logic confirming the impossibility of overcoming gender traces), but to achieve a more indeterminate state: female, yet male, organisms occupying an ironic, ambivalent and paradoxical state of sexual identity. To be androgen insensitives floating in the nowhere land of sexual identity.

The Third Sex

Intersex states, then, as the third sex. Neither male (physically) nor female (genetically) nor their simple reversal, but something else: a virtual sex floating in an elliptical orbit around the planet of gender that it has left behind, finally free of the powerful gravitational pull of the binary signs of the male/female antinomies in the crowded earth scene of gender. A virtual sex that is not limited to gays and lesbians but which is open to members of the heterosexual club as well and one that privileges sexual reconciliation rather than sexual victimization. Intersex states, therefore, as a virtual sex that finally is liberated from sacrificial violence.

In the artistic practice of medieval times, the privileged aesthetic space was that of anamorphosis. The aesthetics, that is, of perspectival impossibility where the hint of the presence of a vanishing whole could only be captured by a glance at the reflecting surface of one of its designed fragments. A floating perspective where the part exists only to intimate the presence of a larger perspectival unity, and where the whole exists only as a momentary mirage captured for an instant by a mirrored spinning top. Now, anamorphosis returns as the privileged perspective of virtual sex, of intersex states. Virtual sex occupies the aesthetic space of anamorphosis: never fully captured in its full seductiveness by its fractal fragments, and always dispersed and exaggerated by its mirrored counter-images. And just as the impossible space of anamorphosis can only be illuminated by the shiny surface of perfectly calibrated objects (spinning mirrors, musical instruments, silver pipes on glittering surfaces), so too are the outward signs of anamorphic sex found everywhere. Heterosexuals fleeing the violence accompanying the decline of the empire of the hysterical male, drag queens rubbing shoulders with sorority sisters at Club Park Avenue in Tallahassee, Florida, top dykes who flip easily between being Philosopher Queen for a day and practitioners of the pleasures of SM, women survivors in Stories from the Bloodhut who present a litany of war stories about male violence in voices and gestures that speak of human love. The outward signs are different: different genders, different sexual preferences, but the anamorphic space revealed by the stories told or the lives lived is always the same. And it is that new sexual horizon, post-male and post-female, that we now call the perspectival world of the last sex.

AGAINST ORDINARY LANGUAGE: THE LANGUAGE OF THE BODY

Kathy Acker

Preface Diary

I have now been bodybuilding for ten years, seriously for almost five years.

During the past few years, I have been trying to write about bodybuilding.

Having failed time and time again, upon being offered the opportunity to write this essay, I made the following plan: I would attend the gym as usual. Immediately after each workout, I would describe all I had just experienced, thought and done. Such diary descriptions would provide the raw material.

After each workout, I forgot to write. Repeatedly. I...some part of me... the part of the 'I' who bodybuilds... was rejecting language, any verbal description of the processes of bodybuilding.

I shall begin describing, writing about bodybuilding in the only way that I can: I shall begin by analyzing this rejection of ordinary or verbal language. What is the picture of the antagonism between bodybuilding and verbal language?

A Language Which is Speechless

Imagine that you are in a foreign country. Since you are going to be in this place for some time, you are trying to learn the language. At the point of commencing to learn the new language, just before having started to understand anything, you begin forgetting your own. Within strangeness, you find yourself without a language.

It is here, in this geography of no language, this negative space, that I can start to describe bodybuilding. For I am describing that which rejects language.

Elias Canetti, who grew up within a multitude of spoken languages, began his autobiography by recounting a memory. In this, his earliest remembrance, the loss of language is threatened: "My earliest memory is dipped in red. I come out of a door on the arm of a maid, the door in front of me is red, and to the left a staircase goes down, equally red..." A smiling man walks up to the child; the child, upon request, sticks out his tongue whereupon the man flips open a jackknife and holds the sharp blade against the red tongue.

"...He says: 'Now we'll cut off his tongue.'"

At the last moment, the man pulls the knife back.

According to memory, this sequence happens every day. "That's how the day starts," Canetti adds, "and it happens very often." [1]

I am in the gym every three out of four days. What happens there? What does language in that place look like?

According to cliché, athletes are stupid. Meaning: they are inarticulate. The spoken language of bodybuilders makes this cliché real. The verbal language in the gym is minimal and almost senseless, reduced to numbers and a few nouns. "Sets", "squats", "reps",... The only verbs are "do" or "fail" adjectives and adverbs no longer exist; sentences, if they are at all, are simple.

This spoken language is kin to the "language games" Wittgenstein proposes in his *The Brown Book*. [2]

In a gym, verbal language or language whose purpose is meaning occurs, if at all, only at the edge of its becoming lost.

But when I am in the gym, my experience is that I am immersed in a complex and rich world.

What actually takes place when I bodybuild?

The crossing of the threshold from the world defined by verbal language into the gym in which the outside world is not allowed (and all of its languages) (in this sense, the gym is sacred) takes several minutes. What happens during these minutes is that I forget. Masses of swirling thought, verbalized insofar as I am conscious of them, disappear as mind or thought begins to focus.

In order to analyze this focusing, I must first describe bodybuilding in terms of intentionality.

Bodybuilding is a process, perhaps a sport, by which a person shapes her or his own body. This shaping is always related to the growth of muscular mass.

During aerobic and circuit training, the heart and lungs are exercised. But muscles will grow only if they are, not exercised or moved, but actually broken down. The general law behind bodybuilding is that muscle, if broken down in a controlled fashion and then provided with the proper growth factors such as nutrients and rest, will grow back larger than before.

In order to break down specific areas of muscles, whatever areas one wants to enlarge, it is necessary to work these areas in isolation up to failure.

Bodybuilding can be seen to be about nothing but *failure*. A bodybuilder is always working around failure. Either I work an isolated muscle mass, for instance one of the tricep heads, up to failure. In order to do this, I exert the muscle group almost until the point that it can no longer move.

But if I work the same muscle group to the point that it can no longer move, I must move it through failure. I am then doing what are named "negative reps", working the muscle group beyond its power to move. Here is the second method of working with failure.

Whatever way I chose, I always want to work my muscle, muscular group, until it can no longer move: I want to fail. As soon as I can accomplish a certain task, so much weight for so many reps during a certain time span, I must always increase one aspect of this equation, weights reps or intensity, so that I can again come to failure.

I want to break muscle so that it can grow back larger, but I do not want to destroy muscle so that growth is prevented. In order to avoid injury, I first warm up the muscular group, then carefully bring it up to failure. I do this by working the muscular group through a calculated number of sets during a calculated time span. If I tried immediately to bring a muscle group up to failure by lifting the heavist weight I could handle, I might injure myself.

I want to shock my body into growth; I do not want to hurt it.

Therefore, in bodybuilding, *failure* is always connected to counting. I calculate which weight to use; I then count off how many times I lift that weight and the seconds between each lift. This is how I control the intensity of my workout.

Intensity times movement of maximum weight equals muscular destruction (muscular growth).

Is the equation between destruction and growth also a formula for art?

Bodybuilding is about failure because bodybuilding, body growth and shaping, occurs in the face of the material, of the body's inexorable movement toward its final failure, toward death.

To break down a muscle group, I want to make that group work up to, even beyond, capacity. To do this, it helps and even is necessary to visualize the part of the body that is involved. Mind or thought, then, while bodybuilding, is always focused on number or counting and often on precise visualizations.

Certain bodybuilders have said that bodybuilding is a form of meditation.

What do I do when I bodybuild? I visualize and I count. I estimate weight; I count sets; I count repetitions; I count seconds between repetitions; I count time, seconds or minutes, between sets: From the beginning to the end of each workout, in order to maintain intensity, I must continually count.

For this reason, a bodybuilder's language is reduced to a minimal, even a closed, set of nouns and to numerical repetition, to one of the simplest of language games.

Let us name this language game, *the language of the body*.

The Richness Of The Language Of The Body

In order to examine such a language, a language game which resists ordinary language, through the lens of ordinary language or language whose tendency is to generate syntax or to make meanings proliferate, I must use an indirect route.

In another of his books, Elias Canetti begins talking from and about that geography that is without verbal language:

> A marvelously luminous, viscid substance is left behind in me, defying words...
>
> A dream: a man who unlearns the world's languages until nowhere on earth does he understand what people are saying. [3]

Being in Marrakesh is Canetti's dream made actual. There are languages here, he says, but I understand none of them. The closer I am moving toward foreignness, into strangeness, toward understanding foreignness and strangeness, the more I am losing my own language. The small loss of language occurs when I journey to and into my own body. Is my body a foreign land to me? What is this picture of "my body" and "I"? For years, I said in the beginning of this essay, I have wanted to describe bodybuilding; whenever I tried to do so, ordinary language fled from me.

"Man," Heidegger says, "is the strangest." [4] Why? Because everywhere he or she belongs to being or to strangeness or chaos, and yet everywhere he or she attempts to carve a path through chaos:

> Everywhere man makes himself a path; he ventures into all realms of the essent, of the overpowering power, and in so doing he is flung out of all paths. [5]

The physical or material, that which is, is constantly and unpredictably changing: it is chaotic. This chaos twines around death. For it is death that rejects all of our paths, all of our meanings.

Whenever anyone bodybuilds, he or she is always trying to understand and control the physical in the face of this death. No wonder bodybuilding is centered around failure.

The antithesis between meaning and essence has often been noted. Wittgenstein at the end of the *Tractatus*:

> The sense of the world must lie outside the world. In the world everything is as it is, and everything happens as it does happen—in it no values exist, and if they did, they'd have no value.

For all that happens and is the case is accidental.[6]

If ordinary language or meanings lie outside essence, what is the position of that language game which I have named *the language of the body*? For bodybuilding (a language of the body) rejects ordinary language and yet itself constitutes a language, a method for understanding and controlling the physical which in this case is also the self.

I can now directly talk about bodybuilding. (As if speech is ever direct.)

The language game named *the language of the body* is not arbitrary. When a bodybuilder is counting, he or she is counting his or her own breath.

Canetti speaks of the beggars of Marrakesh who possess a similar and even simpler language game: they repeat the name of God.

In ordinary language, meaning is contextual. Whereas the cry of the beggar means nothing other than what it is; in the cry of the beggar, the impossible (as the Wittgenstein of the *Tractatus* and Heidegger see it) occurs in that meaning and breath become one.

Here is the language of the body; here, perhaps, is the reason why bodybuilders experience bodybuilding as a form of meditation.

"I understood the seduction there is in a life that reduces everything to the simplest kind of repetition,"[7] Canetti says. A life in which meaning and essence no longer oppose each other. A life of meditation.

"I understood what those blind beggars really are: the saints of repetition..."[8]

The Repetition Of The One: The Glimpse Into Chaos Or Essence

I am in the gym. I am beginning to work out. I either say the name "bench press", then walk over to it, or simply walk over to it. Then, I might picture the number of my first weight; I probably, since I usually begin with the same warm-up weight, just place the appropriate weights on the bar. Lifting this bar off its rests, then down to my lower chest, I count "1". I am visualizing this bar, making sure it touches my chest at the right spot, placing it back on its rests. "2". I repeat the same exact motions. "3"... After twelve repetitions, I count off thirty seconds while increasing my weights. "1".. The identical process begins again only this time I finish at "10"... All these repetitions end only when I finish my work-out.

On counting: Each number equals one inhalation and one exhalation. If I stop my counting or in any other way lose focus, I risk dropping or otherwise mishandling a weight and so damaging my body.

In this world of the continual repetition of a minimal number of elements, in this aural labyrinth, it is easy to lose one's way. When all is repetition rather than the production of meaning, every path resembles every other path.

Every day, in the gym, I repeat the same controlled gestures with the same weights, the same reps,... The same breath patterns. But now and then, wandering within the labyrinths of my body, I come upon something. Something I can know because knowledge depends on difference. An unexpected event. For though I am only repeating certain gestures during certain time spans, my body, being material, is never the same; my body is controlled by change and by chance.

For instance, yesterday, I worked chest. Usually I easily benchpress the bar plus sixty pounds for six reps. Yesterday, unexpectedly, I barely managed to lift this weight at the sixth rep. I looked for a reason. Sleep? Diet? Both were usual. Emotional or work stress? No more than usual. The weather? Not good enough. My unexpected failure at the sixth rep was allowing me to see, as if through a window, not to any outside, but inside my own body, to its workings. I was being permitted to glimpse the laws that control my body, those of change or chance, laws that are barely, if at all, knowable.

By trying to control, to shape, my body through the calculated tools and methods of bodybuilding, and time and again, in following these methods, failing to do so, I am able to meet that which cannot be finally controlled and known: the body.

In this meeting lies the fascination, if not the purpose, of bodybuilding. To come face to face with chaos, with my own failure or a form of death.

Canetti describes the architecture of a typical house in the geographical labyrinth of Marrakesh. The house's insides are cool, dark. Few, if any, windows look out into the street. For the entire construction of this house, windows, etc., is directed inward, to the central courtyard where only openness to the sun exists.

Such an architecture is a mirror of the body: When I reduce verbal language to minimal meaning, to repetition, I close the body's outer windows. Meaning approaches breath as I bodybuild, as I begin to move through the body's labyrinths, to meet, if only for a second, that which my consciousness ordinarily cannot see. Heidegger: "The being-there of historical man means: to be posited as the breach into which the preponderant power of being bursts in its appearing, in order that this breach itself should shatter against being." [9]

In our culture, we simultaneously fetishize and disdain the athlete, a worker in the body. For we still live under the sign of Descartes. This sign is also the sign of patriarchy. As long as we continue to regard the body, that which is subject to change, chance, and death, as disgusting and inimical, so long shall we continue to regard our own selves as dangerous others.

Notes

1.   Elias Canetti, *The Tongue Set Free*, New York: The Seabury Press, 1979, p.5.

2.   Here and throughout the rest of this article, whenever I use the phrase "language game", I am referring to Ludwig Wittgenstein's discussion of language games in *The Brown Book*, (Wittgenstein, *The Blue and Brown Books*, New York: Harper and Row, Publishers, 1960).

3.   Elias Canetti, *The Voices of Marrakesh*, New York: The Seabury Press, 1978, p.23.

4.   Martin Heidegger, *An Introduction to Metaphysics*, New York: Anchor Books, 1961, p. 125. By "man", Heidegger means "human".

5.   Ibid., p. 127.

6.   Ludwig Wittgenstein, *Tractatus Logico-Philosphicus*, London: Routledge and Kegan Paul Ltd., 1972, p. 145.

7.   Canetti, *The Voices of Marrakesh*, p. 25.

8.   *Ibid.*, p. 26.

9.   Heidegger, *An Introduction to Metaphysics*, p. 137.

There has been considerable speculation as to the origin of *suttee*. Some authorities claim that it emanated from a deliberate tampering with Hindu scriptures. The original version ran: '*Arochantu janayo yonim agre*'—'Let the mothers advance to the altar first'. By a minor alteration the line becomes: '*Arochantu janyo yonim agneh*'—'Let the mothers go into the womb of fire.'

There is Considerable Speculation/
Joan of Arc, 1992
Louise McKissick

VIOLENCE AGAINST VIOLENCE
AGAINST WOMEN:
AN AVANT-GARDE FOR THE TIMES

Dianne Chisholm

In a "culture of violence" against women, is feminism's best strategy to cultivate counter-violence?[1] A powerful affirmation of this strategy could be drawn from such notable political theorists as George Sorel, whose *Reflections on Violence* (1906) justifies the use of collective violence in socialist revolution,[2] and Frantz Fanon, whose *Wretched of the Earth* (1961) argues passionately and humanely for native violence against colonialist terror.[3] Counter-violence has also been advocated by feminist political analysts. Reading "the battle between the sexes" in 1974, Ti-Grace Atkinson concludes:

> A 'battle' implies some balance of powers, whereas when one side suffers all the losses . . . that is called a *massacre*. Women have been massacred as human beings over history, and this destiny is entailed by their definition. As women begin massing together, they take the first step from *being massacred* to *engaging in battle* (resistance).[4]

After twenty more years of massacre, Andrea Dworkin urgently reiterates this "fighting back" in 1991:

> We are in a war. We have not been fighting back to win this war. We are in need of political resistance. We need it above-ground. We need it with our lawmakers, with our government officials. We need it with our professional women. We need it above ground. We need it underground too. . . . I am asking you to organize political support for women who kill men who have been hurting them. . . . I'm asking you to stop men who beat women. Get them jailed or get them killed. . . . I am asking you to look at every single political possibility for fighting back.[5]

Counter-violence has even been advocated by feminist psychotherapists who recognize that healing alone is not enough. In *Woman and Madness*, Phyllis Chesler argues that without mobilizing a capacity for violence of their own, women will never be able to confront and overcome the society that abuses them: "women, like men, must be capable of violence or self-defense before their refusal to use violence constitutes a free and moral choice, rather than "making the best of a bad bargain."[6] More recently, Sandra Butler has argued that "skillful, empathic healing work" cannot be seen as an end in itself. "Now it is time," she insists, "to ask whether feminist therapy became too much therapy and not enough feminism. . . . Recovery is an important first step, but must not be an ending." Women must use psychological skills in the service of *social change work*: "our world must begin to expand into building community, redressing our hurts and wounds, and confronting our oppressors."[7]

Feminism has and does advance women's violence against violence against women, contrary to a weakening conservatism which believes that violence is not feminine and contrary to a prevailing liberalism which places faith in humanist institutions governed primarily by men. Even groups of "established" women have advocated fighting back. For instance, an international workshop for women politicians, administrators and educators held in Ottawa in 1984 to discuss "strategies of power" slated the use of guerilla warfare on their future agenda.[8] Is the writing on the wall? While women's responses to the slaying of the fourteen women at Montreal's *École polytechnique*, as collected in Louise Malette and Marie Chalouh's anthology *The Montreal Massacre*, express initial horror and outrage none advocate counter-violence.[9] But, as the period of mourning passes . . . ?

One astute reader of our times, Grant McCracken, Head of the Institute of Contemporary Culture at the Royal Ontario Museum, reported to the *Toronto Globe and Mail* in December 1991 that in such local sidewalk graffiti as "dead men don't rape" he construed an inevitable "women's call to arms."[10] The article stresses that such slogans "could be more than just a passing piece of graffiti," could signal women's "STRIKING BACK," and "the start of a movement in which we [may] see the use of violence against men who commit violence against women." The critic-seer supports his intuition with "salient facts":

> First, we know for certain that violence against women is no accident of our society. It is a structural feature of many domestic relationships. It is also an unmistakable feature in the public relationships between men and women. Public life in North America is marked by an endemic, persistent violence. Men commit it, women suffer it. . . .
>
> Second, we know that much of the violence goes unpunished. . . .
>
> Third, we know that North America has a tradition of 'self-help' in certain public matters. When the police and the courts fail effectively to contain a public menace, people seek remedies of their own. Vigilante action stands ready to fill any vacuum left by the law.

He concludes that "under the circumstances, counterviolence inflicted by women on men may be inevitable."[11] And, he is not alone in spouting this sort of augury. Another cultural analyst, writing with American public security in mind, predicts that as feminist and socialist demands "should exceed society's capacity to deliver reform, then violence or threat of violence is probable" and women's involvement in terrorism will "increase dramatically."[12]

But while McCracken's graffiti may be a sign of the times and may indeed incite women's more aggressive responsiveness, I am not convinced that women's mobilization of physical counter-violence is inevitable—otherwise why must feminists repeatedly, decade after decade, attempt to convince women that mounting violence, that militant fighting back, is a vital, therapeutic if not politic, strategy of survival?[13] While it may seem logical, it is not very probable (despite what men say) that women will respond *en masse* to domestic violence with a deployment of arms and militant terrorism; in a culture that normalizes men's violence and women's passivity, women more "naturally" respond to femicidal violence with vociferous calls for peace and ambivalently aggressive if not hysterical formations of "peace activism."[14] Despite McCracken's claim that women no longer defer to the "argument that violence on the part of women would be answered by still more violence by men," women *are* acutely aware of men's anti-feminist backlash.[15] A glance at Susan Faludi's *Backlash: The Undeclared War Against American Women* will verify this.[16]

To reconsider: what "social change work" could women accomplish by deploying an armed attack on the "culture of violence" aimed against their sex? Is it possible for women to militate against their patriarchal endocolonization by entering what Fanon, in a moment of tragic reflection, describes as the "circle of hate," the vicious circle of "terror, counter-terror, violence, counter-violence."[17] Have women not learned from their more or less voluntary participation in wars of decolonization such as that waged by black militants in South Africa and the U.S. that, to quote Fanon again, "in all armed struggles, there exists what we might call the point of no return"?[18] Moreover, how can any armed rebellion deploy an effective counter-violence when violence has been discovered at the very centre of the machinery of this age of post-structuralism, and to be endemic to the machinery that operates the entire social system? Feminist readers of Michel Foucault cannot help but see violence at work everywhere in the administration of power and knowledge, and even in the most "civilized" constructs and discourses. How do women mobilize a militant front which could, even after overcoming a pronounced muscular timidity, openly challenge something as unconsciously entrenched and rigorously ordained as the violence of humanism which, as Foucault says, "prohibits the desire for power and excludes the possibility of power being seized"?[19] How, except as he suggests, by mobilizing an attack on the notion of the humanist subject itself—"by a 'desubjectification' of the will to power (that is, through political struggle in the context of class warfare) or by the destruction of the subject as pseudosovereign (that is, through an attack on 'culture': the suppression of taboos and the limitations and divisions imposed on the sexes . . .)."[20]

In a feminist analysis which acknowledges such systemic violence against women, how can women's vigilantism and counter-terrorism be promoted as anything but a pseudoinsurrection? It would seem that women's only choices are to conduct a class warfare against men's administration of society to which they, as women, are more violently subjected than any other social subject OR to destroy the very construct "subject," including the feminine as well as the masculine subject and the entire humanist culture from which it arose. And at what cost to women?

Yet, when men's violence against women is discovered *to be an effect of not a cause for* the intervention of the (father's) law, is it not timely for women to perpetrate a counter-violence against the whole social order, to master a pen that will blow a nation of swords to smithereens? When the spokesman for the Canadian federal panel on violence against women calls for an end to "this culture of violence" does he have *women's violence against culture* in mind?

Feminist Avant-Garde Art: Aesthetic Activism?

According to Charles Russell, author of a recent book on the literary avant-garde, "the radical feminist investigations of literary form and social discourse have the potential to be the most significant expression of a revitalized avant-garde sensibility in the postmodern era, precisely because they bring together an aggressive aesthetic activism and a social collectivity that sees itself acting in society and its history."[21] Despite critics like Peter Bürger, who condemn the artistic avant-garde to historical obsolescence,[22] or, like Leslie Fiedler, to the consumer decadence of late capitalism,[23] a very strong case can be made to confirm the existence, at least since the seventies, of a vital, feminist avant-garde. Supposing she needs to make such a case, a critical supporter of the contemporary feminist avant-garde might demonstrate its continuation of the first artistic avant-garde movements and their activist commitment to social and cultural transformation. According to Russell, "the avant-garde wants to be more than a merely *modernist* art, one that reflects its contemporary society; rather, it intends to be a *vanguard* art, in advance of, and the cause of, significant social change."[24] While modernists express a disaffection for their times, devoting ingenious textual innovation to mirroring perceived social and psychological symptoms, avant-gardists act on the "belief that innovation in the form and language of art have social significance, either by their independent effects on the individual's or group's perception, knowledge, and behavior, or in association with the work of other activist members of society."[25] The aesthetic avant-garde acclaims "the special attributes of imaginative language which make it a particularly powerful form of *instrumental* discourse," and is determined to use it to "make us see the world differently and act to transform it."[26] However far in advance of popular and/or traditional culture the avant-garde perceives itself to be, it remains "in touch" with the main body of society.[27] While it "adopts an explicitly critical attitude, and asserts its distance from, the dominant values of that culture," the avant-garde also "reflects the writers' and artists' desire that art and the artist may find or create a new role within society and may ally themselves with other existing progressive or revolutionary forces to transform society."[28] "Invariably," Russell observes, "avant-garde writers turn toward the examples of science and radical politics to find support for their activist aesthetics."[29]

Like the historical political avant-garde, the aesthetic avant-garde conceives of itself as a "*vanguard*"; but unlike most socialist vanguards (except perhaps George Sorel's) the aesthetic vanguard adopts a *strategy of violence*. The term "avant-garde" is military in origin and enters into modern usage shortly after the French Revolution. Serving as "shock troops," the military avant-garde "advanced before the main body to disrupt the enemy's lines, and, usually with great loss to themselves, insuring the success of those who followed."[30] When later appropriated by utopian socialists, the term lost its violent cutting edge. "The socialists' theories lacked the aggressive aspects of the military metaphor," Russell notes, invoking an "organic evolution of the new society" instead of targeting "the enemy to be vanquished."[31]

The artistic avant-garde advances battle on two fronts: *against* the establishment and *for* a future culture, with emphasis on destruction rather than reconstruction. An avant-garde artist deploys his primary strategies of disruption and disorientation, hoping that "the experience of disorientation may in itself provide the desired perceptual and conceptual freedom, if he believes as did many of the dadaists, that there are not adequate grounds upon which to build an alternative system of art."[32] Moreover, the artistic avant-garde directs its violence not only against cultural convention and complacency but also against itself, disbanding before degenerating into vanguard*ism*. "If it is to be activist," the avant-garde "must lead beyond itself."[33]

Following Russell's reconstruction, a critic of today's feminist avant-garde would expect to find an aesthetic activism which militates violently and effectively against established culture, targeting not just conventions and expectations of the artistic establishment, but more broadly, the entire "culture of violence" against women. Moreover, she would expect to find that in such a "culture of violence," feminist avant-garde disruption and disorientation would *expose* and *exceed* social norms and audience expectations of violence. She would expect this feminist avant-garde to forge brave new alliances with other politically progressive cultural, technological, and scientific movements. Finally, she would expect this movement to advance on two fronts, negative and creative, and to clear out after articulating the arrival of a new body politic for the main corps of feminist social change workers to cultivate.

Symbolic Violence

I therefore contend that the most effective counter-violence a feminist movement could advance against a "culture of violence" against women would be *symbolic*: a symbolic revolution. While direct attack on male bodies has become a legitimate strategy of self-defense and survival for desperately battered women, for feminism to amass such a tactic as a general counter-strategy would turn more than one lethal weapon on women themselves. Because sexual oppression in Western societies is administered through symbolic violence, an effective confrontation must also be symbolic. To explain what I mean, I refer to the French sociologist, Pierre Bourdieu. According to Bourdieu—

> the symbolic revolution, which overturns mental structures and deeply upsets people's minds—which explains the violence of the reactions of bourgeois critics and public—may be called the revolution *par excellence*. The critics, who perceive and denounce the avant-garde painter as a political revolutionary, aren't altogether wrong even if the symbolic revolution is doomed, most of the time to remain confined to the symbolic domain.[34]

Bourdieu understands Western society as being comprised of "fields" of power and dominance, a "field" being a "competitive system of social relations which functions according to its own specific logic or rules."[35] Organized through "'objective relations between individuals or institutions who are competing for the same stake,'" a field may more accurately be called a "*battlefield*."[36] The aim of any social agent in the field is "to *rule* the field, to become the instance which has the power to confer or withdraw *legitimacy* from other participants."[37] Every social field, including the intellectual, educational, and cultural fields, have their own specific mechanisms of selection and consecration by which symbolic value is produced and recognized. What makes the field *work* is a "habitus" of shared competitive or combative "dispositions," generated by the play of stakes and structured by an "*unspoken* and *unspeakable* set of game-rules for what can be legitimately said" and spoken for.[38] It is the unarticulated habitus of the ruling class, not the explicit codes of law, which conduct the play of competition, legitimizing some bids for power, and delegitimizing others. In its function as censor "every discourse within the field becomes at once an enactment and an effect of *symbolic violence*." Toril Moi explains:

> a field is a particular structure of distribution of a specific kind of capital. The right to speak, *legitimacy*, is invested in those agents recognized by the field as powerful possessors of capital. Such individuals become spokespersons for the *doxa* and struggle to relegate challengers to their position of *heterodoxa*, as lacking capital, as individuals who cannot *credit* with the right to speak. The powerful possessors of symbolic capital become the wielders of symbolic power and thus of symbolic violence.[39]

Only when a social field or society is thrown into "crisis" by explicit ideological or political struggle is symbolic violence of the ruling class unmasked, its legitimacy radically called into question.

For Bourdieu, culture and the arts form a particularly embattled field of competition for power and legitimacy. "'*Taste* or *judgement* are the heavy artillery of symbolic violence,'" he claims, denouncing "the 'terrorism [of] the peremptory verdicts which, in the name of taste, condemn to ridicule, indignity, shame, silence . . . men and women who simply fall short of their judges, of the right way of being and doing.' There is terrorism 'in the symbolic violence through which the dominant group endeavour to impose their own life-style, and which abounds in the glossy weekly magazines.'"[40]

Bourdieu, moreover, regards sexual oppression to be "the paradigmatic form" of "symbolic violence": "the case of gender domination shows better than any other that *symbolic violence accomplishes itself through an act of cognition and of miscognition that lies beyond—or beneath—the controls of consciousness and will,* in the obscurities of the schemata of habitus that are at once gendering and engendering."[41] In other words, sexual oppression "is structured by a habitus which makes male power appear legitimate even to women."[42] While gender or sex never emerges in a field of its own, we may assume that "under current social conditions and in most contexts maleness functions as positive and femaleness as negative symbolic capital."[43]

When women begin to question and confront this legitimate dominance, symbolic violence is replaced by more overt forms of violence, as witnessed in the backlash against feminism. Physical violence against women signals the effectiveness of a feminist move to *expose and delegitimize* symbolic violence; a move which Bourdieu can only affirm:

> the liberation of women can come only from a collective action aimed
> at a symbolic struggle capable of challenging practically the immediate
> agreement of embodied and objective structures, that is, from a
> symbolic revolution that questions the very foundations of the
> production and reproduction of symbolic capital and, in particular,
> the dialectic of pretention and distinction which is at the root of the
> production and consumption of cultural goods as signs of distinc
> tion.[44]

Advancing Bourdieu's sociological praxis for a revolutionary feminism, Monique Wittig reiterates that "sexuality is not for women an individual and subjective expression, but a social institution of violence."[45] Women, she explains, are primarily oppressed by the social and political category of sex, their categorical hystericization: "for the category of sex is the category that sticks to women, for only they cannot be conceived outside of it. Only *they* are sex, *the* sex, and sex they have been made in their minds, bodies, acts, gestures; even their murders and beatings are sexual."[46] Moreover, the category of sex covertly *legitimizes* sexual violence against women across the entire social field: "for the category of sex is a totalitarian one, which to prove true has its inquisitions, its courts, its tribunals, its body of laws, its terrors, its tortures, its mutilations, its executions, its police."[47] Symbolic violence produces and sanctions actual, sexual violence; in the absence of feminist struggle which exposes the legitimation of this violence, women accept "being murdered, mutilated, physically and mentally tortured and abused, being raped, being battered, and being forced to marry [as] the fate of women. . . . Women do not know that they are totally dominated by men, and when they acknowledge the fact, thay can 'hardly believe it.'"[48]

Wittig warns oppressed groups against relegating symbolic violence to the "the domain of Irreal Ideas" lest they "forget the material (physical) violence that they do" and she urges them to consider specifically the "violence produced by the abstract and 'scientific' discourses as well as by the discourses of the mass media"[49]–"scientific" discourses in the intellectual field and "pornographic" discourses in the cultural field having enough symbolic capital to dictate categorically what is/is not tasteful to the production and consumption of feminine minds and bodies.

An effective feminist intervention for Wittig must initiate symbolic counter-violence. While it takes only one traumatic experience of sexual violence followed by an equally traumatic encounter with judicial passivity for a woman to recognize how male dominance is legitimized in this society, it takes massive feminist action to make this recognition public. Feminism must struggle to make sexual opposition and oppression visible:

> For as long as oppositions (differences) appear as given, already there, before all thought, 'natural'–as long as there is no conflict and no struggle–there is no dialectic, there is no change, no movement. The dominant thought refuses to turn inward on itself to apprehend that which questions it.[50]

What feminism needs most, she concludes, is an avant-garde armed with a "political semiology" to "work at the level of language/manifesto, of language/action, [as] that which transforms, that which makes history."[51]

Violence and Audience

A responsible feminism must jolt us out of our complacent complicity with this culture of violence. More precisely, feminism needs a cultural avant-garde which knows how to target audiences as strategically as it knows how to explode the social text. As Russell Berman observes, avant-garde violence works *on* an audience as well as *in* the art work itself:

> The specific characterizations of avant-gardist aesthetic activity share this tone: provocation and shock. The relationship both to the established institution and to the contemporary public is in no way peaceful . . . . Provocational artists, destroying traditional aesthetic values, antagonize a threatened public which responds with violence.[52]

A feminist avant-garde must be especially rigorous in selecting audiences, aiming its most provocative and shocking de(con)structions, its violent negations, not at women who perhaps suffer from an over-sensitization to cultural barbarism by a reckless media but at sexist institutions and their administrators who capitalize on women's socio-symbolic intimidation. Such an avant-garde runs the inevitable risk of a violent backlash, but as Ruth Roach Pierson puts it, "one lesson that might be drawn from the Montreal killings is that, as there is no more risk involved in being a self-identified feminist than in being a woman, one may as well speak up, as a woman, for women's rights and against women's wrongs."[53] As head of Ontario's Centre for Women's Studies in Education, Pierson observes that education is one such established institution which could use feminist disruption, noting that the journalists who continue to mask endemic violence against women as the workings of madmen and the justices who acquit male defendants of violent crimes have university, if not post-graduate, degrees.

"What is the record of our institutions of higher learning with regard to combatting racist and sexist attitudes?" she asks. "What is the institutional backing given to the Ethnic and Women's Studies programs that have trailblazed the research revealing, and the courses sensitizing students to, the deeply embedded racism and sexism in our culture?"[54]

Luce Irigaray is a feminist avant-garde theorist who aims her explosive negative critique of male symbolic dominance at a philosophical readership. She specifically targets a philosophical audience in an attempt to intervene in the reproduction of a master discourse where the category of sex is most perniciously inscribed.[55] In her essay "The Power of Discourse and the Subordination of Woman," Irigaray analyzes the rhetoric of "sexual indifference" and "the logic of the same" at work in the discourse considered foundational to legal, political, medical, economic, scientific, and educational discourses on woman. She demonstrates that this rhetoric/logic figures "woman" as man's sexual "other" with devastating effect on women in the intellectual and cultural, if not all social, fields. As the repressed, phantasmatic object of his self-conscious, epistemological subject, or as dark, inchoate, chthonic matter to his luminous form and transcendent soul, "woman" functions discursively to enrich and empower men's positive sense of their being and becoming at the expense of women's self-representational capacity. "The 'feminine,'" she observes, recalling Simone de Beauvoir, "is always described in terms of deficiency or atrophy, as the other side of the sex that alone holds a monopoly on value: the male sex."[56] Irigaray exposes the masterful systematicity with which philosophical discourse employs a rhetoric of feminine inferiority and a teleo-logic of sexual opposition to legitimize male supremacy. Moreover, she exposes "the power of its systematicity" and "its position of mastery"[57] *systematically*, mirroring the method of philosophical critique: in this way, she reserves a portion of recognizable symbolic capital with which to appeal to her masculine judges while offending their self-serving good taste to the extreme.

But Irigaray's subversion of the audience does not stop with the exposure of legitimization devices in masculinist discourse: "what remains to be done," she announces, "is to work at 'destroying' the discursive mechanism."[58] She calls for a feminist writing which would "play up" the rhetoric of "the feminine," deploy the figure of female atrophy or irrationality by miming its function in philosophical discourse to "*disruptive excess*,"[59] thereby detonating as well as demonstrating the mechanism of masculine ascendency. This deployment of "feminine" writing, she announces, "tends to put the torch to fetish words, proper terms, well-constructed forms" which serve men's symbolic capacity for self-fashioning and social empowerment. Her "feminine" style of philosophical commentary "resists and explodes every firmly established form, figure, idea, or concept."[60] Elsewhere, in "Any Theory of the 'Subject' Has Always Been Appropriated By the 'Masculine,'" she is even more terroristic:

> Turn everything upside down, inside out, back to front. *Rack it with radical convulsions*, carry back remiport, those crises that her 'body' suffers in her impotence to say what disturbs her. Insist also and deliberately upon those *blanks* in discourse which recall the places of her exclusion and which, by their *silent plasticity*, ensure the cohesion, the articulation, the coherent expansion of established forms. Reinscribe them hither and thither as *divergencies*, otherwise and elsewhere than they are expected, in *ellipses* and *eclipses* that deconstruct the logical grid

of the reader-writer, drive him out of his mind, trouble his vision to the point of incurable diplopia, at least. *Overthrow syntax* by suspending its eternally teleological order, by snipping the wires, cutting the current, breaking the circuits, switching the connections, by modifying continuity, alternation, frequency, intensity.[61]

Irigaray's advance against male symbolic dominance is more negative than creative though she does contend that "every operation on and in philosophical language, [including the 'feminine' one . . .] possesses implications" and that "the first question to ask, therefore, is the following: how can women analyze their own exploitation, inscribe their own demands, within an order prescribed by the masculine? *Is a women's politics possible within that order?* What transformation in the political process itself does it require?"[62] But given the secondary and inconclusive nature of this contention, we might first inquire after the effect Irigaray's violence might have on the philosophical reader who identifies herself as a woman. As Margaret Whitford puts it, what becomes of the violence she provokes in women readers? The questions Irigaray urgently asks of Jacques Derrida could be asked of Irigaray herself: "Where has the violence gone when the deconstructor deconstructs? . . . Does it allow another violence to continue unchecked?"[63]

The analytic violence with which Irigaray provokes her women readers may be precisely the force which mobilizes an effort to synthesize women's *identity*. "Both Derrida and Irigaray would see male identity—the construction of the male subject—as 'violent' and hierarchical," Whitford observes; "but for Irigaray it is not just a question of deconstructing, but also of reorganizing the economy. . . . of constructing the fragmentary feminine, binding together the scraps into a cohesion that is less destructive for them."[64] Does the creative front of the feminist avant-garde then entail the reconstruction of women's identity?[65] Is the reconstruction of women's identity a function of the feminist avant-garde or is such a project more appropriately assigned to the main body of feminism?[66] Then again, just as feminist psychotherapists have concluded that healing is not a sufficient end in itself, feminist theorists may also conclude that reconstructing women's identity is not the ultimate goal of political solidarity. But to return to the question "where goes the violence a feminist avant-garde might provoke in its audiences of women?" Should we not wish to answer: into their *empowerment?*[67]

A Poetics of Empowerment?

A feminist avant-garde deploys a negative symbolic violence *against* the culture of violence against women and a positive symbolic violence *for* the cultural empowerment of women. African-American poet, Audre Lorde, and French prose-poet, Monique Wittig are two activist artists who deploy this double front of violence and whose writings are exemplary poetic representations of the feminist "fight back" rhetoric of the seventies. The seventies were an explosive time for radical feminist publications: political manifestos were produced everywhere, in Italy, the broadsheets of *Carli Lonzi, Rivolta Femminile, Movimento Femminista Romana, Movimento de Liberazione della Donna*[68]; in France, the pamphlets and periodicals of the various fronts of the *Mouvement de Libération des Femmes* coalition, later known as "the new French Feminists"[69]; and in America, the manifestos of Radicalesbians, among others, and the two best-selling anthologies, *Fight Back: Feminist Resistance to Male Violence* and *Sisterhood is Powerful.*[70] Of the American manifestos, the most memorable are also the most violent: Ti-Grace Atkinson's *Amazon Odyssey* with its chapters, "Declaration of War" and "Strategy and Tactics," the latter presenting over fifty pages of flow charts outlining the penetration, occupation and destruction of territory ruled by men[71]; and Valerie Solanis's *S.C.U.M. [Society for Cutting Up Men] Manifesto*, whose title really speaks for itself.[72] But while using language to signal a call to arms, map guerilla war zones and shock college bimbettes with terrorist fantasies, these manifestos do not perform a symbolic revolution. They use language to muster anger, if not armies, whereas the poetic avant-garde uses *anger in language* to expose the symbolic violence of canonical writing, explode master discourses, and prefigure a new body politic. The efficacy of an avant-garde must be measured in its capacity, not simply to incite women to combat, but to breakthrough categorical thinking, to empower, transform, and collectivize their subjective agency.

In *Sister Outsider*, Lorde outlines her use of anger and eroticism in poetry to liberate and empower black women readers.[73] These are the mobilizing strategies of *The Black Unicorn: Poems.*[74] From the heraldic title poem "The Black Unicorn" to the climactic lyrics of "Power" near the end of the collection, Lorde intensifies her discourse of arousal and outrage. Each poem functions as manifesto, declaring war on "the oppressor's language"[75] and displaying a growing awareness of the power of poetry to mediate and organize black women's rage: "I am lost, without imagery or magic/ trying to make power out of hatred and destruction," she writes,[76] and in "The Women of Dan Dance With Swords in Their Hands To Mark the Time When They Were Warriors":

> I do not come like a secret warrior
> with an unsheathed sword in my hand
> hidden behind my tongue
> slicing my throat to ribbons
> of service with a smile
> while the blood runs
> down and out
> through holes in the two sacred mounds
> on my chest.
>
> I come like a woman
> who I am
> spreading out through nights
> laughter and promise
> and dark heat
> warming whatever I touch
> that is living
> consuming
> only
> what is already dead.[77]

With blazing fury this verse sets the reader burning, but not without an "objective correlative." In the first stanza, a figure of the poet-warrior rises phoenix-like out of a destroyed image of domestic femininity, whose unmasked "service with a smile" reveals her brutally desecrated body. In the final stanza, she announces her "coming" with a volatile passion which simultaneously fires her will to live and torches what is most dead(ly) about the enemy, the cold, abstracting reason of his enlightened white mythology. When the poem ends, her passion is not consumed but spreading, entreating the reader to bask in the holocaust of a black woman's armageddon. Such inscription of anger *figures* rather than *incites* the readers' violence, igniting outrage against a socio-symbolic order instead of sparking indiscriminate riot.

Like Lorde's warrior poems, Monique Wittig's *Les Guérillères* uses poetic language to mediate and mobilize the power of women's wrath. A sequence of prose poems flanked by pages bearing names of female guerilla fighters in phalanxes of bold capitals, *Les Guérillères* deploys simultaneously an anti-discursive front and an allegorical revolutionary corps. This is more than utopian fiction, spurring the reader's deconstructive imagination. The initiation of violence is at first slow, but gradually accelerates into global war:

> The women say they have learned to rely on their own strength. They say they are aware of the force of their unity. They say, let those who call for a new language first learn violence. They say, let those who want to change the world seize all the rifles. They say that they are starting from zero. They say that a new world is beginning.[78]

Mobilization does not come easily. First, the women must reclaim their bodies through the dithyrambic eroticism of dance until step by step their rhythmic footwork articulates their collective, nihilistic fury:

> Begin the dance. Step forward lightly, move in a circle, hold each other by the hand, let everyone observe the rhythm of the dance. Spring forward lightly. The ring of dancers must revolve so that their glance lights everywhere. They say, It is a great error to imagine that I, a woman, would speak violence against men. But we must, as something quite new, begin the round dance stamping the feet in time against the ground. They say rise, slowly twice clapping your hands. Stamp the ground in time, O women. Now turn to the other side. Let the foot move in rhythm.[79]

This process is bolstered by sacred writings called "feminaries," whose symbolic "use of the erotic" emblazons the vulva in ritual arousal:

> The women say that the feminaries give pride of place to the symbols of the circle, the circumference, the ring, the O, the zero, the sphere . . . as symbols of the vulva. . . . Sun that terrifies and delights/ multicolored iridescent insect you devour yourself in night's memory/ blazing genital/ the circle is your symbol/ you exist from all eternity/ you will exist for all eternity. At these words the women begin to dance, stamping the ground with their feet. They begin a round dance, clapping their hands, giving voice to a song from which no coherent phrase emerges.[80]

Testimonials of phallogocentric brutality[81] raise the women to such a pitch of anger, they are able to activate and voice violence against their oppressors, destroying oppressive habits of feminine deference and maternal solicitude:

> The women menace they attack they hiss the men they revile them jeer at them spit in their faces scoff at them provoke them flout them apostrophize them mishandle them are abrupt with them they speak coarsely to them execrate them call them down curses on them. They are possessed by such utter fury that they boil with anger tremble choke grind their teeth foam blaze rage and fume leap vomit run riot. They call them to account admonish them put a knife to their throats intimidate them show them their fists they thrash them do violence to them acquaint them with all their grievances in the greatest disorder they sow the seed of discord here and there provoke dissension among them divide them ferment disturbances riots civil wars they treat them as hostile. Their violence is unleashed they are in a paroxysm of rage, in their devastating enthusiasm they appear wild-eyed hair bristling clenching their fists roaring rushing shrieking slaughtering in fury one might say of them that they are females who look like women when they are dead.[82]

Wittig's *guérillères* eventually mounts a battle whose strategies and tactics prefigure those of Ti-Grace Atkinson's "political lesbians," as well as Gilles Deleuze and Félix Guattari's nomadic war machine. For Deleuze and Guattari, as for Wittig, the ancient Amazons present a postmodern model for conceptualizing the movements of a contemporary avant-garde.[83] Against the military establishment and the conscripted labor it commands with heavy-handed discipline and hierarchical rigidity,[84] amazon guerillas deploy an impassioned solidarity with furious speed and shifting angles of action.[85] Against the militia's regimental grid, the nomadic avant-garde "draw[s] a creative line of flight, the composition of a smooth space and the movement of people in that space."[86] And while the militia battles to impose and extend its field of domination, the amazons would wipe the field clean of all formations of dominance.[87]

Les Guérillères also reads as a poetic deployment of the violence Fanon advocates for colonized peoples. Wittig's "women native others" launch absolute war: negotiation with the phallocratic colonizers is out of the question. As Fanon says,

> to break up the colonial world does not mean that after the frontiers have been abolished lines of communication will be set up between the two zones. The destruction of the colonial world is no more and no less than the abolition of one zone, its burial in the depths of the earth or its expulsion from that country.[88]

But Wittig's violent deployment of avant-garde art challenges Fanon's argument that native art only serves to mystify and dissipate energies. Only through armed uprising, Fanon asserts, do the colonized emerge from their "imaginary maze" where they have been "a prey to unspeakable terrors yet happy to lose themselves in a dreamlike torrent." Mobilization, he warns, is averted through ritual theatrics where "the most acute aggressivity, the most impelling violence are canalized, transformed, and conjured away . . . [in] the huge effort of a community to exorcise itself, to liberate itself, to explain itself."[89] In armed rebellion, however, "such a people becomes unhinged, reorganizes itself, and in blood and tears gives birth to very real and immediate action."[90] The instigator of native uprising?—ultimately the abusive violence of the colonizer:

> The native's back is to the wall, the knife is at his throat (or, more precisely, the electrode at his genitals): he will have no more call for his fancies. . . . The native discovers reality and transforms it into the pattern of his customs, into the practice of violence and into his plan for freedom.[91]

Wittig's *guérillères* use precisely ritualized fantasy, theatre, and dance as powerful strategies to mobilize a collective, aggressive front. For them, it is not the oppressor's violence but a violence of their own, which they recover and embody in lyrical and physical culture, to provoke cultural crisis and revolution. Moreover, Wittig's symbolic revolution subverts conventional utopia, ending at the moment of peak mobilization when the women have triumphantly abolished the patriarchal State, destroyed all their captives, and opened a whole new territory for nomadic cultivation. Mourning for their dead and greeting an altogether different breed of sex, they gather sufficient affective power for building a brave new world. Instead of displaying battle fatigue or post-war bliss, the female warriors are fired up with new energy released through demobilization. As with Lorde's warrior-poems, Wittig's writing rouses readerly affects without diffusing them in wistful postfeminist dreams.

Reading Wittig and Lorde, it becomes clear that a feminist avant-garde art must use a medium that is at least as effective as incitant polemic. As Lorde announces: "Unless I learn to use/ the difference between poetry and rhetoric/ my power too will run corrupt as poisonous mold/ or lie limp and useless as an unconnected wire."[92] Unless feminist avant-garde art learns to use poetic revolutionary language to wrench culture out of the vicious circle of master discourse and demagogic rhetoric, only forces of annihilating reciprocity will be raised.[93] What "the women say" in every passage of *Les Guérillères*, what the poet declares in "A Woman Speaks" in *Black Unicorn* are lyrical manifestos that have the power not merely to provoke, but to empower and activate violently anti-violent, anti-categorical counter-formations.

The chapter on the transformative efficacy of feminist manifestos in the history of modernity has yet to be written. And when it is, it will have to consider Julia Kristeva's response to feminism's efforts to mobilize collective cultural resistance in her essay, "Women's Time," which heralds the simultaneous arrival of post-feminism and post-modernism for the eighties.[94] Here Kristeva attacks the new feminist counter-culture[95] while defending Hegel and Lacan for their "true" formulation of the "implacable violence which constitutes any symbolic contract."[96] Equating lesbian motherhood with terrorism[97] and radical feminism with goddess-mongering which, if mass-activated could set ablaze a holocaust whose magnitude the world has never known,[98] Kristeva denies outright the possibility of a feminist symbolic revolutionary front, one capable of overthrowing the patriarchal social order while giving rise to a new sexual politic. After relegating feminism to the cultural imaginary where it is limited to phantasmatic production, she then accuses feminism of wishing to materialize its phantasms in reality. Her discourse betrays the paranoiac logic she displaces on to feminist activism. More disturbingly though, it denies any theory and praxis of women's art as collective subversion of systemic symbolic violence; accordingly, women's only and inevitable form of counter-violence is the individual's giving over to violent crime or terrorism:

> when a subject is too brutally excluded from this socio-symbolic stratum; when, for e.g., a woman feels her affective life as a woman or her condition as a social being too brutally ignored by existing discourse or power (from her family to social institutions); she may, by

counter-investing the violence she has endured, make of herself a 'possessed' agent of this violence in order to combat what was experienced as frustration—with arms which may seem disproportional, but which are not so in comparison with the subjective or narcissistic suffering from which they originate. . . . Since the dawn of feminism, and certainly before, the political activity of exceptional women, and this in a certain sense of liberated women, has taken the form of murder, conspiracy and crime.[99]

Accordingly, the future of feminism lies with an avant-garde which will lead feminism beyond "the idea of difference," forging a break from "its belief in Woman, Her power, Her writing, so as to . . . bring out the singularity of each woman, and beyond this, her multiplicities, her plural languages, beyond the horizon, beyond sight, beyond faith itself."[100]

But such a feminist *écriture*, I would argue, is demobilizing and diffusive, calling for a liberal pluralism in place of collective action, with every woman writing her difference, her language, "beyond sight" of the culture of violence hurled against her. Posing the form a *true* feminist avant-garde should take as a (rhetorical) question—"a factor for ultimate mobilization? Or a factor for analysis? . . . . Imaginary support in a technocratic era where all narcissism is frustrated? Or instruments fitted to these times in which cosmos, atoms and cells—our true contemporaries—call for the constitution of a fluid and free subjectivity?"—Kristeva ushers in the eighties with a cry of retreat.[101]

A Gathering of Forces in the Nineties

Three years after the Montreal massacre, the 1992 October-November issue of Canadian news periodical *This Magazine* features an update on women and violence. The cover story begins with "Rage and Remembrance," a memorial to the Montreal women, before proceeding to the next three articles, provocatively entitled "Fighting Back," "If Boys Will Be Boys, Girls Will Now Take Action," and "Revenge Becomes Her." The back cover advertises the "National Day of Remembrance and Action on Violence Against Women, December 6" while the front cover features a nasty "Fembo" breaking the silence with a gesture of vociferous militancy. Perhaps the period of mourning is passing . . . .

And the new decade of "fighting back" has arrived. The turn of events begins with an explicit recognition by mourners and avengers alike that the justice system simply does not work for women[102] and condones what can be only be called "femicide."[103] The final article in *This Magazine*'s cover story reports the resurgence of women's revenge fantasies in popular literature and theatre, suggesting that, at the level of the cultural imaginary at least, women are responding to femicide with revived violence. The author, Moira Farr, fantasizes the arrival of Clara Kent, "mild mannered reporter by day and amazing fembo at night," and of "Dirty Harriet," the little girl who wanted to be an engineer but who became a mobster instead.[104] Farr also reports the arrival of "Comix Bitch," creation of Seattle artist Roberta Gregory; apparently, "next to her Thelma and Louise look like Lucy and Ethel."[105] In the United Kingdom, Helen Zahavi is disturbing literary audiences with her "dazzling first novel, *Dirty Weekend*" in which a "mousy loser named Bella rises up, stalks and kills a series of creeps." In Canada, Quebec comic artist Julie Doucet is shocking readers with her graphic chronicles of *Dirty Plotte*, a sexy vamp who shows no qualms about dismembering reckless male pursuers. On the theatre front, Beatrice Mosoinier (author of *In Search of April Raintree*) has upset crowds with "*Night of the Trickster*, in which "four native women take revenge on rapists; the play culminates in a horrifying scene during which an attacker is brought to his quivering knees before an angry woman and her knife."[106]

This re-emergence of women's violence in the nineties not only speaks against Julia Kristeva's anodyne alternative to a populist expression of women's anger, but also challenges Elaine Showalter's conclusive pronouncement that such expression in "literature and film offer women little support for fighting back and not much emotional catharsis."[107] Showalter's article "Rethinking the Seventies: Women Writers and Violence," reviews the violent productions of women authors, including, not only the manifestos of Valerie Solanis and Ti-Grace Atkinson, but also Nellie Kaplan's films (*La Fiancée du pirate*, *Papa les petites bateaux*, *Nea*), and novels by Muriel Spark (*The Driver's Seat*), Judith Rossner (*Looking for Mr. Goodbar*), Gail Godwin (*The Odd Woman*), Diane Johnson (*The Shadow Knows*), and Marilyn French (*The Woman's Room*). While at first glance, "women writers seemed at last to be able to express anger and passion, to confront their own raging emotions instead of burying them or sublimating them into madness," a double-take confirms that "feminist fantasies of the liberated characteristic of the seventies . . . have come up against an external limit."[108] "Feminist vigilante action, like the Ellen Jamesians [of John Irving's *World According to Garp*], or Marilyn French's doomed militants, is seen as crazy, futile, and absurd," Showalter surmises. "For feminist writers, disenchantment is imagined as our own newly acknowledged sexuality and anger turned against us in the form of male violence, as if every movement by women pressing towards control engenders a more powerful and opposite reaction against men."[109] But, as it materializes in the collective fantasies of the popular culture of the nineties, the dialectic of women's revolutionary violence gathers a vital, emotional power undaunted by the spectre of men's backlash.

The popular front is not the only place an "angry woman and her knife" can be found. A recent production by the cutting-edge San Francisco press, *Re/Search*, heralds the emergence of *Angry Women*, including provocatively illustrated interviews with Kathy Acker, Lydia Lunch, Diamanda Galàs, bell hooks and Avital Ronell, among others.[110] *Angry Women* is an ecclectic collection of feminist critics, theorists, performance artists, lesbian activists, and pornographers whose only common trait is "anger."[111] Opening the cover, the reader is met with a photograph of Galàs, apparently covered in blood and wielding a knife in her solo performance of "Wild Women with Steak Knives." Thawing the chill of the postfeminist eighties, these angry women passionately reenact the strategies of seventies' avant-garde feminism as well as those of the historical avant-garde—notably Artaud's theatre of cruelty. "Whatever conflicts may obsess the mentality of the times," Artaud had once declared, "I defy any spectator infused with the blood of violent scenes, who has felt higher action pass through him, who has seen the rare, fundamental motions of his thought illuminated in extraordinary events—violence and bloodshed having been placed at the service of violence in thought—once outside the theatre, I defy him to indulge in thoughts of war, riot or motiveless murder."[112]

Angry Women is comprised of "cruel" women who stage for live theatre the bloody violence hurled at women on the streets and in their homes without softening the blows. They present themselves as guerrilla warriors in a war against women which they wage on their own dramaturgical terms. "I'm rallying the troops," performance artist Lydia Lunch declares. "That's my job. Everyone should assume a position in the ranks of this army, because it *is* war, and that's it."[113] In her war against femicide, Galás moves far beyond manifesto rhetoric, "training [her] vocal cords to yield an *ubervoice*" to cast "an immediate extroversion of sound, [which] deliver[s] a pointed, focussed message—like a gun."[114] "I used to talk with my singing teacher in San Diego about guns as *necessity* and *metaphor*," she recalls, alluding perhaps to a passage in Walter Benjamin's "Work of Art in the Age of Mechanical Reproduction": "from an alluring appearance or persuasive structure of sound the work of art of the Dadaist's became an instrument of ballistics. It hit the spectator like a bullet."[115]

At least one of *Angry Women* performs her feminist activism in the university and refers to herself as an "ivory tower terrorist."[116] Avital Ronell delivers a form of feminist critique which is at once "joyous, relentless, outrageous, libidinally charged" and violently subversive: "in a genuine feminist intervention," she testifies, "what has to happen is a Will to Rupture—a Will to Break with these phantasms and divinizations [of feminine monstrosity]."[117] Hers, moreover, is a futurist feminism. Feminism has to make a future for women as well as destroy women's present inhibitions: "true feminism has to investigate and encompass biotechnics, biogenetics, and all fields of technology. A true feminism will stop being phobic about these areas, because it's crucial that women be involved in investigating, exploring and shaping the technological realities of the future."[118]

As *Angry Women* suggests, the prime medium of feminist avant-garde art in the nineties may be performance. *Comix Bitch* may be the most appropriate medium for revenge fantasy, but an avant-garde seeking to waken its audience to the violent reality our culture prescribes for women, would sensibly locate its activism in the action of live theatre. According to Henry Sayre, the American avant-garde has been dominated by feminist performance art since the seventies. Sayre attributes "the rise of women, and of women's art," to the emergence of "a real avant-garde art" occupying a space *outside* museum and gallery and art magazine systems, where it can be politically engaged and engaging.[119] Naming the productions of the "Guerilla Girls" as seventies' prototypes, he proceeds to discuss the prominent works of Carole Schneeman, Faith Wilding, Judy Chicago, Laurie Anderson, and Eleanor Antin in the eighties.

Sayre's argument could be taken much further. Feminist avant-garde art has not only dominated American avant-garde art, but is also spearheading American radical politics since the formation of the Women's

Action Coalition in January, 1992. Organized by New York's leading women artists, including Laurie Anderson, Barbara Kruger, Cindy Sherman, Elizabeth Murray, and Karen Finley, WAC was created in response to the Kennedy rape trial, the Thomas-Hill affair, and Susan Faludi's *Backlash* with a "renewed awareness of the failure of institutional responses to the problem of violence against women."[120] Launching a visual and verbal assault on Republican indifference to violence against women, "WAC has successfully targeted a number of sexual-assault cases, throwing them in the media spotlight through innovative protests."[121] WAC's style of radical civil disobedience borrows from the "Guerilla Girls" of yesterday but also forges allegiance with other activist groups of today, notably the AIDS activist group, ACT UP. Having grown to a corps of 2,500 radical women (who reportedly assemble every Wednesday night in Lower Manhattan in a bid to outlaw misogyny), the New York WAC has set up branches in Toronto, San Francisco, Los Angeles, Boston, and Paris. Together, WAC and other artistic activist groups across the country, amass a cultural front of which the historical avant-garde, its critics and dissentors, never dreamed.

Sexual Politics or Sexual Personae?

But just as feminist avant-garde of the nineties has become thoroughly politicized, there has emerged an apolitical discourse on violence against women which has found equally impressive popularity. In the eighties, feminist avant-gardists had to contend with Julia Kristeva; in the nineties, they must contend with Camille Paglia.

Paglia's internationally bestselling book *Sexual Personae: Art and Decadence from Nefertiti to Emily Dickinson* reinforces the "category of sex" in a revitalized naturalist discourse designed to blow apart social constructionist theories. It is another angry and explosive book, one which makes no attempt to hide the violence between the sexes, or its own violence against feminist activists. Furious with feminist theory for having seriously misdirected women into thinking they are powerless and that political action will redress all power imbalances, Paglia recalls women to their natural power, a power forgotten and repressed by the artifices of civic society and especially distorted and maligned by French language-based feminism. The following passages are taken from her polemical introduction:

Feminists, seeking to drive power relations out of sex, have set themselves against nature. Sex *is* power. . . . Sexual freedom, sexual liberation. A modern delusion. We are hierarchical animals. . . . Nature's cycles are woman's cycles. . . . [Woman] does not have to become but only to be. Her centrality is a great obstacle to man, whose quest for identity she blocks. He must transform himself into an independent being, that is, a being free of her. . . . She has no choice but acceptance. . . . Feminism has been simplistic in arguing that female archetypes were politically motivated by falsehoods by men. . . . Physical and spiritual castration is the danger every man runs in intercourse with a woman. . . . Woman's latent vampirism is not a social aberration but a development of her maternal function, for which nature has equipped her . . . . The male genital metaphor is concentration and projection. . . . Sex is metaphysical for men, as it is not for women. Women have no problem to solve by sex. Physically and psychologically they are serenely self-contained. . . . The sexes are eternally at war. There is an element of attack, of search-and-destroy in male sex, in which there will always be a potential for rape. . . . But women's strange sexual cries come directly from the cthonian. She is a Maenad about to rend her victim.[122]

That the sexes are at war is no news to feminism; but Paglia's announcement that this war is biological and therefore eternal is as old as the patriarchal hills and promises to return women to a thinking predating Kate Millett and Simone de Beauvoir. It is also root-bound in nineteenth-century naturalism and sexology. She contends that since "political equality will only succeed in political terms, it is helpless against the archetypal," and therefore the only by treatment that can transform the body politic will violence be done to the body *natural*: "kill the imagination, lobotomize the brain, castrate and operate: then the sexes will be the same."[123] She might have referred to the nineteenth-century treatment of female sexuality, to its subjection of women to hundreds of thousands of clitorodechtomies and lobotomies executed in the name of sexual good taste as a cure for hysteria and nymphomania.[124] But instead she invokes the inconceivable spectre of mass castration, whose potential horror should convince women to give rape the immediate right of way. And if that is not enough, she blasts women for lacking the virility of will to appreciate rape's real power of horror:

> Feminism's most naive formulation is its assertion that rape is a crime of violence but not of sex, that it is merely power masquerading as sex.

> Rape is male power fighting female power. . . . Feminism, arguing from
> the milder woman's point of view, completely misses the blood-lust
> in rape, the joy of violation and destruction. . . . Women may be less
> prone to such fantasies because they physically lack the equipment for
> sexual violence. They do not know the temptation of forcibly invading
> the sanctuary of another body.[125]

Paglia's *Sexual Personae* might provoke in feminist readers, among less
nobler emotions, a desire to reread Millett's *Sexual Politics*. Turning to
her chapter on "The Theory of Sexual Politics," we find the iconoclastic
thinking that dared politicize the field of sexual relations by lifting the veil
of romance and domesticity. Precisely where Paglia finds a *méconnaissance*
of opposition between sex and politics, Millett presents a recognition of
sexual and political inextricability. Millett's theoretical purpose is explicitly dialectical while Paglia's is crudely manichean: instead of abolishing
sex with an ursurping politics, as Paglia charges Millett-inspired feminism of doing, Millett contends that politics and sex interimplicate each
other at all levels of culture:

> Coitus can scarcely be said to take place in a vacuum; although of itself
> it appears a biological and physical activity, it is set so deeply within
> the larger context of human affairs that it serves as a charged
> microcosm of the variety of attitudes and values to which culture
> subscribes. Among other things, it may serve as a model of sexual
> politics on an individual or personal plane.[126]

Conscious that readers will find her use of politics rather eccentric (ex-
centric), Millett addresses their doubts directly, stressing what she means
by "political" and seeming, perhaps, to underemphasize the "sexual":

> In introducing the term "sexual politics," one must first answer the
> inevitable question "Can the relationship between the sexes be viewed
> in a political light at all?" The answer depends on how one defines
> politics. This essay does not define the political as that relatively
> narrow and exclusive world of meetings, chairmen, and parties. The
> term "politics" shall refer to power-structured relationships, arrange-
> ments whereby one group of persons is controlled by another.[127]

To elaborate what she means by "power-structured relationships,"
Millett refers to Max Weber's notion of "*herrschaft*, a relationship of
dominance and subordination" and to Hannah Arendt's observation

that "government is upheld by power supported either through consent or imposed through violence."[128] Ideological conditioning, she argues, is the violent means by which patriarchal *herrschaft* establishes itself. Patriarchal ideology employs the discourses of biology to naturalize the political order of sexual difference;[129] using biological categories to explain sexual behaviour, including sexual violence against women, it conceals its political complicity in what is presented to women as a natural reign of terror. While Millett speculates on the politics of coitus, lifting the veils of romance and biology to expose the phallus beneath the sheets, Paglia rages against the meddling of feminists, throwing the veil back on the phallus so as to ressurect the penis. The penis, of course, is far easier for women to contend with: one aggressive swipe, or bite, and its finished—and so Paglia would arm her vampire brigade with the myth of the toothed vagina.[130]

Outraged by the prevailing narrowness of state and legal definitions of sexual violence, feminists have reinforced and expanded Millett's conceptualization. The editors of *Femicide: The Politics of Women Killing* write that:

> The concept of sexual violence is valuable because it moves beyond earlier feminist debates over whether rape, for example, should be seen as an act of violence or of sexual assault. The limitations of this debate center on a narrow definition of the term *sexual*, one that rests on whether the man is seeking sexual pleasure. In contrast, the term *sexual violence* focuses on the man's desire for power, dominance, and control. This definition enables sexual aggression by men to be seen in the context of the overall oppression of women in a patriarchal society. It allows feminist analysis to distance itself from legal discourse that is based on discrete and narrow definitions of the sexual and the violent, definitions that can distort and deny women's experience. Such distancing is especially important given the moralistic, racist, heterosexist conservatism that dominated law and order debates in the 1980s.[131]

In a decade so richly inhabited by feminist cultural avant-gardes like the Women's Action Coalition, how can Paglia's extraordinary popularity be explained? She speaks a discourse of power to white heterosexual men who enjoy the culture of male supremacy, and to white heterosexual women who, intimidated by feminist activism and male sexuality alike, wish their passivity to be legitimized. While feminism *agitates*, Paglia *assures,* translating women's fear of male social, political, and physical power into female sexual self-glorification. She tells women they are the object of rape because they have what men have not but would have, or would escape, or would destroy. Men inflict violence on women because they, women, are *overpowering.* Women who would not be troubled by the negative dialectic, and the violence of backlash, perpetrated by a feminist avant-garde can find easy and immediate empowerment in Paglia's inert sexual cosmology.

Moreover, Paglia claims that her reading of culture *is* avant-garde, and that it warrants the same symbolic capital with which anything new and innovative might be rewarded in capitalism's bid to market and recuperate subversion. On this point, she is perfectly sanguine: "to be conscious of the social context of art seems automatically to entail a leftist orientation. But a theory is possible that is both avant-garde *and* capitalist."[132] What sells and compels art/culture is sex, and the bloodier the better since the pornographer's "cruelty" is the commodified form of natural barbarity.

Make no mistake: Paglia is parodying, not imitating, Artaud, whose Theatre of Cruelty was designed to shock audiences into recognizing and confronting the unspeakable horrors of political reality to which they had been inured by an anodyne bourgeois stage. Paglia reverses the intent of Artaud's manifesto, calling for an art which would transcribe the violence of human sexuality so as to allow nature tolerable expression. "We may have to accept an ethical cleavage between imagination and reality," she muses, "tolerating horrors, rapes, and mutilations in art that we would not tolerate in society. For art is our message from the beyond, telling us what nature is up to."[133]

Paglia bases her "avant-garde" on "an aesthetics and erotics of profanation—evil for the sake of evil, the sharpening of the senses by cruelty and torture, [as] documented in Sade, Baudelaire, and Huysmans."[134] But she dismisses women from membership on account of their inferior will to sexuality and creativity. While one might wonder at Paglia's claim that "women may be less prone to [sadistic] fantasies," given the well-documented abundance and proliferation of sexual violence in women's art and literature since the seventies, what is more perplexing is her failure to distinguish avant-garde sadomasochism from the sexual oppression and pathology that mainstream culture and society sanction as "natural." Sade, Baudelaire, and Huysmans exploit the category of the natural not to give vent to the *natural* but to expose and destroy the precious artificiality, propriety, and hypocrisy of an imperialist bourgeois regime. Their so-called "naturalism," revived by Georges Bataille, William Burroughs, Alain Robbe-Grillet and Kathy Acker in the twentieth-century, is a form of critical materialism launched at deadly power regimes which disguise themselves in abstract idealism. This is precisely why Angela Carter suggests, contrary to what Paglia says about women's weakly will to sex and power, that women might best arm themselves for sexual warfare with Sadean counter-violence:

> Sade describes the condition of women in the genre of the pornography of sexual violence but believed it would only be through the medium of sexual violence that women might heal themselves of their socially inflicted scars, in a praxis of destruction and sacrilege. . . . Sade remains a monstrous and daunting cultural edifice; yet I would prefer to think that he put pornography in the service of women, or, perhaps, allowed it to be invaded by an ideology not inimical to women.[135]

One might also remind Paglia that Simone de Beauvoir, six years after publishing her *Second Sex* (1949) prefaced the Gallimard edition of *120 Days of Sodom* with her essay "Must We Burn Sade?"[136] Feminists engaged in a theory of sexual politics are neither so unadventurous nor so prudish as Paglia would have us think.

In the violent nineties, there could be no greater call to arms for feminists, undaunted by the dialectical interminability of the struggle, than Paglia herself. For while she calls herself an "amazon warrior" and locates herself at the forefront of the feminist avant-garde, she rallies but a rearguard of sexually and politically beleaguered personae and relieves responsible social agencies by blaming femicide on women themselves.

Notes

I would like to thank Sarah Westphal and McGill University's Centre for Research and Teaching on Women for inviting me to write and present the original version of this paper.

1.   Though the phrase "culture of violence" now has common currency, in the initial instance it appeared in two news articles: Michele Landsberg, "Killer's Rage Too Familiar to Canadians: Culture Condones Violence Against Women, Children," *Toronto Star*, 8 December 1989, A1, A16; and The Canadian Press, "Mentality of Violence Must Change," *Edmonton Journal*, 16 February 1992, C2. I refer specifically to the latter article: "It's time

to stop the culture of violence in which two Canadian women are killed by their male partners each week, say members of a federal panel on violence against women. 'At some point this tolerance of violence, this culture of violence, must cease,' said panel-member Daniel Lemieux, co-ordinator of the Quebec Coalition of Sexual Assault Centres, at a news conference Saturday. 'The time has come to change the mentality, the people are motivated enough to make an important change of direction.'"

2. "There is something terrifying," Sorel notes approvingly of workers' strikes, "which will appear more and more terrifying as violence takes a greater place in the mind of the proletariat. But in undertaking a serious, formidable and sublime work, Socialists raise themselves above our frivolous society and make themselves worthy of pointing out new roads to the world." George Sorel, *Reflections on Violence*, trans. T.E. Hulme (1906; London: Collier-Macmillan, 1950), 275.

3. Frantz Fanon, *The Wretched of the Earth*, trans. Constance Farrington (1961; New York: Grove Press, 1963); see esp. the chapter "Concerning Violence," 35-106, 93-5. Fanon defends violence enacted by natives in colonial regimes since "it constitutes their only work, invests their characters with positive and creative qualities," and "binds them together as a whole." Accordingly, the violence of decolonization/liberation "introduces into each man's consciousness the ideas of a common cause, of a national destiny, and of a collective history." Such violence "is cleansing. It frees the native from his inferiority complex and from his despair and inaction; it makes him fearless and restores his self-respect." Furthermore, it is demystifying: "illuminated by violence, the consciousness of the people rebels against pacification. From now on the demagogues, the opportunists, the magicians have a difficult task. The action which has thrown them into a hand-to-hand struggle confers upon the masses a voracious taste for the concrete. The attempt at mystification becomes, in the long run, practically impossible."

4. Ti-Grace Atkinson, *Amazon Odyssey* (New York: Link Books, 1974), 49.

5. Andrea Dworkin, "Terror, Torture and Resistance," (Keynote Speech delivered at the May 1991 Canadian Mental Health Association's "Women and Mental Health Conference— Women in a Violent Society") *Canadian Woman Studies/Les cahiers de la femme* [Special Issue on "Violence Against Women: Strategies for Change"] 12 (Fall 1991): 37-42, 41-2.

6. Phyllis Chesler, *Women and Madness* (New York: Harcourt Brace Jovanovich, 1972), 293.

7. Sandra Butler, "Building Mishpocheh," in *Canadian Woman Studies/Les cahiers de la femme* [Special Issue on "Violence Against Women: Strategies for Change"] 12 (Fall 1991): 119-20.

8. The "Strategies for Power" workshop was organized by Dr. Norma Walmsley, Chairperson of the Subcommittee on the Status of Women of the Canadian Commission for UNESCO. There were twenty-six delegates, representing the U.K., France, Italy, Norway, West Germany, Canada, and two international agencies. Participants were politicians, academics, administrators, professionals and leaders of women's organizations, including Judy Erola, Canadian federal minister responsible for the Status of Women, Flora Macdonald, former Canadian minister of external affairs, Lady Trixie Gardner, a member of the British House of Lords, and Eva Rath, founder of the German *Frauenpartie*. See Margaret Gillet, "Strategies for Power," in ed., Yolande Cohen, *Women and Counter Power* (Montreal: Black Rose, 1989), 200-9, 206.

9. Louise Malette and Marie Chalouh, eds., *The Montreal Massacre*, trans. Marlene Wildeman (Charlottetown, P.E.I.: Gynergy Books, 1990). In "Violence, Fear and Feminism: Fragments of a Reflection," Simone Landry argues that regardless of violent anti-feminist

backlash, and despite the cultural double standard which condones violence for boys while teaching girls "to repress it and to turn it inward against themselves," feminist non-violent resistance "must continue in full force" (119-24). Paula Sypnowich observes in "An Incitement to Violence" that, although feminism has made violence against women more intolerable, "every aspect of popular culture implicitly encourages it"; spurring the liberal conscience is not enough but counter-violence would be going too far (128-31). In "The Vicious Circle of Violence," Gloria Escomel condemns violence outright, arguing that to see its absolute abolition, women's liberation must abandon male destructiveness and imitate feminine repression (131-35).

10. Grant McCracken, "A Call to Arms for Women?" *The Toronto Globe and Mail*, 16 December 1991, A16.

11. McCracken, A16.

12. Daniel Georges-Abeyie, "Women as Terrorists," in *Perspectives on Terrorism*, ed. Lawrence Zelic Freedman and Yonah Alexander (Wilmington: Scholarly Resources, 1983), 71-84, 81-2.

13. In her chapter, "On 'Violence in the Women's Movement,'" Ti-Grace Atkinson despairs of arousing an audience of (mostly academic) feminists to armed violence: "I suspect I am making a mistake. Perhaps I am trying to ingratiate myself with you by considering this subject in a serious manner. In fact, I truly believe the discussion of violence as a tactic for the Women's Movement is, at best, absurd. . . . I think that the increasing discussion of violence, as a concept or tactic relevant for us, is a case of 'militancy of the mouth.'" Atkinson, "On 'Violence in the Women's Movement'," *Amazon Odyssey*, 199-211, 202.

14. In another chapter, "Declaration of War," Atkinson observes of American society that "it has been necessary to program women's psychic structure to nonresistance on their own behalf—for obvious reasons—they make up over half of the population of the world." Atkinson, "Declaration of War," *Amazon Odyssey*, 47-55, 51.

15. McCracken, A16. He offers three weak "counterarguments" to women's violence against violence against women: first, "the strong contention of some feminist groups that violence is a peculiarly male way of engaging with the world, that it is simply not an important or characteristic part of the female repertoire"; second, that violence by women would be met with still more violence by men; third, that "women do not resort to violence in the present, . . . so they will not resort to violence in the future." He dismisses all three as being outdated or unimpressive, asserting instead that "the inclination to answer violence with violence may well become a new and quite ordinary feature of femaleness."

16. Susan Faludi, *Backlash: The Undeclared War Against American Women* (New York: Doubleday, 1991).

17. Fanon, 89.

18. Fanon, 89.

19. Michel Foucault, *Language, Counter-Memory, Practice*, ed. Donald F. Bouchard, trans. Donald F. Bouchard and Sherry Simon (Ithaca: Cornell UP, 1977), 221-2.

20. Foucault, 222.

21. Charles Russell, *Poets, Prophets, and Revolutionaries: The Literary Avant-garde from Rimbaud through Postmodernism* (Oxford: Oxford UP, 1985), 251.

22. Peter Bürger, *Theory of the Avant-Garde*, trans. Michael Shaw (1980; Minneapolis: U of Minnesota P, 1984).

23. Leslie Fiedler, "The Death of the Avant-Garde," in *The Collected Essays of Leslie Fiedler*, Vol.2 (New York: Stein and Day, 1971), 454-60.

24. Russell, *Poets, Prophets, and Revolutionaries*, 15-6.

25. Ibid., 16.

26. Ibid., 24.

27. Ibid., 6. The avant-gardist "places himself in an explicit social context and calls the attention of the writer and audience to the inherent social dynamics of their culture, whether those dynamics be represented by other visionaries, scientists, political activists, or even apparently abstract and impersonal forces with which the writer identifies."

28. Ibid., 4.

29. Ibid., 26.

30. Ibid., 16.

31. Ibid., 16.

32. Ibid., 34.

33. Ibid., 38.

34. Pierre Bourdieu, *In Other Words: Essays Towards a Reflexive Sociology*, trans. Matthew Adamson (Stanford: Stanford UP, 1990), 149.

35. Toril Moi, "Appropriating Bourdieu: Feminist Theory and Pierre Bourdieu's Sociology of Culture," *New Literary History* 22 (Autumn 1991): 1017-49, 1020-21.

36. Ibid., 1021.

37. Ibid., 1021.

38. Ibid., 1022.

39. Ibid., 1022.

40. Ibid., 1026

41. Pierre Bourdieu and Loïc J.D. Wacquant, *An Invitation to Reflexive Sociology* (Chicago: Chicago UP, 1992), 172. To illustrate his claim, Bourdieu points to a case study by Lynn Chancer (1987) of "the negative reactions of Portugese women to the highly publicized group rape of another Portugese woman in Bedford, Massachusetts, in March 1983." The comments of the women who marched in defense of the six rapists on trial "reveal the deeply taken-for-granted assumptions about masculinity and femininity as they are socially defined within this community: 'I am Portugese and proud of it. I'm also a woman, but you don't see me getting raped. If you throw a dog a bone, he's gonna take it—if you walk around naked, men are just going to go for you.' 'They did nothing to her. Her rights are to be at home with her two kids and to be a good mother. A Portugese woman should be with her kids and that's it.'"

42. Moi, 1030.

43. Ibid., 1036.

44. Bourdieu and Wacquant, 174

45. Monique Wittig, *The Straight Mind and Other Essays* (Boston: Beacon P, 1992), 19.

46. Ibid., 8.

47. Ibid., 8.

48. Ibid., 3.

49. Ibid., 25.

50. Ibid., 3.

51. Ibid., 32.

52. Russell A. Berman, *Modern Culture and Critical Theory* (Madison: U of Madison P, 1989), 186.

53. Ruth Roach Pierson, "Violence Against Women: Strategies for Change," *Canadian Woman Studies/Les cahiers de la femme* 11 (Summer 1991): 10-12, 10.

54. Ibid., 12.

55. See Luce Irigaray, *Speculum de l'autre femme (Speculum of the Other Woman)* (Paris: Les Editions de Minuit, 1974), *Ethique de la différence sexuelle* (Paris: Les Editions de Minuit, 1984), *Amante marine. De Friedrich Nietzsche (Marine Lover. Of Friedrich Nietzsche)* (Paris: Les Editions de Minuit, 1980) and *L'Oubli de l'air chez Martin Heidegger* (Paris: Les Editions de Minuit, 1983) for deconstructive critiques of male symbolic dominance in Freud, Lacan, Plato, Aristotle, Plotinus, Descartes, Spinoza, Kant, Hegel, Nietzsche, Merleau-Ponty, Heidegger, and others.

56. Luce Irigaray, *This Sex Which is Not One*, trans. Catherine Porter (1977; Ithaca: Cornell UP, 1985), 68-85.

57. Irigaray, *This Sex Which Is Not One*, 74. She would interrogate "the conditions under which systematicity itself is possible: what the coherence of the discursive utterance conceals of the conditions under which it is produced . . . that allows the logos, the subject, to reduplicate itself, to reflect itself by itself," calling for "an examination of the operation of the 'grammar' of each figure of discourse, its syntactic laws or requirements, its imaginary configurations, its metaphoric networks, and also, of course, what it does not articulate at the level of utterances: *its silences.*"

58. Ibid., 76.

59. Ibid., 78.

60. Ibid., 79.

61. Luce Irigaray, *Speculum of the Other Woman*, trans. Gillian C. Gill (1974; Ithaca: Cornell UP, 1985), 142.

62. Irigaray, *This Sex Which Is Not One*, 81.

63. Margaret Whitford, *Luce Irigaray: Philosophy in the Feminine* (London: Routledge, 1990), 131. Irigaray observes that deconstructive philosophical discourse is no less violent to women than traditional philosophical discourse. Whitford explains: "The deconstruction of identity continues to leave women in a state of fragmentation and dissemination which reproduces and perpetuates the patriarchal violence that separates women. Although both Derrida and Irigaray point to the violence of patriarchal metaphysics, for Irigaray, deconstruction seen from women's point of view has not been able to imagine any way of addressing its own theoretical death drive, its own nihilism" (p.121).

64. Whitford, 137.

65. Ibid., 146. Whitford explains that Irigaray's conception of women's reconstruction of community identity would avoid reproducing men's violent formations. "There is a plea here not to imitate the sacrificial violence of men by making other women scapegoats to ensure unanimity within communities of women, but to find other ways of resolving

conflicts. And it is essential that rites be public, social, symbolic—not private, individual, and hidden. Without symbolic mediation, violence always threatens."

66. Teresa de Lauretis's semiotic theory suggests how a feminist cinematic avant-garde might intervene violently in the cultural (re)production of violence without subjecting women to further violence or rehabilitating women's identity. Her project of subversive *imaging* is based primarily upon the notion of "semiosis," and in particular upon the epistemological action of "the interpretant," outlined by that seminal semiologist, Charles S. Peirce. Elaborating Peirce's philosophical pragmatism and applying it to avant-garde film studies, de Lauretis identifies the interaction between spectating subject and the screen as the prime arena for habit-changing interpretative activity or subversive semiosis. With the advent of feminist reading practices, she projects a semiosis powerful enough to resist the naturaliza-tion of patriarchal codes of desire. Given moreover women's entry into the film industry as avant-garde film producers, she foresees a massive transformation of the codification of desire into something quite new—a signifying practice which articulates women's contradic-tory discursive experience as over-represented object and under-represented subject. See Teresa de Lauretis, *Alice Doesn't: Feminism/ Semiotics/Cinema* (New York: Macmillan, 1984).

67. The title of this paper, "Violence Against Violence Against Women," was chosen against the more commonplace "Women Against Violence Against Women" to indicate an emphasis on strategy rather than on identity. "Women Against Violence Against Women" is the name adopted by the U.K. anti-porn group (WAVAW).

68. See Paolo Bono and Sandra Kemp, eds., *Italian Feminist Thought: A Reader* (Oxford: Blackwell, 1991) and Teresa de Lauretis, *Sexual Difference: A Theory of Social-Symbolic Practice* (Bloomington: Indiana UP, 1990).

69. See Elaine Marks and Isabelle de Courtivron, eds., *New French Feminisms* (Brighton: Harvester Press, 1981) and Claire Duchen, *Feminism in France: From May '68 to Mitterand* (London: Routledge and Kegan Paul, 1986).

70. See Radicalesbians, *Women-Identified Woman* (New York: New England Free Press, 1973); Ann Koedt, Ellen Levine, and Anita Rapone, eds., *Radical Feminism* (New York: Quadran-gle Books, 1973); Frédérique Delacoste and Felice Newman, eds., *Fight Back: Feminist Resistance to Male Violence* (Minneapolis: Cleis Press, 1981); Robin Morgan, ed., *Sisterhood is Powerful: An Anthology of Writings from the Women's Liberation Movement* (New York: Vintage, 1970).

71. Atkinson, "Strategy and Tactics: A Presentation of Political Lesbianism," *Amazon Odyssey*, 135-89. "Without this confrontation and a detailed understanding of what his [man's] battle strategy has been that has kept us so successfully pinned down, the Women's Movement is worse than useless," Atkinson argues. "It invites backlash from men and no progress from women" (47).

72. Valerie Solanis, *S.C.U.M. [Society for Cutting Up Men] Manifesto* (New York: Olympia Press, 1967/8); excerpts rpt. in Morgan, ed. *Sisterhood is Powerful*. Solanis calls for immediate criminal (versus civil) disobedience by "dominant, secure, self-confident, nasty, violent, selfish, independent, proud, thrill-seeking, free-wheeling arrogant females, who have free-wheeled to the limits of this 'society' and are now ready to wheel on to something far beyond what it has to offer." She strongly advocates women's mobilization in place of dropping out, since dropping out is precisely what the system wants "the non-participation, passivity, apathy, and non-involvement of women." She calls for mass rebellion by over half of the country's work force that would see the destruction of the patriarchy "within a year." Like

Fanon, she calls for the complete elimination of the colonizer by murder and violent uprising. Violence is foregrounded: "SCUM will not picket, demonstrate, march, or strike . . . . Such tactics are for nice, genteel ladies. If SCUM ever strikes . . . it will be in the dark with a six-inch blade." But unlike Fanon, she advocates only rational violence: "Both destruction and killing will be selective and discriminate, SCUM is against half-crazed, indiscriminate riots, with no clear objective in mind . . . ." Solanis, quoted in Morgan, ed., *Sisterhood is Powerful*, 580-1.

73. Audre Lorde, "Uses of the Erotic: The Erotic as Power," "Uses of Anger: Women Responding to Racism," *Sister Outsider: Essays and Speeches* (Freedom, CA.: Crossing Press, 1984), 53-9, 124-33.

74. Audre Lorde, *Black Unicorn: Poems* (New York: Norton, 1978).

75. This phrase comes from a poem by Adrienne Rich, "The Burning Paper Instead of Children." Adrienne Rich, *The Fact of A Doorframe: Poems Selected and New 1950-1984* (New York: Norton, 1984), 117.

76. Ibid., 108.

77. Ibid., 14-5.

78. Monique Wittig, *Les Guérillères*, trans. David Le Vay (1969; London: Peter Owen, 1971), 85.

79. Wittig, *Les Guérillères*, 98-9.

80. Ibid., 44-48, 52-3.

81. Ibid., 106-7.

82. Ibid., 117-8. "Females who look like women when they are dead" recalls Sylvia Plath's "Lady Lazarus": "Dying/ Is an art, like everything else./ I do it exceptionally well./ I do it so it feels like hell./ I do it so it feels real./ I guess you could say I've a call./ . . . Beware/ Beware./ Out of the ash/ I rise with my red hair/ And I eat men like air." Sylvia Plath, *Collected Poems* (London: Faber and Faber, 1981), 245-7. Both Adrienne Rich, in "When We Dead Awaken: Writing as Revision" (in *Lies, Secrets, and Silences* [London: Virago, 1980], 33-50) and Hélène Cixous, in "The Laugh of the Medusa," (in Marks and de Courtivron, eds., *New French Feminisms*, 245-64) rouse women readers with an image of awakening from the dead, as does Audre Lorde in "The Women of Dan Dance . . . .": "I come as a woman/ dark and open/ some times I fall like night/ softly/ and terrible/ only when I must die/ in order to rise again." Lorde, *Black Unicorn*, 14.

83. Gilles Deleuze and Félix Guattari, *A Thousand Plateaus: Capitalism and Schizophrenia*. Trans. Brian Massumi. (1980; Minneapolis: U of Minnesota P, 1987), 355.

84. Wittig, 94. "The women say that they [the Military men] have a concern for strategy and tactics. They say that the massive armies that comprise divisions corps regiments sections companies are ineffectual. Their exercises consist of manoeuvres marches guards patrols. These afford no real practice for combat. They say that in these armies the handling of weapons is not taught efficiently. They say that such armies are institutions. One refers to their barracks their posts their garrisons. . . . They say with this concept of war weapons are difficult to deploy, effectives cannot adapt to every situation . . . ."

85. Wittig, 95. "Their favourite weapons are portable. They consist of rocket-launchers which they carry on the shoulder. The should serves as a support for firing. It is possible to run and change position extremely quickly without loss of fire-power. There is every kind of rifle. . . . The manoeuvres are raids ambushes surprise attacks followed by a rapid retreat."

86. Deleuze and Guattari, 422.

87. Ibid., 423.

88. Fanon, 42.

89. Fanon, 57. "This is why," Fanon insists, "any study of the colonial world should take into consideration the phenomena of the dance and of possession."

90. Ibid., 56.

91. Ibid., 58.

92. Lorde, "A Woman Speaks," *Black Unicorn*, 109.

93. As we see at the end of "Power": "and one day I will take my teenage plug/ and connect it to the nearest socket/raping an 85-year-old white woman/ who is somebody's mother/ and as I beat her senseless and set a torch to her bed/ a greek/ chorus will be singing in 3/4 time/ "Poor thing. She never hurt a soul. What beasts they are." Lorde, *Black Unicorn*, 109.

94. Julia Kristeva, "Woman's Time," in ed., Toril Moi, *The Kristeva Reader* (Oxford: Blackwell, 1986), 187-213.

95. Kristeva, 207. "Thanks to the feminist label, does one not sell numerous works whose naïve whining or market-place romanticism find the pen of many a female writer being devoted to phantasmic attacks against Language and Sign, as the ultimate supports of phallocratic power, in the name of a semi-aphonal corporality whose truth can only be found in that which is 'gestural' or 'tonal'?"

96. Ibid., 203.

97. Ibid., 205. "In the refusal of the paternal function by lesbian and single mothers can be seen one of the most violent forms taken by the rejection of the symbolic . . . as well as one of the most fervent divinizations of maternal power—all of which cannot help but trouble an entire legal and moral order, without proposing an alternative to it."

98. "If the archetype of the belief in a good and pure substance, that of utopias, is the belief in the omnipotence of an archaic, full, total englobing mother with no frustration, no separation, with no break-producing symbolism (with no castration, in other words), then it becomes evident that we will never be able to defuse the violences mobilized through the counter-investment necessary to carrying out this phantasm, unless one challenges precisely this myth of the archaic mother. . . . Indeed, she does not exist with a capital 'W,' possessor of some mythical unity—a supreme power, on which is based the terror of power and terrorism as the desire for power. But what an unbelievable force for subversion in the modern world! And, at the same time, what playing with fire!" Kristeva, 205.

99. Ibid., 203-4.

100. Ibid., 208.

101. Ibid., 208.

102. *This Magazine* reports that after four years of researching the statistics on violence against women, Maria Crawford, coordinator of the Women We Honor Committee in Toronto, discovered that ninety-eight percent of the women murdered in Ontario were killed by men, that in many cases, they were raped, mutilated and dismembered, or, as one coroner put it, "overkilled." Her conclusion: that "the current system in place to protect women—peace bonds, restraining orders and court orders—clearly does not work." Megan Williams, "Fighting Back," *This Magazine* 26 (October-November 1992):16-18, 18.

103. Jill Radford and Diana E.H. Russell, the editors of *Femicide: The Politics of Woman Killing* (New York: Twayne, 1992) explain feminism's current usage of this term: "Femicide, the misogynous killing of women by men, is a form of sexual violence. Liz Kelly has defined sexual violence as 'any physical, visual, verbal or sexual act' experienced by a woman or girl, 'at the time or later, as a threat, invasion, or assault, that has the effect of hurting or degrading her and/or takes away her ability to control intimate contact.' Underlying [the definition of this term] is a recognition of the dissonance between women's and men's perceptions and experiences of the social world and of violence. It gives women's experiences and understandings priority over men's intentions and as such is consistent with one of the basic tenets of feminism—women's right to name our experience" (3).

In an attempt to break the official silence on nation-wide violence against women, the editors of *This Magazine* notify readers of a "Femicide Register" of names of women violently killed by misogyny across Canada. See Mary Billy, "Those Behind the Count," *This Magazine* 26 (October-November 1992): 17.

104. Moira Farr, "Revenge Becomes Her," *This Magazine* 26.4 (October-November 1992):20-23, 21.

105. Ibid., 21.

106. Farr, 22.

107. Elaine Showalter, "Rethinking the Seventies: Women Writers and Violence," in *Women and Violence in Literature*, ed. Katherine Anne Ackley (New York: Garland, 1990), 237-54, 253.

108. Ibid., 253.

109. Ibid., 254.

110. Andrea Juno and V.Vale, *Angry Women* (San Francisco: Re/Search Publications, 1991).

111. For a sceptical review of this ecclecticism, see Carol Sternhell, "Don't get even, get mad?" *Women's Review of Books* 9 (March 1992):14-5.

112. Antonin Artaud, *The Theatre and Its Double*, trans. Victor Corti (1970; London: John Calder, 1974), 62.

113. Lydia Lunch and Andrea Juno, "Lydia Lunch" [Interview], in *Angry Women*, 105-17, 115. Lunch recalls Solanis when, in responding to a question regarding the feminist future, she answers: "I'd like to see a women's army storm into the White House with Uzis and shotguns and eliminate at least half the population who work in politics. They're killing you slowly—what's the alternative? Kill them quickly, kill them now—before they kill everything else, okay?"

114. Diamanda Galàs and Andrea Juno, "Diamanda Galàs" [Interview], in *Angry Women*, 6-22, 8. Though she aims her ballistic *ubervoice* at men in the audience, it is women's defenceless attitude, she believes, that needs to be most radically changed: "I'm disgusted with the idea of women making themselves invisible as they go down the street—that has to be turned around. The *attitude* is the first thing—whether you back it up with your physical self-defense or a gun is your option, but the attitude needs to be there. Nowadays we're not just about being hassled by one or two men at a time, we're talking about *packs* of men."

115. Walter Benjamin, "The Work of Art in the Age of Mechanical Reproduction," *Illuminations*, trans. Harry Zohn (1968; New York: Schocken Books, 1969), 217-52, 238.

116. Avital Ronell and Andrea Juno, "Avital Ronell" [Interview], *Angry Women*, 127-53, 127.

117. Ibid., 127, 130. In response to the question, "what's 'wrong' with feminism today?" Ronell answers that "it's dependent on what man does. Feminism has a *parasitical*, secondary territoriality . . . subject to reactive, mimetic and regressive posturings. So the problem is, *how can you free yourself?* How can you not be *reactive* to what already exists as powerful and dominating? How can you avoid a *ressentimental* politics? Is it possible to have a feminism that is joyous, relentless, outrageous, libidinally charged—."

118. Ronell, *Angry Women*, 153.

119. Henry M. Sayre, *The Object of Performance: The American Avant-Garde since 1970*, (Chicago: U of Chicago P, 1992), 88.

120. Megan Williams, *This Magazine*, 18.

121. Ibid., 18. Lucie Young of *The Manchester Guardian* reports that one of WAC's tactics was to project huge posters on to the facades of Houston's key buildings. "The 30 posters sport the latest in-your-face graphics and provide facts and figures. One says, 75 percent of women who are raped know their attackers. What is it about the word NO that you don't understand? . . . Based on the credo that actions speak louder than words, this group has so far: Protested successfully against misogynist judges in New York rape trials; Sent TV mogul Ted Turner a 'We are watching' letter about his station's refusal to show pro-choice ads as well as anti-abortion propoganda; Marched on Washington to show their displeasure at Bush's stance on abortion; Shocked White House guards by filling Bush's garden with green tennis balls covered with facts and figures concerning women's oppression and the odd rude rad-fem slogan." Lucie Young, "WACs of women's rights take the battle to Houston," *Edmonton Journal*, 21 August 1992.

122. Camille Paglia, *Sexual Personae: Art and Decadence from Nefertiti to Emily Dickinson* (New York: Vintage, 1990), 2-26.

123. Paglia, 23.

124. See Elaine Showalter, *The Female Malady: Women, Madness, and English Culture, 1830-1980* (New York: Pantheon, 1985).

125. Paglia, 23-4.

126. Kate Millett, *Sexual Politics* (New York: Ballantine Books, 1969), 31.

127. Ibid., 31.

128. Ibid., 33, 35.

129. Ibid., 36.

130. Paglia, 13.

131. Radford and Russell, eds., *Femicide*, 3.

132. Paglia, 36.

133. Ibid., 36.

134. Ibid., 24.

135. Angela Carter, *The Sadeian Woman: An Exercise in Cultural History* (London: Virago, 1979), 26, 37.

136. Simone de Beauvoir, "Must We Burn Sade?" trans. Joseph H. MacMahon, [preface to] Marquis de Sade, *120 Days of Sodom and Other Writings*, trans. Austryn Wainhouse and Richard Seaver (1955; New York: Grove Weidenfeld, 1966), 3-86.

STORIES FROM THE BLOODHUT

*Rhonda Hallquist, Audrey Joy, Jamie Lantz, Kim Lowry,
Cynthia Meier, and Lori Scheer are performing artists living in
Tucson, Arizona, and are the originators of Bloodhut Produc-
tions, a feminist theatre company.*

In the fall of 1991, we began to meet. We knew each other through past
theatrical and artistic ventures. We shared possible themes, searching for our
voices, looking for connections among our experiences. We talked, we argued,
we cried, we listened, we dreamed and imagined and wrote. We emerged with
a series of true stories. These are our stories.

One night at rehearsal, Kim and Esther talked about their friend who fondly
described the bloodhut, a place where women gathered and were waited upon
and cared for; a place where women, set aside from normal time and life, could
talk freely. According to Native American belief, the Bloodhut is also where
women receive sacred visions. The Bloodhhut became our metaphor.

We believe that proclaiming our stories is a powerful and healing act. We
have worked in a collaborative process without the singular direction of one
person. Our vision is richer and stronger because of this. We know that when
we speak the truth about ourselves, the circle of understanding around us
grows.

Perfect Body

Cynthia Meier

I come to the North Rim of the Grand Canyon. I come to watch. I come to write. I come to rest. And an old man and woman are talking about who's fat and who isn't on the veranda and speculating on why.

Now the old woman points out another woman on the veranda with what she calls a big butt. And thank God the man says, "It just fascinates you, doesn't it?"

At nine years old I was on diet pills. I kneel on the floor next to my bed, hand on my heart, trying to slow it down, trying to silence the tick-tick-tick inside me. What happens to a nine-year-old heart on speed? And when does the body forget the torture of years?

We were Sandy and Cindy as long as I can remember. Two years apart in age, we were inseparable. Sandy was petite and dark. I was big and blonde with wide green eyes. On my birthdays, her family came over to celebrate. The bright blinding light of home movies and two little chairs set in the middle of the room. Sandy and I sit in them while I open my presents—little garnet rings and needlework kits. Afterwards at dinner, Sandy slyly places anything she doesn't like on my plate.

We have another, more private game. Whenever we go swimming together or napping together, we play some sort of question and answer game. One day, we are naked sitting in front of my vanity table with the huge round mirror. Whenever one of us gets a question wrong, we have to show our naked bottom to the other in the mirror. My bottom is round and pink. Sandy's is thin and hollow and today she has a large bruise on it. I think that Sandy's bottom isn't much to look at and that she is definitely getting the good view. It was the last time I remember liking my bottom. I was four.

I lost 87 and a half pounds on Weight Watchers, the first time. I was 20. At that time, Weight Watchers, which is owned by Heinz, suggested their dieters eat fish 3 to 5 times a week. I wasn't much of cook at the time, so it was tunafish for me. And since I really wanted to lose weight, I ate tunafish every day—at least once a day. Tuna with low-fat mayonnaise. Hot tuna with peas. Flaked tuna on dry toast. Tuna straight out of the can.

For nine months. 270 cans of tunafish. Is it any wonder that the smell of tunafish now makes me sick?

For awhile I became a certified aerobics instructor. "Fat and fit" was my motto. I was going to inspire other fat women. But these fat women who came to my class would ask, "How long had I been exercising?" and "if I've been exercising for that long, how come . . .?"

Exactly. How come?

Three summers ago when I was home in Michigan, my mother got out some old photos. Now, both my parents are fat. Both my sisters are fat. 5 out of 6 aunts are, 2 out of 6 uncles are fat, 4 out of 9 cousins are fat (3 are skinny; they're adopted), 3 of my grandparents were fat, so why was I surprised to see my great-grandmother in a black and white photo standing in front of her Michigan farm, strong and proud and most decidedly fat? I felt vindicated, freed, proud as I looked at this photo of my great grandmother, yet I heard my mother's voice saying, "See? The fat comes at you from both sides of the family. You didn't have a chance." But yes, mother, I do, just as great-grandma did. I will live life in this body with vitality and strength and gentleness. I have a chance.

There's that word: FAT. Not unlike the word CAT or RAT or VAT for that matter. The F-sound like in flower or fuck or fortune or fun. Not a bad sound-FFF. Although my friend John says all F-words are funny. FAT. A funny word. It's a short word, not unlike tall or black or thin. It's an adjective that describes a noun. Like: "The fat feather floated over the telephone." Or: "The fat moon rose over the tall mountain next to the thin tree." Of course, FAT is also a noun as in "She can have three fats a day," or "This is what a pound of fat looks like." In our world, fat is also an insult, as in, "Hey fatso" or as I cross the street with my bicycle, a man leans out of his truck and shouts, "No wonder your bike has fat tires!" How I wanted to give him a fat lip.

"Warm, sensuous, full-figured blonde . . ." the ad began. I got lots of responses. Men, I soon discovered, had a different idea of what full-figured meant than those of us who have used those euphemisms for years. Euphemisms like "chubby," "Rubenesque," "overweight"—(I always want to ask, over whose weight?)—the list goes on.

But before I met my husband, Tom, I still used euphemisms and "full-figured" was one of them. Seventeen men responded to my ad in the Tucson Weekly. I met nearly all of them. Many were surprised by my size and were politely disinterested and I never saw them again. Some I dated over a period of months. The most amazing experience was with a man who suggested we meet at TGIFridays. I should have taken a clue from that. When we met, he said, "You said you were overweight, but I didn't know you meant that overweight." I burst into tears cursing that I'd bought what was to be our first and last round of drinks, and we sat down to talk about "it." Pretty soon, he was consoling me, saying, "It's okay. I used to be a cocaine dealer." Wait a minute. It's okay that I'm fat because he used to be a cocaine dealer? Since when did being fat become a crime?

In all of these encounters, I learned three things:

1. Never use euphemisms.
2. Rejection has nothing to do with who I am.
3. Never go to TGIFridays.

I have a long history with gay men. Probably longer than I realize. When I was in college, I began to think of my body as a kind of opening—a closet door, as it were—that gay men would pass through right before they discovered they were gay. Perhaps the Goddess was using me for her purposes. I thought it was because I was fat. They were turning gay because I was fat.

I know better now. I know that these men—all 7 of them—were gay long before they met me. They chose me as a lover not because they were afraid of other women, not because I represented a kind of mother-womb, not because I was a fag hag. They chose me because we had so much in common. Because we longed for the same thing. Because deep inside we were ashamed of who we were.

Not long ago I watched my dear friend John get dressed for a party. He stood in front of a mirror for half an hour taking his belt off and on, rolling his cuffs up and down, sucking in his stomach, trying out different poses. And I suddenly realized that all the beautiful gay men I've known with their impeccable dress and three showers a day, smoking to avoid eating, were trying as hard as I was to deny their bodies and their bodies' appetites, trying to create an image which was as false as it was thin.

How can we advocate for gay rights, for women's rights, for any rights until we acknowledge the diversity that comes in human form and we stop trying to look like some ideal which doesn't even exist?

The Nutritionist. The nutritionist is 5'10", maybe 120 pounds with a silk dress cinched at the waist with a silver buckle. She tells me what to eat and why and every other week I return and she weighs me and we look at how well I filled in my weekly menu chart, and we devise new strategies for those weak moments—at parties, after a stressful day at work, when friends from out of town want to go to a Mexican restaurant. I lose weight. For six months, I lose weight. 40 pounds. Losing weight slowly is best. Moderate exercise spaced throughout the week is best. If you're hungry at 4 pm, take some non-fat crackers and non-fat yogurt to work for a snack. No eating after 7 pm. If 1400 calories a day isn't working, we'll go down to 1200. If 1200 isn't working we'll go down to 1000. Are you measuring your portions? What's this candy bar on Wednesday afternoon? You didn't fill out your whole chart. Come in once a week now that things are slipping. You know, I can't continue to see you if you're not losing weight. Intergroup and your doctor need to see progress.

I was gaining weight. One year after the nutritionist stopped seeing me, I had gained 60 pounds. 20 more than when I started. And I was not alone. 95% of all people who diet regain what they lose, the statistic goes. And I bet the other 5% weren't fat to begin with.

Diets. Diets with friends. The knowing nod of the friend. The accomplice. "If we do this together, we'll stick to it." We eat cottage cheese, we take powdered drinks, we pop pills, we cut celery. We know our bodies are wrong. We exchange lists and charts and tips. And we secretly together hate ourselves. We know each other's pain. We know each other's hatred.

As the years continue, our dieting, our dying, our killing becomes more sophisticated. We make long lists of reasons why we eat. We attend lectures. We see therapists. We analyze our "Problem." We spend billions of dollars every year. All the while the hate is fed. While the hate is fed, we starve.

I am so angry. Angry that this bullshit I've listened to my whole life was ever even said to me:

Cindy, I care about you. If only you'd lose weight . . . BULLSHIT.
Cindy, you have such a pretty face, if only . . . BULLSHIT.
Cindy, you have so much talent, if only . . . BULLSHIT.
Cindy, if only for your health . . . BULLSHIT.

Being pulled aside by well-meaning friends, approached by strangers in the grocery store, counseled by teachers, lectured by relatives, talked to by theatre directors, "How much weight could you lose by opening night?" BULLSHIT.

I am an actress. Whatever else I may be in the world, I am an actress. I probably would have been a great classical actress. I lost 100 pounds to play Blanche DuBois. The reviewer in the city paper said I was too hefty for the part. What do you do when you have the soul of Juliet in what others perceive as the body of her nurse? There are a few successful fat actresses. But they are, by and large, comic figures. I am not. Perhaps in classical Greece or in the time of Sarah Bernardt, the great tragic actress who was fat—perhaps then I would have made it. Here and now, I don't even try.

I have a recurring dream. I am on a table and a thin silver knife trims all the fat off my thighs and hips. The knife traces a slender path and the skin is quickly folded over before my spirit can leave. I never wake from this table or stand or move. I am unable to move. The knife continues to trace over the new lines of my body and the fat is neatly removed.

I have many friends who are fat-phobic—who love me and respect me and are fat-phobic. People who would never tell a racist joke tell the one about the fat guy. These friends sit in the chairs of my house and talk about how they don't like these ten pounds or how so-and-so let himself go and is now fat. They sit in the chairs of my house and say this. I lower my eyes and change the subject. When I don't change the subject and say, instead, "If you think you're fat, what does that make me?" They quickly respond "Oh, no. You are fine. That's fine for you," indicating that it's okay for me to let myself go. They do not realize the shape of hate in their condescension.

Last fall I went to the Arizona Theatre Company to see "Ain't Misbehavin'." I had no idea what to expect. All of the promotional photographs were of the two thin cast members. The other three members of the cast were fat. When the two fat women came on stage and began to sing and swing and dance and be sexy all over the place, I began to cry. Sitting on the steps of the balcony in a packed house, I wept to see such beauty, such possibility.

I love to swim. I love to swim in the turquoise blue of warm water. My sister who is really my twin, sits on the beach and reads while I jump over waves with her daughters, my nieces. She is afraid to let anyone see her fat legs, so she hides on the beach where people can see her fat legs covered with thick cloth. I love to swim.

So, I went to a waterpark with these same nieces in Pennsylvania, and went down a huge curving slide. As I slid, I went dangerously close to the edges, not realizing that these slides are not built for my size. My life flashed before me as I bounced into the air and thought of the crowd surrounding my fat and broken body underneath the long slide. When I splashed into the pool at the bottom, a woman asked if I was all right. Stinging with embarrassment, I talked with my nieces later. They said all the kids said, "Wow. Look at her go!" with admiration and longing for my speed.

I love to swim, so I went to a second waterpark with these same nieces here in Tucson. This time, not wanting anyone to admire my speed, I paddled around in a kind of parent pool looking for spots of shade. As I floated—one of the most wonderful advantages of being fat—my 8-year-old niece came crying to me. She was standing in line at a slide when another kid called her "fat" in that ugly way. I held her, crooning to her that I know. I know. I hold her floating in the water, watching the water bead on her perfect body.

I sleep in the nude. Considering I come from a family where we used two towels after a bath, one for the top half and one for the bottom half (because it was dirty), this sleeping in the nude is quite radical. It means touching the folds and rolls of my body. Of waking with only sheets around me. Of travelling to the bathroom naked and catching my body, my body in the mirror. Slowly I begin to know my body. I begin to trust the desire Tom has for this body, my body. I begin to know that this is my body. This is my fat body. This is my own body. And she is perfect.

Lying Down

Kim Lowry

Lying down my breasts are
full enough and point to the ceiling.
My stomach is admirably flat
and my thighs paint
a line of muscle to my abdomen.
Lying down in the dark
I am a pen and ink of sensuality.
I believe that you can't feel my
imperfections in the blackness.
I choose to believe that your
hands are not as sensitive
or critical as my discerning eyes.
Lying down in the dark
I am a poem much more overwhelming
than this.

Dancing for Dollars

Lori Scheer

Economics! Economics! Economics!
That's it—that's why I put it on the line—
I tried it all before—every job that comes to mind!
In just two weeks the rent would be due
—And what about necessities, utilities, food?
With fifteen dollars to my name, I felt I had to play the game.
I put my fear upon the shelf and went to see for myself.

Money, money, money, money. . . MONEY!

Here's the rules of the game if you want to play:
Two-inch heels, at the least, and some lingerie.
Dancing two songs at a time when you're on the stage—

And you better do it right 'cause it's your only wage—
Unless you strike it rich with a solo show
—That's more private, in a booth —
But you're always safe, in truth!
Because there's always glass between him and you
with a slot for him to pass the money through.
Now this is how it works when you're dancing for the jerks.
(I mean the customers, ya know—
the guys who come to see the show)
They go into a stall, drop a token in the slot:
They see onto the stage — they check out what you got!
For song one: take off your top.
For song two: your bottoms drop.
And make sure you always smile —
Cash makes it worthwhile!
It's a peep show
    freak show
You're dealin' with some creeps so
      let 'em take a peek!
            You'll get the cash you seek.

My dancin' name is Krystl. I would prefer not to see anyone I know here at my new job. It is strange; I don't know how I'm able to do this.

But the C.D. system sets the pulse, and the dancing is what I come here to do. — And I do it because

I NEED MONEY

and I've been unable to land any other jobs. No one else has ever hired me the very day I applied. — The lady who hired me has a bachelor's degree in music and psychology. I have a degree in theatre.

First night on the job, I wear a black camisole and black panties. Gigi says to me, "Honey, you're too covered up, you won't make any money." But she's wrong! I make $15 that night. The next night I wear a T-bar and a lace boustier: I make $80 that night — that's because I score my first solo show.

These are weird. Men actually pay money to masturbate while looking through a glass at a naked woman. They pay $10 for every 5 minutes, and of course the more they pay, the better the show.

There are rules. (And I am glad of that.)

In Arizona it is illegal for a dancer to touch her nipples or pubic area. Also, she may NOT insert anything into any orifice of her body.

That means no chewing gum, either.

You have to be creative to fill the time.

On my side of the glass is an over-sized mattress on a platform. And a timer. The walls are mirrored.

On the customer's side is an ashtray, a wastebasket, and a box of kleenex. We can talk through a small panel of holes in the glass, just below the tip-slot.

After the show's over, the dancer changes the sheets on the mattress, and cleans the customer's side of the booth. So often, you see a lady in spike heels and lingerie: donning a pair of plastic gloves, thrusting a roll of paper towels under her arm, marching bravely—ammonia bottle in hand:

going to clean the customer's semen from the glass.

We lovingly call it: SPOOGE....

Money, money, money, money...

The rest of my earnings come from the enclosed stage. Gigi says to me, "Honey, if you're sweatin' you're workin' too hard..." But I don't mind sweating because I've always loved dancing! I like getting paid for it. Of course, a lot of the customers are just here to look at pussy.

That is a word that previously referred to a cat, and NOT my vagina. ...But I'm learning to adapt to the jargon.

The customers are all different. There are regulars who come in several times a week, know all the girls' names, have their particular favorites... like Pen-Light-Man: he always chooses the fourth stall facing the stage, drops a few tokens, drops his trousers, and holds a pen-light over his penis... We are not aroused.

I like the little red-haired man. Very courteous. He bought a $30 solo show from me—after making sure I was unmarried (he didn't want to feel disloyal, he said), then halfway through the show, he started a conversation and we talked about self-discovery books until the time went off. Why is such a man paying women to talk to him?

Some of the men are just lonely. I try to remember that. —To me, a man looks vulnerable with his trousers at his ankles.

But some of the customers are just pigs, let's face it.

I came off the stage one night to find the D.J. kicking a guy out for pissing in the booth.

Once I had a $40 solo show, and the guy asked me to talk dirty to him... I couldn't do it—but I worked my way out of it—I said, "It would really turn me on to hear *you* talk dirty!"

Well, what would you do? You wouldn't work there in the first place? Well, I don't know a better way to raise this much cash in a day.

Once a customer said to me, "Ever seen one this big?"

I hated to break it to him.

I've learned that a man's eyes can be a lot scarier than his dick.

The bald man in the tan jacket: smoking his cigarette while stroking his shaft—watches me, then lets the lights go on so I can see his face as he narrows his eyes and flicks his tongue and makes kissing and moaning sounds... This man is paying my rent.

What is erotic?

Sounds like, "neurotic..." Let me tell you about my co-workers...

I've met some wonderful, bold, colorful women. Several have been dancing for years. But there is only one answer when you ask any of them (and I've asked all of them): Why are you here?

Money, money, money, money...

Once a dancer ran off the stage and threw the tokens at the man who'd put them through the slot instead of money, screaming, "HOW'M I SUPPOSED TO FEED MY KIDS WITH THIS?!"

The job gets stressful. The place can crawl with frustration. I mean, for one thing, your naked body is on display for strangers. You feel like you're under a microscope. It's no wonder several of these women have eating disorders ...and other problems. ...A lot of these women have been abused—one girl came in here with cigarette burns on her breasts! ...So drugs and alcohol medicate the pain and fuel the bravado...which you need for this job. Then you find yourself in competition with the other women for the daily dollars.

Incidentally, menstrual periods can be a nuisance, but we strippers have a way of dealing: use tampons, but cut the string first. It becomes a very private joke. The customers never suspect.

You know, when you spend time with a group of women — all in your underwear—an interesting camaraderie can develop. I once conducted a survey: I asked each woman how she felt about men.
Only one woman said she hates men.
Inevitably, she makes the most money every night. I'm talking $300 a night! She wears a blond wig, has a Barbie-doll figure.
One night this lady had a solo show and the customer purposely ejaculated through the holes in the glass. It got on her back and in her hair. She told me, "Krystl, these men would just as soon piss on you as come on you."

I wonder who's really in control here. Most of the women say they're in control—it's their show, their body. But I see the dollar in control, and that comes from the men.
Gigi says, "I'll sell 'em a peek...ya gotta sell it: ice to the Eskimos or titties in their face for a minute..." I know what she means...you have to play the game...feed the fantasy—and you have to play a game with yourself to play the game with them.
But I wonder: Why do these men prefer this transaction to a relationship?

I've been unable to sleep at night since I started this job. When I close my eyes, I see the strange images from work. I'm not comfortable with this job, but I've done so many other different jobs—till I burned out on each one—and none of them paid this kind of—

At least the rent's paid, bills are paid; there's gas in the car and food in the fridge...and I've seen every dollar of it pass through the slot.

But at this point I'm in constant physical pain. My lower back, my rotators are badly strained.

The art of dancing is getting lost because of the required grinding and pretending to fit the most superficial image of femininity! My anger does not enhance my earnings: nobody likes an angry stripper.

So Gigi says to me, "You're an actress...when you come in here, Krystl takes over. The only time Lori and Krystl meet is to handle finances."

That's a fine plan. But it's Lori's face beneath the drag-queen make-up, and Lori's body within the flimsy lingerie. Lori's sensitive skin endures the daily razor to keep Lori's pubic hair within the boundary of the T-bar which is stretched against the crack of Lori's ass.

And I see Lori's eyes in the mirrors that surround me.

Lori looks tired. Lori thinks: "Men are looking at my vagina for a buck..."

A very old man buys a solo show from me. I'm quite sure it's an uninspired performance; the minutes seem like hours to me. Afterward he says, "Thanks for reminding me what it's all about."

I say, "Mister, it is not about this."

He slides an extra $20 through the glass.

One night I'm home, not sleeping, and a vision comes to me. I see a little girl in a little dress, dancing in a grassy field.

Suddenly the scene changes and she's dancing on the stage at work— the little girl is bending over, about to assume the most degrading position—where your face isn't visible, only your pussy—

and I am shocked.

I know the little girl is me, and I know I belong in the grassy field. I quit that night.

You know, I had never seen my own body or my own genitalia so clearly as I did in those mirrors—I really saw it—an actual reflection of my vagina as I danced and moved.

And you know, it does resemble a flower.

The Women in My Family

Kim Lowry

What I remember most about my family is women who moved things. I don't mean things as in a pencil, or you move that box there. Women who moved lives. Who still move my life. What I remember most about the women in my family is this: backs of hidden sinew bearing the weight and the stories behind the red, red heartbreaking lips.

Story: 1948. My grandmother.

If I can't have you no one will, he said, as he pulled the gun from the glove box. I imagine she felt her heart lurch in her chest and like she was going to float away. I imagine she didn't quite believe it, but she did because she struggled with him and I wonder how long it seemed as she reached to turn the gun around, to resist this 285 lb. man who had raised his hand to her and let it fall on her cream colored, dark light flesh so many times. I feel, but I don't know, that she must have believed that if she was going to die she could at least fight, and she was thinking of her children, my mother and my aunt and what would become of them when she didn't return from the drive to discuss with daddy the fact that she never would go back to him. What I wonder did she feel as the gun went off and the bullet passed into him, not where he had intended at all. Relief? Remorse? Madness? Did she bolt from the car to find help or had help arrived? When they did why did they take her, arrest her, put her in jail?

They put her in jail because she fought back and the bullet pierced his jealous heart. She was stunned into silence in a cell as she waited and was brought to trial and found not guilty, SELF-DEFENSE. Wasn't it obvious? It was not her gun, not her car, not her idea to drive to discuss the fact that NO she would not come back to him. Not with promises to the stars.

See, I heard when the story was given round at first, out of shame, that my grandfather died of a heart attack. I heard that he was so big he could carry his two daughters one on each arm as he walked his family home from the restaurant they owned. I heard he drank a quart or two of milk with his eggs or waffles or bacon and biscuits and gravy each morning.

Later I heard of how my mother, perhaps sixteen, already dating my father, a wild charming boy from a respectable family, my mother faced her father in the driveway. In front of my now cowering, unable to rise, bloodied and bruised grandmother. Faced him holding a rake, tines on the defense, like the claws of a large metal cat. She spit out the words "I'll kill you if you touch her again, I'll kill you myself," till he backed away with perhaps fear or maybe just not wanting it so badly in the driveway, backed to one side of the drive where the pecan tree had dropped its overripe fruit to stain the concrete and crunch like bones under his shoes. And I hear their voices. My grandmother silent but for the heaving of her chest as she tries to breathe with broken ribs through blood and saliva. And my aunt, the pretty one, already throwing up each day, after each meal, to maintain the slim beauty that would be her ticket out of hell, can only weep to one side. My mother's voice, sharp with rage, her eyes steeled to a point protecting her mother as she would later her children.

My mother decided then that no one would ever get her down or hold her back. My mother, beautiful like a swan later on the ice far away from her childhood, with me and my sister, long legs in black, blue coat ringed with white fur in silhouette against the black green trees and we are silent but for the clump clump and kshook kshook of our skates. And you Mother look down at me all beauty and tall and love, would I ever be that tall? And you rise against the black green trees in blue black clothes with red red lips over white teeth. Now I know the colors of bruises new and healing and of the blood and the bone.

Story: 1963. My Aunt/My Mother's Sister.

I asked, Mother, may I have some of these pictures or get copies?

You said, darling take whatever you want—voice dipping low—I don't need pictures. I have her here—elegant finger to your temple pointing out the invisible memory that is so clear behind your own eyes.

Here are the facts as I know them:

My aunt was 27-years-old. She was married to a man 20 years older, currently in process of divorcing him. She knew something he didn't want her to say. She had something (a $35,000 trust fund for her children) that he wanted. She had been on a date with Ronnie Blankenship and had come home—Had probably been drinking—she was found nude in front of the living room bar—her head was bashed in—skull fractured—weapon: metal ashtray—weight: 3.2 lbs.—the house was set on fire—Ronnie Blankenship was found nude with smoke inhalation in the bedroom—my aunt died of smoke inhalation—she may or may not have lived had there been no fire—she may have been a vegetable had she lived—someone poured gasoline all over the house—the paperboy on his route saw the fire and reported it—my cousins were staying with a nanny.

My mother said to me—there is not a minute of a day that goes by that I don't think of her—There is not a night before sleep that I don't speak to her.

My mother's sister was 27-years-old. She was beautiful. I did not get to talk to her. I was 3. I miss her.

Drum Dance For...

Jamie Lantz

(In celebration of the body and in honor of the passion and vibrancy communicated through it, this dance is dedicated to the women.) Beginning with the fast low tone of the sacred Tarahumara drum, joined by the sharp Middle Eastern doumbek drums, and finally the crashing of the African shakare (shaker), the circle of sound is set. With a spinning leap into the center the dancing begins. Moving through the space, the stalking animal, the dervish, Our Lady of the Pelvis, slaps hand and foot to floor, charging in and out of rhythm. Placing on the altar an invocation of the body unfettered. Flirting with the drummers, praising the space, giving body to the face of Women.

That's What Mothers Are For

Rhonda Hallquist

I never feel smarter or more knowledgeable than when I learn something about myself. I rejoice in that learning, which allows me to sort through and understand memories that have remained a mystery to me. Memories from childhood or from last week. It wasn't until I was about twenty that I finally understood why I always thought of my third grade friend, Mary, with such fondness. It wasn't until then that I knew why I'd had a crush on Barb Jones in seventh and eighth grades. Other memories take longer to understand. They float around my head trying to find a home, but they lack that one learned thing that would link them together. So they resurface now and then to appear before me as clearly as if all that time, eighteen years, had never passed.

He is a man. I've been asked not to use his real name, but I always knew him by a false name: George. He is my mother's lover, at our apartment a good deal of the time, because if my mother were to go out, she'd have to leave me alone, which was out of the question, or find a sitter, also out of the question, since she didn't trust anyone with my life. I was and probably will always be the most important thing in her life.

So George. George sometimes ate with us, sometimes cooked for us which was nice if you like the kind of exotic food he cooked. My mom made stuff like Kraft Macaroni and Cheese, and my favorite, Swanson frozen dinner of Salisbury steak with corn and mashed potatoes and a brownie. I loved Kraft Macaroni and Cheese and Swanson frozen dinners. He sat at our table and called to me.

"Come here baby, come up on my lap. How was school today, huh? What did you do today." Up on his lap I sit, thinking at nine years of age that I am too old for this. He kisses me on the cheek, holds me tight around the shoulders or waist. He comes into my room to kiss me goodnight and tells me how much he adores my mother. He always kisses me several times, on the cheek, on the nose, on my forehead, on my mouth. I watch him kiss my mother a lot, too. Or rather, I start to watch them kiss then I turn away. I never liked his kisses. Soon, I learned to pretend I was asleep when he came to my door.

One night, I woke up, as usual, hungry for sweets. I got up to get my usual ration of cookies to eat in bed, and as I slipped past my mother's door hoping not to wake anyone, I see their silhouette against the light of the window. I hear murmurs. Then I'm in the kitchen, trying like hell to be quiet so I can get back to my room undetected. They would be so embarrassed, I think, to find I know what they are doing.

He calls to me.

"Hey babe come on in here."

Suddenly I am afraid. Very afraid. The thoughts flying through my head don't even have a theme, they are simply the thoughts of a child who fears to be found out, to be found.

More murmurs, my mother's voice, slightly audible, "No."

She appears in the kitchen. She glides, she is so gentle.

"Hungry?"

She spies the cookies on the napkin. She touches me softly somehow on the face or head. "Let's get you back into bed." He calls to her. Again I am terrified. I fear he will come out that door and there will be a confrontation, of what sort, I am uncertain. She ignores him. There is nothing I remember more strongly about that night than the importance I feel as she silently escorts me back down the hall to my room, past the now closed door. She tucks me safely in bed with my cookies, kisses me on the cheek and says, "Goodnight my baby, sleep tight." She gently closes my door.

Years later, we sit, my mother and I, in a bar, getting silly on Planter's Punch, and I ask her,

"Why did you stop seeing George?"

After she tells me he was kind of a jerk, that he drank too much, and was very likely connected with the Mafia, she says,

"One night he told me what he wanted more than anything. A threesome."

I try to imagine my mother involved in a threesome. I ask,

"Well, what would he do, find someone off the streets or did he have someone in mind?"

She prepares herself for what she will say now, and I can see I've asked her one of those questions she hoped I would never ask.

"What he told me was, nothing would make him happier than a threesome with me and you."

She told him then that they would no longer be seeing each other and that if he tried to see her or me she would kill him.

Soon all my memories of him made sense. More importantly all the feelings I had about him made sense. Why I never wanted to get up on his lap. Why his arms around me made me uncomfortable. Why I would pretend to be asleep when he came to my door. Why I hated the kisses he put on my cheek, on my nose, on my forehead, on my mouth, kisses that were always too wet.

My Dad Rolled Queers

Kim Lowry

My dad rolled queers.

"Me and the boys," I imagine him saying, "Me and the boys, we waited outside of one of their watering holes—pushed 'em down, kicked 'em around, took their money and had us a little party."

When I was nineteen, I fell in love with a woman. Before that I didn't know what to call it. I called it magic. See, when I would get a crush on a girl in school she would always get a boyfriend about two weeks later. It wasn't like I ever went up to the girls and said "hey, I love you," most of them I didn't even know very well—just something—I don't know—I couldn't stop looking and wanting to touch just a little. As this kept happening, I came up with my quasi-scientific, actually, magic theory that if I loved a girl her life would be so much better. A theory that got me into no small amount of trouble later.

Anyway. Magic. I fell in love with a woman—women.

My dad rolled queers

To Save, To Embrace, To Love

Audrey Joy

Last year, 29 states set all time records for the number and rate of rape. Number: the amount of womyn who endure rape.

(She puts on a pair of fishnet stockings.)

In 1990, more womyn were raped than in any other year in United States history—exceeding 100,000 for the first time ever.

(She puts on a snakeskin leotard.)

Rate: the number of rapes per hour.

(She puts on a girdle.)

In 1989, according to the Federal Bureau of Investigation, there were 10 rapes every hour. In 1990, according to the FBI, there were 12 rapes every hour—nearly 300 every day.

(She puts on a bra.)

Out of 100 womyn sitting in this room, approximately 40 have been sexually abused.

(She puts on white silk panties.)

Rape means your body is penetrated without your consent by a penis
or an object
or a finger
or a pencil
or a rifle
or a bottle
or a piece of glass
or a knife
or

(She puts on a red slip.)

Acts of sexual violence are planned. What this means is that the perpetrator chooses someone and manipulates the situation to his advantage, whether this is days or moments prior to the attack.

(She puts on a black mini skirt.)

Most victims of sexual violence are attacked by someone they know and trust.

(She puts on a wide red vinyl belt.)

Among incest survivors, 33% are runaways.

(She puts on a black halter top.)

Among female drug addicts, 44% have been sexually abused.

(She puts on a black pump.)

Among female psychiatric impatients, 50% have been sexually abused.

(She traces red lipstick up her left inner arm.)

Among female prisoners, 100% have been sexually abused.

(She puts on a black sandal.)

Therapy groups, support groups, and workshops are held addressing the following:

Adult Survivors of Incest and Child Molestation
       Survivors.
Healing from Rape
       Survivors
Parents of Sexually Victimized Children
       Survivors
Male Survivors of Incest, Child Molestation or Rape

                Survivors
        Survivors who are Physically Challenged
                Survivors
        Lesbian Survivors
                Survivors
        Multiple Personality Disorder Group
                Survivors
        Daughters and Sons United
                Survivors
        Anger
        and Grief
        and Death
        and Love
        (She removes the excess clothing.)

My mother's story:

It is 1964. I am 25 years old. I have two beautiful children: Audrey Joy, 3 years old and Jeffrey Allen 4 years old. I do my best to be a good mother. I read Parenting Magazines. Doctors say it is a good idea for fathers to bathe their little girls. I decide it is a good idea for my husband, father of my children, to bathe my daughter once a week. Saturday night–a night off for me from the bathing routine.

"Time to get ready for bed. Time for a bath."

I took a bath with my father. He'd dry me off. He'd wrap the towel around me. He'd rub different parts of my body, as you do when you're drying yourself off.

Eight months. Different variations.

Fingers up me in the bathtub.

Fingers up me outside the bathtub.

Fingers up me in my bedroom while he helped me put on my pajamas.

In my fourth year of life I developed urinary tract infections and uncontrollable vomiting. During this same year, my mother decided she didn't care what doctors in Parenting magazines said. She resumed bathing me on Saturday nights.

In my 26th year of life, I developed the ability to question my family about my past.

"Mom, why did you stop the bathing routine?"

Absentmindedly she responds, "Something just didn't feel right to me."

In my 6th year of life, I developed a chronic fear of being violently abused or killed.

Fear.

Fear of dying in an elevator.

Fear of dying on a roller coaster.

Fear of dying in a car accident.

Fear of being killed by kidnappers.

Fear of being killed by a stranger who is lurking in a dark hallway of my house.

Fact: My father consistently threatened to kill me if I ever told anyone about the things he did to me.

Fact: Ten years ago, my father tried to kill my brother with a knife.

Fact: My father might want to kill me for telling these stories.

Fact: I save my life by telling these stories.

I was beaten by my father.

This means many things.

It means my father leaving a welt the size of his fist on my face.

It means his belt flying across my small body as I watched him lose all sense of control.

It means compulsive crying or horrifying silence.

I was raped.

This means many things.

It means my father's mouth.

My father's fingers.

A penis.

It means vaginal infections at age 5.

Only wear clean cotton underwear.

A new washcloth every time I bathe.

Clean bathtubs.

Only use dermatologist's recommended soaps.

It means my body banging against my bed as I tried to rock myself to sleep.

My father says it is impossible that any of this happened.

My father says he never touched me inappropriately.

My father says there was no bathing or bedtime routine in my family.

My father says he was never inappropriately violent.

My father says I live in the historical past.

My father denies my mother.

My father denies me.

My father is dying of cancer.

How we suffer.

We are crazy mad-women, worse than bitches, although some of us are that too.

We live in secret—Shhh—Don't tell.

We are uncontrollably angry, throwing bricks through windows, tearing schoolmates to shreds.

We have no sexuality—not really.

We are uncontrollably promiscuous or uncontrollably frigid

But we're just out to save our life, our body, our spirit

To save, to embrace, to love.

Last December, I was in San Francisco. I went to Muir Woods with my friend Paul. For awhile, we followed a paved path. But then we climbed over a wooden guardrail and hiked up into the hills.

We stopped at a clearing. I told Paul I wanted to climb further up, so I could spend time alone.

The hike up was very steep. The earth crumbled each time I took a step. I had to grab on to the trunks of trees to pull myself up.

I found a grove of four trees. Each one a different type of pine. I sat in the middle of them, in the dirt, and I took off all my clothes.

The sun sparkled through the needles. It was low in the sky and it hit my body.

I felt the rich black-brown dirt under me.

I felt the trees—huge, protecting.

I felt completely protected, completely safe, as if the inside of my body and the outside of my body were one—are one.

I felt the roots of my body connect with the roots of the Earth.

I lay down in the dirt and felt the Earth hold me and rock me.

Welcome Home

Kim Lowry

In the bathroom at the dorm, stoned, I am bending, though I can barely bend for the fullness of my stomach. I am bending to the white bowl and pushing my first two fingers down my throat, like fucking my mouth, till I vomit and again and again and again until I am sure my stomach is empty and I can suck it back up under my ribs. Only this once—just so I won't have blown my diet—and then the next day and the next. Humbled, I am, in front of the toilet puking in my own hand so no one will hear me. Trying to wash away the cloying smell of half-digested food. Again and again and again until I don't have to suck my stomach back under my ribs—it's just back there.

Then in fear of being found out, I cease to eat. Well, a carrot, half an apple a day and exercising, running in place, basketball every day. I am so thin. I am pure muscle. Muscle that my body can eat since I do not. Organs that my body can eat since I do not.

And what is this, this eating of our own flesh? Self cannibalization. Why? So we can be Madonna with our rotting teeth and brittle bones; hair loss, deadly dull eyes, the broken veins in our noses and cheeks, so rosy?

One day I stood up and said—NO MORE. I am a woman and I have hips and breasts and I am soft though I can be hard and I can hold out the darkness for you or I can swallow you into a darkness that will scare you to death. I am beautiful and I desire. I desire myself, my company. I am seeking a piece of soul and my journey has begun. It was never out there. It was never at the mall or in the movies. The princesses didn't have it, the movie stars couldn't give it. I am not my body or my possessions or my education. I am not my grandmother, my grandfather, my mother, my aunt, my father. I am simply—I am Home. Welcome Home.

FINDING THE MALE WITHIN AND TAKING
HIM CRUISING
"Drag-King For-A-Day" at The Sprinkle Salon

Shannon Bell

Les Nichols in *Linda/Les and Annie—The First Female to Male Transsexual Love Story,* says that the most amazing thing about being a man (Les is an F-to-M) is "the respect."

"I get much more respect as a male."

I kept hearing this as I was getting my surface manhood at a recent "Drag-King For-A-Day" workshop facilitated by Diane "Danny" Torr (New York performance artist and gender critic) and Johnny Armstrong (F-to-M cross-dresser and editor of *Rites of Passage* Magazine) at The Annie Sprinkle Transformation Salon in New York.

As a veteran cross-dresser, I am wondering how this "drag" experience is going to differ from my day-to-day gender fucking. I teach a course "Gender, Sex and Politics" and because for me performing theory is where sexual and gender politics are challenged, I dress as a femme one day and wear men's clothing for the next lecture: men's suits, full leather gear—the snap-up pants were custom made for a male stripper who moved into lace and left them on the rack—and cowboy boots. The Drag-King flyer promises:

> We will teach you simple, repeatable techniques for changing your appearance and creating your own male persona. Moustache, 5 o'clock shadow, bushy eyebrows and flat chest are easily achieved. You will pick a new name, and VOILA! you're ONE OF THE BOYS! You will also learn specific gestures, phrases and tones-of-voice; and you'll be coached on the best ways to convincingly: DRESS/ACT/TALK/WALK/STAND/MOVE/DANCE/ETC. LIKE A REAL MAN!!

As he is doing my make-over, Johnny tells me "Cross-dressing is different when you get the hair on your face; you cease to be a woman wearing male attire and can pass as a man." I got a moustache and sideburns, creating not the kind of guy I like to fuck, but SAM. SAM is a small, tight, SM top of few words and cruel sneers. SAM is not a boy like my more surface male part. SAM is a man. He is in his mid-to-late thirties, modelled on my cowboy twin cousins Harry and Hugh: same sideburns, same moustache, different hat—an SM leather hat. Why? Well, because the only sort of man I'd want to be is a gay man and the sort of gay man I want to be is a slightly (though not much) more masculinized version of Sue, the hottest butch female SM top I know. Gender fucking is a composite activity. SAM is a simple but composite character, a postmodern guy, a blend of my cowboy cousins, homosexualized and urbanized, and a really butch female SM top.

We learn to talk slow: "take all the time in the world, talk low, say few words," instructs Torr in an authoritative low commanding voice. Torr shows me and nine others how to stroll into a room as a man, how to sit, how to hold power, just hold it. It is interesting the different types of guys that we transformed into: in addition to SAM, there are a couple of corporate types, two hippy-like bros who spent some time cruising Washington Square Park, dude friends, and a sensitive intellectual in vest and tie. Torr herself has evolved through cowboy, leather boy to businessman and then the quintessential male: a 1950s Dad/Uncle character complete with fifties suit, tie, cufflinks, watch, felt hat, and cashmere overcoat. Who was Torr's inspiration for the "quintessential male?" President Bush. In the circle of power that we as a group form to talk about being male, Torr tells us about her study of quintessential male power. "I looked at Bush's State of the Union address over and over

"Danny" Torr
Photo:Annie Sprinkle
Annie Sprinkle
Photo: Johnny Armstrong

again. I wanted to see what it was that he was doing with his body so that he could convey a sense of importance and authority while the content of his speech itself was idiotic. (If you remember, Bush came up with such profound words of wisdom as "If you have a hammer, find a nail" and "If you can read, find someone who can't.") Torr tells us that she realized that Bush's "behaviour, the way he uses his body, is opaque; you can't read his face, nothing is given away. You can't read him." And then for the big disclosure: "His whole body is an exercise in repression"; Torr continues, "And I realized this is what it means to be the quintessential man. It is an exercise in repression."

SAM is very glad he is a gay guy. But boy something odd is happening to SAM's cock/pussy. Annie who is in girl clothes (she has done male drag a number times and is hosting this Salon as a girl), smiles at SAM; he melts. SAM is processing this: when he came in as Shannon, she talked to Annie, but didn't melt; now that he is a gay guy, SAM thinks Annie is the most beautiful woman he has ever seen. Well, gay guys have always had impeccable taste in women; I should know, my lover is one. And Annie has always had a sexual way with gay guys. Later, as Annie is doing photos for each of us, she flatters SAM by telling him he's really sexy and that he sort of looks like Les Nichols. SAM is in heaven; Les is his kind of man. Wow! SAM knows he doesn't really look like Les, but boy this gets him grabbing his crotch and doing really sexy male poses for his photos. Annie can make a man out of anyone.

Back to the circle of power: The hippy bros tell us how they had been repeatedly approached in Washington Square with the words, "Hey man, or hey bro want some smoke?" They had passed! Annie, holding onto the extra large icicle dildo that is being handed from speaker to speaker, tells the group about a previous "Drag-King For-A-Day" Salon where the passing activity was to go to a strip club on forty-second and watch the babes. Annie, a veteran strip club performer and a sometimes female audience member, said it was a totally different experience when she went as a guy. She said "these beautiful goddesses were on stage and the men, although they might be turned on, didn't appreciate them." Annie felt "sick and embarrassed to be a man."

Torr had arranged a passing event for us bros. An arts benefit just above the village (in the teens). We head off, occupying maximum space on the walk over. SAM is conscious of being a leather fag; especially after some helpful soul says to him "Man, you belong in the village." SAM knows he has an affinity group over on Christopher, but hey, he is going dancing with the bros. We get to the club, lots of good-looking girls and guys talking and dancing, some good-looking men dancing with one another. People stare as we come in: it is not often that a leather guy, two corporate fellows, everybody's uncle, a couple of hippie bros and fellow dudes, and a sensitive intellectual go out together. SAM looks around, he looks at one of the hippie bros: the one that looks like a young Robert DeNiro with long black hair and beard. Whoa, what a hunk of guy! "Wanta Dance?" Oh, Oh SAM and his partner don't know how to dance like guys. Better find Uncle Danny Torr. Torr in a paternal bored way mumbles: "It's all about holdin' your hips still." Hey, he is right. Uncle Danny gives us the approving nod as he chats with some important looking people.

SAM has arranged to meet his gay lover G.; oh boy, what will G. think of SAM's moustache, sideburns, and attitude? G. walks into the club looks at SAM and says "Ohh boy!" SAM goes with G. for a late night dinner. Two gay men together at a sushi bar on Avenue A. My lover looks like Genet and acts like a blend of Genet, a masculine Jewish mother, prince of the patriarchs, and a hustler. It is the first time in eight years that there has been no sexual spark between us: two tops out for eats. We sneer at each other a few times; say "yep," "nope." The big thing about being a guy with a moustache is getting to perfect that male smile. I sneer at the sushi makers a couple of times. Set them at ease. "Yep, I'm a guy."

Outside, two lesbians, a platinum blond in a leopard skin print coat and a brunette in vinyl, stop me. They pat my arm and ask me questions to which I have to answer more than three words. Ever wonder why really cool stereotypical guys don't talk much? Their voices would go up. "Why, Yeah, I (voice rising) know where the Pyramid is." Oh what the hell, I ask: "Going to the Clit Club, huh? There is a really gorgeous stripper called Trash on at midnight." They smile (actually laugh); they know how hard it is to be a man.

SAM strokes the side of his moustache and thinks 'those sure were beautiful funky lesbians.' They liked SAM; they thought he was cute. Huh, "cute." Okay, so its hard to trick funky lesbians. Let's see how SAM does with your regular kind a guy: Mr. Hegemonic Heterosexual. Mr. H.H. for short.

G. and I are making our way home; SAM tells the cabbie where to go — "7th and West 24th, buddy." "Okay man," replies the driver. G. and

I stop at an Italian restaurant in Chelsea for dessert to take home. The restaurateur (Mr. H.H.) says to SAM "What can I do for you, sir?" SAM likes that. Yep, he's a sir. SAM says "Well, I'll have one of them and one of them." Later, I notice G. halves the pastry with SAM fair and square; none of his usual sneaking a bit more. "Thanks, buddy." G. rolls his eyes. SAM's not his favorite among my parts. We swagger home. I have a plan for G. SAM takes his clothes off, looks at G. and says, slowly because tough guys always say it slow: "bring that cock here." G. does. I've always wondered what it is like to suck cock with a moustache. It's a riot. "Put your cock inside," commands SAM. G. does. SAM turns around to sneer at G. a bit, let him know he is doing an okay job; feeling affectionate SAM says "Hi, little buddy." G: "That's it." SAM decides to flatter G: "Nice Cock you got." G's had it: "That's it. SAM's just not my type." SAM's not insulted. "Oh yeah, your loss buddy." G. tries sweetness with me: "Come on Puggy, take the moustache off; let's go to bed." I do because I want to talk. "What to you think of SAM? SAM's the greatest isn't he?"

SAM had arranged to meet Danny Torr's alter ego Diane Torr a couple of days later to find out how such a hot woman knows so much about being a man. It turns out Torr has been working crossing gender and crossing continents in her performances since the early eighties. Torr has performed all over the U.S., in Canada and in Germany, Holland, Belgium, England, and Italy. Her most recent show (March at P.S. 122 in N.Y.) "Ready Aye Ready," subtitled "a standing cock has *nae* conscience," is a refurbishing of eighteenth-century Scottish poet Robert Burns as a cross-dresser. Torr, who teaches movement and dance, is a Shiatsu masseur, and has a blackbelt in Aikido, offers a weekend Sexual Transformation workshop. She takes people back to the amoeba stage where there is only one sex; she then brings them through evolution to the gendered beings they are today. Torr says that in the amoeba space people tend to become polymorphic: "beings with thoughts and gestures that are not encoded in Western civilization." This is quite unlike the "Drag-King For-A-Day" Workshop which is based on the acquisition of the gendered movements and gestures that are socially constructed in the male body.

I ask Torr what she thinks the Drag King workshop does for the women who take it. Diane tells me that "part of what happens at the Drag King workshop is that women learn certain things: we don't have to smile, we don't have to concede ground, we don't have to give away territory." She pinpoints the moment when she realized that all women would benefit from developing a masculine alter ego and using it in their lives to get ahead: it occurred when she was in male drag visiting a female friend in the hospital. Torr could get answers from the doctor that her female friend couldn't, just by virtue of the fact that she was a man. "These gestures that get results are available to everyone; they are just gestures of authority, that men have claimed as masculine."

Diane tells this great story about Danny out on the town, passing. Danny went to the big bi-annual event at the Whitney Museum. "I saw some of my girlfriends, I waved to them. They just ignored me and walked straight past or they looked through me. I thought "Oh my God, I am incognito, I am in disguise, nobody recognizes me. I am a man. I am passing as a man." Then I began to sweat, I really began to feel a bit nervous because I thought "Oh, God can I pull this off?" But people just seemed to accept that I was a man and that was it. Then the real test came: this woman came around and started chatting me up. I was dumbfounded, completely speechless. I didn't want to talk because I didn't want her to hear my female voice, so I kind of turned away. Then I realized that this was the correct thing to do to engage her even further. She just accepted it as perfectly normal behaviour that I should be disdainful and contemptuous and she continued gesticulating madly, obsequiously. She wasn't the kind of woman Danny or Diane likes. I made some sort of grunting gesture and split."

LOSING IT

Shar Rednour

"Shar!" Randi punched my name out like it was a cheer. She finished drying her hair and threw the towel onto the bed. "I hope you Heartland girls make good coffee."

"Oh, sit down and eat." I smiled, then turned to take the coffee off the stove. She sat down in front of the plate of biscuits and gravy with potatoes and eggs on the side—my standard breakfast after a night of indulgence. And had she indulged me! San Francisco was proving to do me well. I didn't know about her, but I was famished.

"You know, babe" she said, pointing a biscuit covered fork at me, "you still got your hymen." Randi's New York-style bluntness hadn't bothered me until this.

My mouth dropped open "I what? Randi, look, I've been squatting over mirrors since the first edition of *Our Bodies, Ourselves*. I know my vagina."

"Babe," she said between bites, "I've seen and felt a lot of cunts. You still got your sacred shield. You're a virgin."

I sipped my coffee, controlling an urge to shriek. "This is nuts," I said.

"I'm a budding sex guru. I'm the one who tells my friends about their bodies. I teach *straight* chicks how to give head."

But Randi did know women. She was proud of her 32-year-old butch bachelorhood; she'd never dated the same woman for more than six months. That floored me—I was not quite 24, had just moved away from a four-year relationship, and had had a mere handful of other girls.

"I'm...I'm...I've always been... I'm just tight," I stammered.

"You're not tight," Randi said through a mouthful of eggs. "Tight can stretch. Hasn't anybody ever popped your cherry?"

After she'd gone, I squatted over a mirror. My cunt lips don't swing down like a lot of women's. I hardly have inner lips at all, as a matter of fact, just a slightly framed slit and a large clit. I spread myself open and looked at the V-shaped membrane just inside my vagina. I touched it. It felt like the thin membrane that connects the tongue to the bottom of your mouth. Thinking of it that way gave me the creeps.

I slumped down onto the bathroom floor. "No," I admitted to myself, "I don't guess anyone has popped my cherry." The phrase brought back ugly memories of a grade school slumber party where older girls had teased me because I didn't know what a "cherry" was. I'd gotten very upset about being ignorant, though I kept insisting, I knew. I pretended I had to pee and went to the bathroom to cry. My mom heard me from the bedroom next door and called me in. I told her what was wrong and she told me what "popping your cherry" meant. I sauntered back to the bed games and nonchalantly slipped my definition into the conversation the first chance I had.

Another memory flooded my vision: the image of my ex-lover emerging from the bathroom. She had taken a shower after a hard fuck session, and was all warm and wet in her towel robe. "I know why I bled," she'd said. "I'm not on my period—you popped my cherry."

"I did not!" I shrieked like that grade-school girl.

"Yeah, honey, I think that was it."

"Are you sure you're okay? You don't hurt?"

"I'm great." She smiled and went back to the bathroom. I had never thought about it again.

I tried to remember encounters when I could have possibly ripped my hymen. I had never fucked a guy and had never wanted to; I just wasn't much into penetration. I had fucked my ex every which way, then climbed on top of her face and rode into heaven. She'd rarely slipped one finger into me, much less two. The couple of times I had asked for more or for the dildo she would try, but then say she was afraid of hurting me. And although I had fucked a few women since moving to San Francisco, when I thought about it I recognized a pattern: women getting one finger inside me, then shying away. I hadn't minded, until Randi. No one made me want to be fucked like Randi did. She was a seasoned butch—I had begged for more and apologized for being tight. Her voice haunted me: "Tight can stretch."

I absent-mindedly traced my fingers around my slit as the memories kept coming forward to be a part of the scenario like witnesses in a trial. Things noticed but ignored as unimportant until now. One of the first memories of my life is sitting in a pan filled with warm salt water. Years later, I asked Mom why she would sit me in the salt water. It took her awhile to remember—she had taken me to the doctor, I was only a baby, to find that I had an infection. She doesn't remember what kind. She only remembers him looking at my vagina and saying, "Oh, I see the problem. This will fix her right up." Then, he got a scalpel and cut me, right there on the table and sent us home to salt water soaks. What did he cut? Didn't he cut enough?

Randi called me that afternoon from work, "Hey Shar. How do you feel about what I told you this morning? You know, I was thinking about how I lost my virginity." She paused. "I don't know. I think that it's very special that you get to *decide* how you want to deal with yours. With so many women, something just happens one night with some guy. Then it's done. I think you should really decide what you want to do." Her tone softened. "Maybe this is my chance to share some kindness that I didn't get."

I had already been thinking about what I was going to do. It seemed like such a ritual at 24. I began my quest.

I told all my close, and even not so close friends. The women's responses ranged from "Are you sure?" to "That's a patriarchal myth." One sex journalist scoffed at me, sure that I was confused. Only one woman shared her "first time" story with me. She had been with a kind gentle boyfriend who went very slow with the sexual progress of their relationship, so slow that by the time he got around to penetration she was positive that she wanted more. More.

In contrast to the women's responses, my fag roommates were intrigued. Their "How did it feel?" questions were prefaced with excited, "Oh wow's", unlike the skeptical, "oh yeah's" of the women. They instantly believed me, and we sat for hours at coffee shops discussing the pros & cons of virginity loss, and ways to go about doing it.

I did consider simply keeping it. I had gone this far with just one finger, and thought it would be kind of neat to die "pure" at 80. Well, I kicked that idea out pretty fast: I wanted to have more, know more, do more.

Susie Bright, the editor of *On Our Backs* at that time, gave me a complimentary personal ad with the condition that I share every juicy letter. It ran two issues—seeking a woman to "Pop my cherry." No one replied. *No one*. From my contacts with *On Our Backs* I knew that having no one answer an ad is weird. I placed an ad in a local lesbian newspaper; once again, not one response. All my experiences with lesbians regarding this issue were adding up— backing off after one finger, denying memories of their own virgin loss, disbelieving I hadn't lost mine, not responding to my ad. *Women were afraid of hymens.*

While the ads were running I was still dating and fucking. And, women were still stopping at one finger without even a whimper of pain from me. Randi had gone on to other women but was periodically checking on the situation like a big butch sister.

Months passed as did the excitement. My guys stopped asking for my date details with eager eyes. I stopped getting my hopes up. My body was at a stand still while my mind was racing with sexual growth. Ideas, fantasies, goals. When would I get *more!* Following the old adage—I decided to do it myself. Yes, a brilliant idea. I planned a night to fix a nice dinner, have some wine, then take my own virginity. Well....it didn't quite work out that way. After a few drinks, the guys talked me into going out with them instead.

"You wanna drink?"

I had been flirting with her best friend all night, therefore talking to *her* all night. She was butcher than her best friend and smelled sexy and tough.

"No, but we could still talk."

"You wanna fuck?"

"You got money for a cab?"

She bonded with my dog, made conversation with the two guys fucking on the living room futon, laughed at the moans coming from one of the bedrooms, and asked, "How many people are in this fuck palace?"

I put her in my bedroom and gave her a beer. "Three guy couples plus us."

"Seriously? Are they going to be able to hear us. I can hear them." She sat on the bed.

"Yeah." I kicked off my shoes and stood between her knees.

"That gonna freak you out?" She slowly ran one finger down the middle of my chest, then ripped open my shirt with one hand.

"We live for it."

When we got down to fucking she became belligerent with my tightness. She thought I was nervous. She slapped me on the ass and said, "Cool out, chick. Loosen up!"

I told her that I was just tight and to just get over it. She called me "nasty" because she saw how much I liked being spanked. She shoved my face into the pillow, and growled, "Keep your ass in the air, girl, and shut your fucking mouth or your gonna get a whipping." I obeyed but had to moan and whimper as she fucked harder which earned me more spankings.

She jabbed three fingers into me. I cried out. I felt myself tearing—there was a burning and stinging in my cunt while the smacks rained down on my ass. A warm sensation spread throughout my genitals, but the relief was brief because she kept adding more fingers and fucking harder. I was crying, literally, into the pillow while I moaned. More tearing, more burning as her knuckles slammed my clit. The intensity rose with the pain. I wavered on that plane before coming, was pulled back by the pain, then rose to a higher plateau until finally the crest broke and I came— crying, shaking, my body heaving. I curled up and pulled away from her as shudders of leftover orgasm passed through me. I had turned into snot and juice and burning ass and begging cunt.

I bled for just one day, but pissing stung horribly for three.

*   *   *

Randi and I shared a Spuds-O-Rama at Spagetti Western while I told her the whole story. She felt slightly sad. "It could have been so romantic.

A one night stand? I feel bad—it didn't have to hurt. Maybe I should have done it. She sounds like an asshole."

"Don't you see? It did have to hurt." I exclaimed. "She probably is an asshole. She didn't give a shit that I was bleeding. Or maybe she didn't know. I don't care. I got what I wanted and I got off. So many women have rejected me when I begged for more. It hurt and I don't know that you could have hurt me, Randi."

She knew that I was right.

Overall I felt great. I was very proud of my escapade and the guys loved my story. Talking to Randi did leave me feeling a little sad with the whole situation. But not disappointed—I wanted more, and I got it. My body was finally able to catch up with my mind—only for a while, though, it's been a race between the two ever since.

Addendum: A few months after losing it a gynecologist noticed a few jagged bumps on me and treated them as genital warts—with strong warnings of cancer. I was torn between feeling very scared and thinking that this was ridiculous. I knew those bumps. I spent $175 before getting a second opinion from the Women's Needs Center. Phoebe, the nurse practioner, said there was no way she would treat me for warts, "These are your own personal tags. They're great. They're yours."

KATE BORNSTEIN: A TRANSGENDER TRANSSEXUAL POSTMODERN TIRESIAS

Shannon Bell

Gender School

"Sex is fucking, everything else is gender," Kate told us on the first day of gender school, a four part, sixteen hour Cross-Gendered Performance Workshop which was part of Buddies in Bad Times Theatre (Toronto) summer school program. Kate is a Buddhist M-to-F transsexual perform-ance artist and gender educator. Kate has been both male and female and now is neither one nor the other, but both-and-neither, as indicated in the title of her play *The Opposite Sex ... is Neither!*

The Cross-Gender Workshop aimed at deconstructing gender. The two different phases consisted of shedding gender, and trying on a new gender; and getting to zero point and then constructing a new gender. The first phase dealt with gender theory. During this part of the workshop we learned how to build gender cues such as: physical cues—body, posture, hair, clothing, voice, skin, movement, space, weight; behavioral cues—manners, decorum, protocol, deportment; textual cues—stories, histories, associates, relationships; power dynamics—top, bottom, entitlement/not; and sexual orientation (to whom am I attracted?).

This part of the workshop prepared us for constructing a character which we would work on for the following three sessions. During the final class we did a one hour Zen walk across the theatre stage. For the first half-hour of the walk we shed all our acquired gender characteristics; for the second half, we took on our character's gender traits.

The only constraint on selecting a character to perform was that it be some version of the opposite gender. I decided on the male object of my desire: I had done male drag before, but I had never stood in the shoes of the object of my desire: a butch chickenhawk. I had usually done boy: the crossover from woman to boy is pretty easy for a butch-femme and besides when women do male, our male often comes out boy due to similarity in skin, size, weight and energy. This time I was going to do the sort of male that brings me to my knees: the sardonic, gruff, older boy lover in the tradition of Jean Genet, Allen Ginsberg, and a couple of less famous, but no less impressive boy lovers whom I have had the pleasure of sharing with boys.

Hair and clothing—no problem: the striped prison T-shirt that Genet was famous for, leather jacket, cords, police boots, hair slicked straight back. I practiced leaning, hands in pockets like Genet on the cover of *Querrelle*. I got the sardonic smile. I practiced walking in the footsteps of a gay friend who is into young men; modelled his body, his deportment, mannerism, voice; lifted some authentic boy loving poetry, borrowed some of Genet's personal history and took Ginsberg's age and his presence.

Locating myself in Genet's stomping grounds of the 1930s and 1940s, the Barrio Chino in Barcelona, I reminisced and cruised imaginary young men. I spit my words: "There was the French language and there was me. I put one into the other and now it is finished—C'est fini!"; gruffly solicited company: "Got some time? Want to go?" I also recited poetry fragments to the phantom boys of previous years:

> Child of Michelangelo
> Turn On
> Light the world.

Soft hard sphinx, emerald wild rose,
They won't domesticate you.
Glowing defiant soft green,
Excellent Brat.

Dear Chicken

Delicate brown-eyed boy,
Body full of charm.
Mischievous, funny boy,
Big tits of iron.

Funny young boy,
Beautiful bulging eyes.
Funny young boy,
Beautiful boy growing old.

I disclosed my bisexual desire, so common among chickenhawks: "The powerful whores, the rough, hairy sailors, the smooth-skinned boy-beauties, we ate together, drank together, fucked together. God, how I miss them."

I never did fully get the character; I got the form and the voice for the first performance, and as the character continued to elude me I got glimpses of the inside of a desire which, although frequently enjoyed, isn't accepted in this society of same-age, same-class, mirror-self sexual narcissism. I got the sorrow of someone who knows the beauty and knows society's corruption of it: "I saw the beautiful chickens turned off by the state." As Kate was directing me: 'you are old, feel the arthritis in your hand, the burning in your prostate,' 'you haven't scored for a while feel the desperate desire,' 'cruise with your eyes,' 'walk with the weight lower in your body,' 'show us a glimpse of the time you had with the sailors, boys, and whores and how much you miss those days,' 'I want you to go hangout on the Second Cup's steps in Boy Town and watch the hawks cruise the young guys, see how constant it is'—the gender of my character, like my own gender, was dissipating, devolving. Kate kept asking each of us what our character was fighting for. Mine was fighting for the right to be. This is Kate's fight too and a fight she wages for fellow sexual outlaws. Her San Francisco theatre company is named Outlaw Productions.

Shannon Bell as the
Object of her desire
Photo: Petra Chevrier

The Opposite Sex ... Is Neither!

The Opposite Sex ... Is Neither! is a one-woman performance piece written and performed by Kate Bornstein.

Maggie, a goddess-in-training, "has taken a wrong turn at the moon and ends up in late twentieth century North America." Her current goddess training exercise is to allow her body to act as a conduit for seven people who are "neither male nor female, neither here nor there, and neither dead nor alive." Maggie is to hold the gateways of higher awareness open for them as they each tell their own story of crossing gender. The gateways are "no-space, no-time" where truth can be experienced.

There is Ruby, the she-male drag queen performer: "tits, big hair, lots of make-up and a dick,"[1] who is dying, her body ripped apart by AIDS lesions. There is Kat who enters Maggie's body as she is waking up from sex change surgery (M-to-F); Kat, a compulsive support group joiner, concludes that "gender's just something else to belong to." Along comes Billy Tipton, the passing he-she jazz musician, who lived her life as a man because "swing is for men." Billy is dead but has been waiting in trans-space to tell his story. Mary, who used to be Peter, drops into Maggie's body on her way to her surgeon's office. Mary is a devoutly religious transgenderist afraid she'll end up in hell for her transgression. And there is Anaya, a post-operative M-to-F who passes through Maggie as she is dying from being beaten for never passing, for always being outside. Anaya confesses: "I honestly never believed I was a man. I don't think I ever really believed I was a woman. Right now, I don't think I am one or the other." Then there is Dean, a pre-op F-to-M, who at the point of surgery decides to stick with her pussy: "Fuck the penis—who needs it?" Dean had been told by society and by lovers that he couldn't be a man because he didn't have a penis: "they never said it was because I have a vagina. No! It's always about penises[.]"

As Maggie coaxes the no-show seventh gender outlaw to enter her body, she realizes she is the seventh: "Not dead, not alive! Not here, not there! Not one, not the other! ... it's me?!?!?"

Kate Bornstein, in *The Opposite Sex ... Is Neither!*, has provided a typology of difference in gender difference and has presented the spiritual side of that state of ambiguity occupied by transgenderists, transvestites, transsexuals, cross-dressers, and all those between one thing and the other.

Kate on Kate

Shannon: In the Cross-Gender Performance workshop you gave some very right-on definitions of gender.

Kate: Gender is simply a way to classify people. Depending on the time and the culture, there are different criteria for the classification. In this culture, at this time, it is genital. Gender assignment happens at birth when the doctor inspects for a penis. The infant is assigned gender corresponding to the presence or absence of the penis.

Shannon: How does one go about deconstructing gender?

Kate: The first thing to do is to ask the question: What is gender? This is a question that does not get asked; people mostly ask "What is the difference between men and women?" They begin by presupposing a specific bi-polar gender system. The first step in taking gender apart is to ask the question; the second step is to get other people to ask the question. As Maggie says in *The Opposite Sex ... Is Neither!*, "a civilization is more well-known by the questions it asks than by the answers it comes up with." I don't think "What is gender?" is an answerable question. I think the answer is that there is no such thing as gender, other than what we say it is.

Shannon: I really think gender is something to play with. Maybe this is because over the last eight or nine years I have hung with a lot of people who have been playing with gender. What is shocking to me is when you see people totally genderized who aren't playing; gender is such a parody of itself.

Kate: I love watching people play with gender and I think that is great. Camp could be the leading edge in deconstructing gender.

Recently, I have begun to feel the sorrow that comes from oppression based on gender. So I am not in a playful mood these days. I have been playful and I am sure I will be again. But right now I am meeting more and more people who have been crushed not as men, not as women, but as neither. When people have been crushed all their lives for being an effeminate man and then they get crushed for being a drag queen and then they get crushed for being a transsexual woman, where do they go? It gets really sad to see these people dying.

I like the idea of playing with gender. I do it in my art. But in my life it is not as playful right now. I am hoping enough people ask the question about gender so that I am free to play with gender again.

Shannon: I guess it is kind of a privilege to be able to play with gender.

Kate: In a way, yes. The stakes are a little bit higher when you get frightened, if you don't have a safe base to come back to. It can get really frightening. You can't say "Oops, I was playing." Because when you go home at night there is nothing to return to except what you have been playing at.

Shannon: In your performance piece *The Opposite Sex ... Is Neither!* Maggie, the goddess-in-training who finds herself in the twentieth century finds the societal importance ascribed to gender very funny, and the fact that there are only two genders equally silly. Kate, you are pretty strongly female looking: you are gorgeous, have long honey-red hair, a husky sultry voice, large breasts, and big green eyes, I mean WOW. Do you really think of yourself as both male and female?

Kate: Oh yeah. I don't think my breasts are large. You know, no one has said I have really large breasts, but since I came to T.O., about six people have told me "you have really large breasts." I didn't get implants or anything, they grew. It is not like I decided this is the size I want. Do I really think I am not a man and not a woman? I know that I am not a man and most of the time I feel like I am not a woman. I keep one foot in the place called woman because otherwise sometimes you can blow away into madness. There is no other place to touch down in this culture, except among people who are laughing about gender: the drag-queens, the cool butches, and other transgenderists who are laughing and not trying to be one or the other.

Shannon: When you are neither are you a mix of the two? What does it mean to be neither?

Kate: It means I am not bound by the social constrictions of either gender. To be a man or to be a woman for me at this point in my life would be one closet or another.

Everyone I have talked to has conceived some sort of dissatisfaction with gender, be it what they feel they are required to do in this culture, or what they feel they are being inhibited from doing. Most people have a bone to pick with gender in some form. When that dissatisfaction can't be cured by buying enough gender-specific products or when it can't be silenced by the state or the medical profession or by religion or peer pressure, then it becomes known as gender dysphoria. I make it clear that I am a transsexual by choice and not by pathology.

There are more and more people who are questioning gender, and not by dint of Gender Studies Programs. There they mainly focus on what is the difference. They don't study gender. There is one field that is questioning gender, however, and that is ethnomethodology. Kessler and McKenna—An Ethnomethodological Approach (1982) deserves tons of credit. Part of the dedication in the book that I am writing is to them.

Shannon: Do you have a title for your manuscript?

Kate: The working title is *Gender Terrorism Made Easy*. It is an analysis that places gender in the same arena as apartheid, scientology; it places it as a class system, not something that is natural; it analyzes all the cult phenomena associated with gender. I know cults from the inside. For years and years I was a leading spokesperson for a cult: Scientology. I was a big time Scientologist for a long, long time.

Shannon: That is amazing. You seem perfectly normal.

Kate: Four people from my past in Scientology came to the show last night. We all went over to their house after and stayed until 1 a.m., reminiscing. I left Scientology about ten years ago. I was a male when I was with Scientology. I was in sales. I used to go around and give sales lectures. I studied Jerry Fallwell and other televangelists.

Gender is a cult. Membership in gender is not based on informed consent. There is no way out without being ridiculed and harassed. There is peer pressure that is being brought to bear on everyone in this cult.

There is no humor about gender. The only humor is from the people who transgress gender. My book will be the first written on gender by a twentieth century transsexual.

Shannon: You could really popularize Scientology.

Kate: Please!

Shannon: No wait, can you imagine? You could appeal to a whole new set of recruits. A male spokesperson for Scientology ending up an SM Lesbian Transsexual. How Cool.

Shannon: What sort of process did you go through to become a female?

Kate: That is the subject of my next show—*How To Be A Girl in Six Easy Lessons*. I went to a voice teacher, for example. Every person I went to in order to learn how to be a woman, to learn how to act and appear as a woman, took me too far into the construct, too far into the lie, into the closet. At voice lessons I was taught to speak in a very high pitched, very breathy, very sing-song voice and to tag questions onto the end of each sentence. And I was suppose to smile all the time when I was talking. And I said, "Oh, I don't want to talk like that!" The teachers assumed that you were going to be a heterosexual woman. No one was going to teach you to be a lesbian because lesbian was as big an outlaw as transsexual. I actually learned how to talk by listening to Laurie Anderson. If you listen to my voice, I do hit my end consonants very strongly, like Anderson.

Shannon: What about your female mannerisms, how did you acquire those?

Kate: It is a matter of juggling cues. Passing is the whole thing. Cultures from time immemorial have always had people who have been neither one nor the other. It is our culture that is telling them to be invisible. All therapists, as good and as noble as they might be, counsel transsexuals to tell a little lie. They say don't ever say you are a transsexual; you are a real woman (or real man) now. You have a whole new past. People are going to ask you about when you were a little girl and you are going to say "when

I was a little girl." *Transsexuality is the only condition in Western culture for which the therapy is to lie.* Every transsexual is counselled not to reveal their transsexuality, but to devise a past for themselves.

Transsexuals (M-to-F) get a lot of shit for walking into women's bars and into gay men's bars (if they are F-to-M transsexuals). They don't talk, they try to pass, and that pisses off a lot of lesbians and gay men. There is friction. And I think there is responsibility on both sides. It is not just those cold-hearted lesbians or gay men, how dare they pick on another minority group. No. They see people who are lying. I would be offended if some transsexual comes up to me and says "I'm not a transsexual." And they have. I get real offended. I say "go live your life," I can't deal with lies. I have to temper this with realizing that not only does the entire culture say that they are invisible and don't exist, but their therapists for years have drummed it into their heads that they had to lie.

So how did I learn to be a woman? I never did. I learned to be a passing transsexual. I learned that if I am on the phone with someone and they say "Good-afternoon sir," I will take my voice up a little bit higher and say "Hi, it's not sir." I balance and juggle my cues constantly. How did you learn to be a woman?

Shannon: Gay men taught me to be the kind of woman I am now. And more recently, I learned how to be a goddess from Annie Sprinkle: I took her ten hour Slut and Goddess Transformation Salon. And also from just being her friend.

Shannon: You were a het guy until what age?

Kate: Yo, what do you want to know for? Until I was thirty-five or thirty-six.

Shannon: That's amazing. You look younger than thirty-six now. When did you have your change, last year?

Kate: I'm forty-four.

Shannon: Did you look young as a het man?

Kate: No, I looked a lot older.

Shannon: How do you account for looking younger as a woman than as a man?

Kate: Part of it is hormonal. I'm on daily estrogen which smooths out the skin quite a bit. In this culture woman is equated with young, woman is equated with child; it is the wide-eyed innocent look for women. It says child. More exposed skin says child. Longer hair says child.

Shannon: You changed genders and you became a lesbian. Did your taste in women change?

Kate: No, but I was finally able to be with the women I really wanted to be with. I can't tell you how many women I approached when I was a straight man only to find out they were lesbian.

Shannon: What is your taste in women?

Kate: I like really creative women. It doesn't matter butch or femme. I get really attracted to femme—not particularly high femme. I like three-quarters of the way in either direction. This is real sexy to me. I like a little bit of danger. I'm into SM and I am a switch. I appreciate someone who is into switching.

Shannon: Were you into SM as a guy?

Kate: No, only in fantasy. It took quite awhile after I was a woman to come to terms with SM because to me, topping was equated with being male. I had to get over that before I could top.

Shannon: What did you like about being a male?

Kate: My stock answer is I like being able to write my name in the snow. I like the safety. You can walk through the streets with impunity pretty much as a guy.

Shannon: What do you like about being a woman?

Kate: The freedom, the freedom to play with roles, the freedom to play on a whole spectrum, the ability to talk and the ability to listen.

Shannon: And what do you like about being a lesbian?

Kate: The ability to be on par with a lover.

Shannon: Kat, in *The Opposite Sex ... Is Neither*! says "no matter who wins your revolution, I am still an outlaw." What does it mean to be a sexual outlaw?

Kate: A sexual outlaw is a person who breaks sexual, or in this case, gender rules. The prime directive of gender in this culture is, if you are a woman, thou shalt not be a man and if you are a man, thou shalt not be a woman. And in sex, thou shall be heterosexual.

Shannon: The nineties' concept of Queer, Queer Theory and Queer Identity is supposedly more inclusive. Are transsexuals still pretty much outlaws within Queer or are they more accepted?

Kate: There has been a lot of debate recently about inclusion. In Minneapolis and Seattle this year (1992), Gay Day was renamed Lesbian, Gay, Bisexual and Transgender Day; whereas, the big National March on Washington had a huge debate and ended up being Lesbian, Gay, and Bi—not bisexual just Bi—and not Transgender. Apparently, there were cheers when people heard that it wasn't going to include transgender. I was kind of hurt by this at first and I made several calls to the Coalition. They haven't returned my calls. But I stopped to realize: wait a minute, wait a minute, why should lesbians and gays include transgendered people? Not all transgendered people are lesbian and gay. In fact, the majority probably are not.

The majority of people who play with gender are probably straight. I am including male and female heterosexual cross-dressers. This being the case, why do transgendered people gravitate to and expect inclusion in the Lesbian and Gay Community? Because lesbians and gays are a sexual minority and the words sex and gender have been used interchangeably for so long. No, this is too analytical. But then I realized where these two groups, transgenderists and lesbians and gays overlap; it is scary where they overlap and no one is going to like my answer.

The definition of gender in this culture includes the mandate of heterosexuality. To be a woman means to love men, to be a man means to love women. So in fact, every lesbian and every gay man is transgressing gender roles and gender rules. Whereas not all transgendered people are lesbian and gay, all lesbians and gays are transgendered. It is not a matter of lesbians and gays including transgendered people. It is a matter of transgendered people including lesbians and gays, and no one is going to like this.[that]

What this does is call into question identity and it could be seen as making light of the lesbian and gay movements. It's not. It is just saying what it is that we have in common. It is saying yes there is a lesbian movement, yes there is a gay movement, yes there is a lesbian and gay movement, yes there is a transgendered movement. What do these four movements have in common? They fuck with gender roles. Nothing else do they have in common.

I know why transgendered and transsexual people aren't included. It gets back to passing: you have to be a man, you have to be a woman. But my existence within a lesbian and gay community is threatening to the very foundations of that community. Here I am: I am saying that I'm not a man and I'm not a woman. So what happens when a lesbian is attracted to me? I call into question her lesbian identity.

It is a problem for anyone whose identity is wrapped up in a bipolar gender system. It is fascinating that we would pin all of our sexual orientation on the gender of sexual partners rather than a person's age or the sexual activity—what the person does in sex. This is why I really like the SM world. People into SM are pinning their sexual orientation on what they do and not who they do it with, necessarily. This is a tidal wave about to crash.

I have had lovers who would say to me "you are such a beautiful woman." I thought 'Oh, that is so great,' and we'd have wonderful sex. But then I would start to talk, I'd say "I just realized ..." and start talking about some of the stuff I have been discussing here. The lover would go "No, no, you are a woman now!" And I would say, "Well, no I am not.

And I do want to talk about being a boy and playing Davey Crockett with the little boys in the neighborhood."

It wasn't only when I'd talk about my past, but when I would do a play like *Hidden: A Gender* where I played a chiefly male character. The character I played was a villain. He was basically the voice of all my internalized fears about my "gender disorder." I made this character a cross between Geraldo Rivera and a nineteenth-century medicine show barker. He is peddling this stuff called Gender Defender: the pink bottle is for the girls and the blue bottle is for the men. I had studied the barkers; they would invent illnesses. I asked myself what is a horrible name for this illness and I called it *gender blur*. This name has caught on. I see it surfacing in articles around the Bay Area and I saw it in a book. The term came from this horrible character.

Shannon: This is one of the things I really like about postmodernity. No one can hang onto a term or an idea for more than a minute because someone else is already onto it. And often in the next usage the whole meaning is inverted or subverted.

Kate: There is a transgender liberation happening. Leslie Kleinberg writes about it in her book *Transgender Liberation*. Within the transgender movement there is a hierarchy: at the top of the heap are the post-operative transsexuals who pass, next down are those who don't pass quite as well but are post-operative and then down and down and down, depending where you are standing. If you are standing in the shoes of a she-male, that is the top of the heap. At the bottom of anyone's heap is the closet case who puts on his wife's panties when she is away on a business trip.

Sandy Stones's theory, in *The Empire Strikes Back—A Post Transsexual Manifesto*, is that the next step in the evolution of the transgender movement is the transsexual who does not pass, the transsexual who does not assimilate, the transsexual who is not ashamed. Marjorie Garber, in *Vested Interests*, has pegged the position of the transgendered person, the cross-dresser, whatever you want to call it, as a signifier of boundary crossing, as existing at the point of an identity of crisis. Garber proceeds to examine plays, books, films, paintings and performance, and finds that at the intersection of other identities—race, class, nationality, religion, there is the crossdresser.

I think the place of the transgender person in our culture today is the place of the *fool*: the jester, the trickster, someone who can laugh. This is where performance art fits in. It is here that we can find a lot of fools.

Shannon: When did you begin gender performance or performing gender?

Kate: I went from being male to not-male, to female, and now to not-female. I started performing when I found out people were interested in the question of gender.

Shannon: What is the condition of being not-male?

Kate: In this culture it would be called androgyny but still on the male side of it.

Shannon: After you became female did you embrace femaleness for awhile?

Kate: I tried to. I tried it all on. Like my character Kat says:
"I tried on your names, I sang your hit parade..." I thought, I am a woman so I'll buy the clothes, I'll be a power dresser. I was at IBM when I did my changeover.

Shannon: How did people react?

Kate: For the most part supportively. It was headquarters that flipped out. They sent vice-presidents up once-a-week, three weeks in a row, to check me out, to see if I was wearing purple eye shadow and feather boas.

Shannon: What is the state of not-female?

Kate: I'm kind of treading water. I think it is more fluid for me now. It goes into a spiritual space. There is no way to pin that down except to say "it is not here, it is not there, it is not one, it is not the other." That is the whole point of *The Opposite Sex ... Is Neither*!

Shannon: This is a real cross-over between Buddhism and postmodernism because you get to the not-I, the not-gender.

What wisdom have you acquired by living as both a man and a woman?

Kate: I gained the ability to question gender. Being not-one and not-the-other is a space where you can make a lot of realizations. It's what Maggie says at the beginning of *The Opposite Sex ... Is Neither!*

> See—there are these gateways in time and space. They're not here. They're not anywhere... This is no-space, this is no-time. It's where we can really experience truth...

> In my last life as a human, I would look for these gateways. And whenever I'd find one, I'd stay inside it as long as I could.

I constantly do that, I constantly look for this point of light, this point of being neither.

I do rituals before each performance. One of the most joyful times is when there is really no boundary between me as a performer and the audience. That adds to the no-boundaries of the script and the no-boundaries of my life. I like to include the audience in the performance. From my SM background it has to be consensual. So I try to give the audience a role that is okay for them to play. In *The Opposite Sex ... Is Neither!* it is "please witness." When the audience is included and acknowledged, constantly acknowledged for being there, the boundary breaks down.

Shannon: Do you miss your penis?

Kate: No, not at all.

Shannon: God, I would really miss my pussy if I had a sex change. You know if you put a speculum sideways in a woman's pussy you can see the erectile tissue and muscle surrounding the female urethra. It looks very much like an internal cock when it is erect.

Kate: That is what mine is like. What they do for a M-to-F sex change is cut the penis open, scrape out the inside and then turn it inside out so that the outside of my penis is now the walls of my vagina. The head of my penis is now my cervix. You have more sensation in your clitoris than I do because mine is reconstructed from my perineum. It has lots of nerves and is fine, but yours is more sensitive. However, the walls of my vagina are more sensitive than the walls of your vagina.

Shannon: What about your cervix or previous penis head. Is it sensitive?

Kate: Yes, we have been searching and have just found the right sized dildo, which is great because pounding hurts. What I have is a cul-de-sac which just goes so far. I still have a form of ejaculation from the Cowper's glands. It comes out of my urethra.

After the interview I go to see *The Opposite Sex ... Is Neither!* again. I wanted to see Kate channel Billy Tipton, the passing he-she 1920s jazz musician, one more time. Kate can read her audience. As Billy says:

> My wife left me after sixteen years. See, I never told her I was a woman. After I died, and word got around, she swore she never knew. That's a mighty big regret I have, mighty big. If you see her, you tell her I am so goddamn sorry I never told her. Her name is Kitty. [Billy looking straight at me] You tell her that, please. Please?

I whisper "yes," in a sort of inaudible hoarse whisper that carries into the space between her words and my mind. Can Kate tell that there is something about Billy, his voice, his maleness, channeled through her gorgeous female body, that ignites a sense of awe in my clit and continues up the back of my spine and out the top of my head? Maybe it's because Billy is such a mind-fuck, a trickster through and through. Billy begins his exit:

> I had to be a man ... I have been readin' all the newspapers since I died, and they like to make it out I did it for my music. I love my music, but lookin' back, it wasn't everything. Maybe I just simply loved my Kitty. Maybe I was just one ornery old bulldagger who got away with it all.

Endnote

1. All references from *The Opposite Sex...Is Neither!* are from Kate Bornstein's script, copyright 1991, 1992.

GAY LIFE/QUEER ART

Frederick Corey

I

I used to be a gay man. Now, I am a queer. What used to be a private matter of personal relationships, friendships, and enculturation is now a public matter of cultural politics, allegiance to my values, and an examination of the fluid boundaries between being *in* and *out* of the closet, *in* and *out* of the margins, *in* gay culture and *in* queer politics. My *coming out*, as it were, was grounded in a personal experience, and my transition from being gay to being queer was shaped by performance art and my desire to get *in*side my own body.

On Wednesday, December 18, 1990, my boyfriend, Kim, had to go to the doctor's office for another test of some sort, and since his mother was in town, she would take him. I could spend the day at the office getting ready for the final exams I would be giving on Thursday. I was relieved— I had read every magazine in every doctors' office in Scottsdale, and this would give Betty something useful to do.

I talked to Kim in the early afternoon, we did not say much, but then, around 5:30, he called me from the doctor's office. He had to go to the hospital right away. I remember only three words: liver, bone, and cancer. I stopped thinking.

I went home and went into the bathroom where I started to pack an overnight bag: hair dryer, gel, bathrobe, hair spray, wrinkle cream. I heard the front door open. Kim entered the bedroom, closed the door behind him. He was wearing a purple mock neck from the Gap, a pair of faded inverse silhouette Levi blue jeans, London Fog black loafers, a black belt, white socks, and he said to me in a voice that could not have been more clear, more precise, more terrified, "I have cancer."

He started to cry. As I held him, I knew everything was changed. I began living on two simultaneous planes: the first, the survivor, the task master, he who packs an overnight bag, remembers the toothpaste, an extra toothbrush, a list of phone numbers and the insurance card; the second plane, the knower, the sad one, he who now understands everything in life will not be okay, will not be good, will not work out, no matter how much planning, trying, manipulating or hoping, no matter how good things may seem, life is a tragedy punctuated by a few pleasant moments.

Twenty-five days later, Kim died from what the doctor spent four months calling the stress of a new job, from what turned out to be a quick and ferocious cancer in the brain.

And in the spring, I had to come out of my emotional coma and get back to work. I study performance. On occasion, I perform. I specialize in the study of literature as an act of speech, of taking a poem by Gerard Manley Hopkins, scanning it, analyzing it, memorizing it, and "doing" it for an audience. A lot of fags "do" things like this: focus on some delightful obscurity because, after all, we cannot really talk about who we are or what our bodies know. But with Kim dead and suicide on my mind, I could not concentrate on sprung rhythm or the latest developments in semiotics. Such stuff was completely irrelevant to my life.

I ended up in Los Angeles, exploring the world of performance art. What I discovered was a whole new world, an arena of broken silence, body knowledge, political intervention, and cultural consciousness. I found people who, like me, engage themselves with performance, but while I opted for academics, they chose sociopolitical art. I became especially intrigued by gay and lesbian performance art.

II

I wanted a ticket to Tim Miller's *Sex/Love/Stories*. It was sold out. In a big way. I really knew nothing about the show and nothing about Miller, this being before he became one of the famous NEA Four, but my intuition was strong. I wanted to see this performance. That afternoon, I wrote an impassioned letter to Miller begging for a ticket. He left a message at my hotel. A ticket was waiting for me at the door.[1]

Is it pathetic of me to liken my first encounter with Tim Miller's *Sex/Love/Stories* to Joseph Conrad's *The Secret Sharer*? Is my comparison nothing but a hangover from my literary days, or did I feel like the narrator/captain who, quite by surprise, stared at the naked Leggatt and saw himself, his double, risen from the bottom of the sea? "And suddenly I rejoiced in the great security of the sea as compared with the unrest of the land."[2] The comparison is absurd. I was not within the great security of the sea, but rather in the unrest of California, in the Highways Performance Space in Santa Monica.

I sat toward the back on a folding chair, and I watched the people enter. How nice, I thought, to be able to go to a performance with my own people. This is a mostly male audience, a few women here and there, but mostly guys, and all gay. The audience-as-community takes on a new dimension, different from the traditional view of the "collective audience." Group laughter is irrelevant here. I am bored by the interesting nonverbal system of codes that set the space as a theatre space. Instead, I am intrigued by the cultural norms and values *given* in the space: the guys hold hands without being self-conscious or conspicuous; men who might otherwise be nervous about male/male affection kiss casual acquaintances on the lips; everyone touches everyone, and here, it is *in* to be *out*. It is as though we are in a bar, but no, a theatre is very different from a bar, because in a theatre, the audience acts as a collective in the communication processes inherent in aesthetic performance. As a group, we listen, watch, laugh, or sit in silence together, but here heterosexual privilege is non-existent. Maybe we are within the great security of the sea.

The house lights dim and now we are in the dark. A voice shoots from the back: "SEX. LOVE. AIDS." And then a more calm tone, "We're here now in the dark. We're all in it together." I appreciate the ambiguity. "It" refers to both AIDS and the darkness of the theatre, to the complications and comfort of community, and as though the script is a reflection of my imagination, Miller continues talking about being in a dark performance space with a bunch of gay men. "We're sitting very close to each other," he says, "a little afraid of the person next to us. Grab that person's hand to remind us we're in it together." He is building his audience as a community of queer consciousness. The lights come up on the stage.

I am taken aback, not in a large way, but more as a matter of slight surprise. Miller looks like me. Not entirely, but I look at the program searching for a date, and yes, he was born in 1958 (*I in 1957*), and he is around six feet tall, *as am I*, white, brown hair, brown eyes (*mine are blue*), thin, and he must be from a suburb. He has that I-was-born-in-a-suburb look about him. Whittier, California. *Birmingham, Michigan*. I try not to think about it. But for all the theatre and performance I have seen, I cannot get it out of my mind that I have never seen a performer who reminded me of me.

"Stop it," I say to myself. "You are a formalist. You do not believe in subjective criticism. You do not accept post-structuralism. Look for the metaphors. Distance. You need distance."

Miller is alone on the stage, and he begins to tell us his life story. He is eighteen when he breaks up with his first boyfriend. *I was afraid to be gay when I was eighteen*. He goes to work for the May Company, selling wrist watches. *I went away to college*. Miller moved to New York. *I moved to Carbondale*. He has lived the life I wanted to live.

"Time passes," Miller says. "You get a little older. Try to create a queer identity for yourself." Suddenly, I am struck by sadness. At one point in my life, I was going to be a performance artist. *1983. Living in downtown Chicago. Applying to the School at the Art Institute. Changed my mind. Went to get a Ph.D. instead. Time passes.* Miller meets Doug. Tim and Doug. They are still together. Almost eight years. Miller tells us about his coming out, discovering himself, falling in lust, having sex, finding a boyfriend, becoming politically active, doing performance, and embracing his queerness. While I was in graduate school studying SPEECH, Miller was breaking silence.

There's that old saying, If every lesbian and gay person suddenly turned lavender, discrimination against us would cease because everyone would realize just how many of us there are. This is a futile saying, though, because we are not going to turn lavender. We need to speak out. This whole idea of speaking out and breaking silence has become something of a fashion, thanks in no small part to the television talk shows where the intimate details of personal lives are broadcast coast to coast: how it feels to be a woman, silenced by men; how it feels to be African American, oppressed by white people; how it feels to have been abused by a parent, or an uncle, or the local minister. Breaking the silence of homosexuality is different from these other forms of silence, though. When we tell people we are gay or lesbian, we are talking about something that is in no way visible or obvious, nor are we talking in order to *recover* from something. Furthermore, when we tell the world who we are, we invite stigmatization. As a gay, white man from a privileged class, for example, I enjoy a luxurious duality. I can be gay *and* powerful; I can tell selected people about my being gay but appear straight in oppressive contexts; I can go in and out of the closet at my leisure; I can be with my boyfriend at night but be promoted at work. In short, I can be a happy hypocrite.

Queer theorists deconstruct such hypocrisy in the context of "outing" others or being "out" by choice. In the conventional heterosexual/ homosexual binary, to be straight is to be inside the power structure, while being gay or lesbian is to be outside, in the margins, or without power. Diana Fuss critiques this convention, though, presenting a paradox:

> To be out, in common gay parlance, is precisely to be no longer out; to be out is to be finally outside of exteriority and all the exclusions and deprivations such outsiderhood imposes. Or, put another way, to be out is really to be in—inside the realm of the visible, the speakable, the culturally intelligible.[3]

Being out, then, authorizes the insider's view of marginalization, and this in itself becomes a source of power.

This power is more than a point of privilege. For queer activists like Miller, speech is a responsibility. Tired cliches like "the love that dare not speak its name" or being "in the closet" have been replaced by new slogans like "SILENCE=DEATH" or "in-your-face" lesbian politics. Thus, breaking silence through performance goes beyond the personal and into the political.

"I don't have to work very hard to get into trouble," remarks Holly Hughes, one of the NEA four. "I'm a lesbian, and expressing homosexuality artistically is illegal in this country."[4] Here, Hughes is given to hyperbole, but her point must be taken to heart. "Sodomy" laws are still on the books; national political conventions are filled with hateful rhetoric towards homosexuality; many gays and lesbians who are dis-criminated against in employment or housing have no legal recourse; performance artists who discuss openly being gay or lesbian risk having NEA funding pulled. In his promotion of the highly political perform-ances of ACT UP, Douglas Crimp underscores the importance of art that does not somehow rise above obstacles such as homophobia or the fear of AIDS, but rather confronts such fears. Through performances that challenge existing legal and social codes, he argues, art has

> the power to save lives, and it is this very power that must be recognized, fostered, and supported in every way possible. But if we are to do this, we will have to abandon the idealist conception of art. We don't need a cultural renaissance; we need cultural practices actively participating in the struggle against AIDS. We don't need to transcend the epi-demic; we need to end it.[5]

Miller is a member of ACT UP, and political rhetoric is central to *Sex/Love/Stories*. At one point midway through *Sex/Love/Stories*, Miller reenacts a performance that took place in front of the Los Angeles County General Hospital. "The biggest hospital in the world," he says as he sets the scene. "Right here is a big mean iron fence." He tells the audience that as a member of ACT UP, he has been asked to perform a protest speech, and in his meta-performance, Miller reads the inscription from the facade of the County Hospital, a long and noble statement about how no citizen shall be deprived of health or life due to social apathy. The inscription is cast as an irony against the reality of what goes on inside the building, a place where people with AIDS look at "blood-stained walls" and sit on "a hard bench getting their chemo and throwing up from the side effects in full view of all."

Miller uses his meta-performance as an example of performance as political activism and a call for more political intervention from the audience before him. The AIDS crisis must be seen as important to us, he says, using the inclusive pronoun to refer to bourgeois gays, "as it is to shop for a new leather jacket or to make yet another performance piece." Thus, Miller implicates himself along with the rest of us. Everyone who cares about people with HIV needs to ACT UP, Miller says, and "maybe we fags and lesbos can become a model for how Americans can stop forgetting." He acknowledges this is a difficult task, because it is easier to go shopping than it is to remember how many friends are dead, and in the most compelling scene in the performance, Miller expresses this difficulty through a postmodern, panic integration of his body, the performance, and the gay male culture. He begins the scene by saying he has to find a way "to remember AND to be here in my body." He pauses, and then, as he is talking about the bodily experience of being gay, he begins to touch his own body. Within moments, he is disrobed and while his black jeans bind his ankles, his tank top has become a sling holding his hands over his head. His arms are stretched upward and backward, and his head is tilted to expose his jugular. As I watch the image, I am reminded of Guido Reni's portrait of Saint Sebastian, echoed not only here but also in Kishin Shinoyama's portraits of Yukio Mishima, deepening the allusion of bodily vulnerability/persecution.[6] Miller holds this pose motionless for about 90 seconds, and then he talks to his penis. "Come on," he says, "get hard." He then establishes a dialogue between his body and the act of performance when he says to his penis, "Don't talk to me about performance anxiety." He plays the humor of the scene through and then begins a poetic discourse using the ambiguity of the word "hard" as being both a symbol of being a queer male and the difficulty of social consciousness. "Get hard," he says, "because it still feels good to be touched . . . get hard because the world can be a fine place . . . get hard because there's work to be done . . . get hard because I am a queer and it is good and I am good and I don't just mean in bed . . . get hard because it is time to make a move." This entire scene creates tensions between the body as a house of knowledge, the body as a contested zone in contemporary society, performance as an act of speech, and the need to be political.

Miller is in a state of *panic performance* now, and he is making every effort to reclaim his body and let his flesh appear (or re-appear) in the hyper-modern condition. The body is the source of power, agent of change, and topic of public discourse over individual rights versus social policy. In this scene, is Miller articulating what the Krokers call "body aesthetics for the end of the world"?

> Indeed, why the concern over the body today if not to emphasize the
> fact that the (natural) body in the postmodern condition has *already*

disappeared, and what we experience as the body is only a fantastic simulacra of body rhetorics?[7]

Miller is on the stage virtually nude, looking for a direct connection between the phallus and the penis, looking for a metaphor between the necessity to be hard in order to create change and the potential hardness of the male sex organ. The construction of the metaphor is in the hands of the audience, and Miller pulls his pants up.

But the body rhetorics are in motion. The *economic* rhetoric "that would target the body as a privileged site for the acquisition of private property."[8] The *political* rhetoric of the body as an argument against mediated images of gay men as sex mongers. The *psychoanalytical* rhetoric of one man on the stage trying to recover sexuality in the age of AIDS. The rhetoric of *desire: queer rhetoric.* Indeed, the gay man's body is different from other bodies. He knows he is different from others at a very early age. A secret passion, an extra glance at the lifeguard, the electrician, a haunting feeling lurks deep inside. He is six, maybe, or thirteen, but in any case, he is silent. This is, to be sure, the thought that stays in the body.

At some point, the gay man learns language that describes what the body knows. Faggot. Queer. Fairy. Sissy. None of the words is too appealing. The body is excited about what it knows, but the mind is horrified by what the body feels. He looks at his penis. The villain. Cut it off and be done with it.

But the penis is not the source of body knowledge. It is only the instrument. The *panic* point.

As I watch Miller perform, I think: *I shall learn to let my body speak for itself in its own language.*

III

I returned to my hotel and started to think about creating a performance about my life with Kim. He was the start of my life as a gay man, and his death shook my very being into a state of vulnerability and honesty.

Six months later, I was ready. For 90 minutes, I told stories, showed slides, and engaged in a little political intervention in a performance titled *The Death of a Married Man.* The driving force behind my performance was my new maxim, "speak out." As an assistant professor in a huge public American university, I was accustomed to speaking out about cultural sensitivity, the rights of the individual, new conceptualizations of 'family', and other liberal issues, but I had always remained notably silent on the topic of gay relationships. I was a coward. When I first arrived at my university, I felt quite confident about myself and actually considered integrating my personal life with my professional life, but my then-Dean suggested (kindly) I remove all of my service related to the local AIDS project from my file. "I appreciate your work," said the Dean, "but some people in the college, some people in high positions, have an attitude." And one of the most prominent professors at the university told me, kindly, not to mention the fact that I am gay. "My god," she said, "are you crazy? Wait until you get tenure." Fine, I thought, I will be like all the feminists before me: plod along, do a series of banal studies on dead straight white people, get tenure, and then, maybe, I would abandon my cowardly ways and shout: Surprise! I'm a fag and I will write on Queer Theory.

And then Kim died.

I don't know if I stopped caring, or if Diana Fuss is correct when she says, "recently, in the academy, some would say that it is 'in' to be 'out'."[9] In any case, I had a new Dean and I went ahead with my performance. So much for Gerard Manley Hopkins.

"I would hate to be a straight white Christian man trying to get tenure right now," I said in passing to one of the senior professors in the Department. She looked at me as though I were some kind of kook, and she marched off to a personnel meeting.

My performance was a political move. Either I positioned myself as marginalized, searching for my voice, or as a straight white guy—doing what? Shedding new light on the orality of poetry by Milton? I could not even imagine. And would I be tenured? In the politics of academia, a quasi-democracy operates. Committees vote on issues such as promotion and tenure, and administrators dread ferocious memos from angry professors. During the two-month run of my performance, I carefully noted my support and determined without qualification that my greatest support came from straight faculty who practice or advocate strongly feminist theory and criticism. Their support was open and vocal; they brought friends to the performance, wrote letters, talked to people in high places about my work, and let me know that if I ran into "trouble," I could call upon them (and their powerful heterosexuality). A less public, more personal level of support came from openly gay faculty. These were the people who helped me rehearse, move set equipment, and arrange my performance spaces before the shows. The difference between these two levels of support is important: while openly gay faculty were supportive, they were less likely to make a public display of their relationship to me and my performance. The vocal feminists, however, acted as political billboards.

Students, surprisingly, were completely indifferent. They did not much care or even note that their professor was a gay man engaging in a splashy performance about his dead lover. Since I was not openly gay before the performance, I braced myself for a backlash from this largely conservative group. I thought I would find FAG spray painted across my office door, encounter rude graffiti in the bathroom, or hear snickers as I walked down the hall. Nothing of the sorts happened.

The most delicate response to *The Death of a Married Man* came from faculty who are gay but discreet about their sexuality. "Courageous," I heard, "Courageous. Bold, too." That they would find my move courageous (read: foolish?) should have come as no surprise, but it did. I failed to recognize the omnipresent Homosexual Code of Honor. Inside the networks, everyone knows who is gay, who is married and gay, who is repressed, and who is dangerously out. Privately, inside information is shared, but publicly, the Code holds confidentiality as the precious rule. *Time passes. Another friend is dead, and we are keeping secrets.* The Code belongs to a culture different than mine, and any caution offered must be filtered through generational growth. *Time passes.* No one openly refers to the Code. It rules our lives, but it is not discussed. Instead, straw arguments are put forth about how queers should *understand* the dynamics of oppression. To wit, I was told that I was unfair to my parents and to Kim's parents for my open critique of their unwillingness to accept our being gay and in a marital relationship. I was told to understand and accept our parents' inability to accept or understand us, to recognize the Christian messages they have been fed about our "decadent" lifestyles, to realize they cannot hear about the facts of our lives and deal with it. These provisions create a communication labyrinth in which no one ever gets anywhere, no understanding is ever reached, and half the parties are dead and dust before progress is made and lives are shared.

IV

My reading of *The Secret Sharer* is misguided. I am not one who sees Tim Miller (who has a body far cuter than mine, I note enviously) and is the narrator/captain in Conrad's novella. I am Leggatt. I am he who is naked, who has killed a man, who arrives on deck in need of help. I am he who appears to be, for all the world, a naked man from the sea, sitting on main-hatch, glimmering white in the darkness, my elbows on my knees and my head in my hands.

My body fails me. I have the body of a structuralist. When clothed, I adorn my body from the outside-in: my tie must be thin falling into width, my slacks—100% worsted wool—have pleats that shape my hips and give me a little ass, my shirt must be baggy enough to hide my little gut, and the sleeves must be long enough to take attention away from my skinny wrists. I trim my body hair, and when I wear shorts, I drop my socks carefully so that I appear to have calves.

I reveal all of these details about my clothes with tremendous embarrassment. I want to be *inside* my body so that I may speak *out*, but I can describe only how it feels to stand in front of 50, 100, or 250 people and talk about being gay. *Panic:*

1. I use my body as a shield. As I stand in front of the audience, my muscles tighten to form an impenetrable force that protects me against rejection. I try to appear relaxed, but the truth is every part of my physical presence is on guard.

2. My mind keeps on talking. I want to occupy all space and time with language. If I can code everything and explore everything through semantics, I will be able to avoid the truth of the body.

3. My body wants no applause. I physically reject the notion of people clapping when the performance is over. My very best performance is only a commodity. The audience is a passive consumer of my life, and ultimately, nothing has changed.[10] I am angry at the very concept of applause.

4. My mind and body agree on one thing only: I have nothing to lose. *What-the-fuck:* caution to the wind. Become confessional. Get queer.

Notes

1. My discussion of Miller's performance is based on two viewings, the first on 4 April 1991 at Highways Performance Space in Santa Monica, California, and the second on 14 September 1991 at Kerr Cultural Center, Scottsdale, Arizona. All quotes are taken directly from the manuscript, kindly provided by Miller.

2. Joseph Conrad, *The Secret Sharer*, 1912, rpt. in *Classics of Modern Fiction*, ed. Irving Howe (New York: Harcourt, Brace & World, 1968), p. 287.

3. Diana Fuss, Inside/Out," *Inside/Out: Lesbian Theories, Gay Theories*, ed. Diana Fuss, (New York: Routledge, 1991), p. 4.

4. Holly Hughes, "The Archeology of Muff Diving: An Interview with Holly Hughes," by Charles M. Wilmoth, *The Drama Review* 35.3 (1991): 220.

5. Douglas Crimp, "AIDS: Cultural Analysis/Cultural Activism," *AIDS: Cultural Analysis/Cultural Activism*, ed. Douglas Crimp, (Cambridge: MIT Press, 1988), p. 7.

6. Reni has two paintings of St. Sebastian, one in the Museo del Prado, Madrid, and the other in the Galleria di Palazzo, Genoa. Here I am referring to the Genoa rendition.

7. Arthur and Marilouise Kroker, "Theses on the Disappearing Body in the Hyper-Modern Condition," in *Body Invaders: Panic Sex in America*, ed. Arthur and Marilouise Kroker (New York: St. Martin's Press, 1987), pp. 21-22.

8. Kroker and Kroker, p. 22.

9. Diana Fuss, p. 4.

10. I struggled with the source of my anger long after my performance, and then late one evening, I was reading an interview between the poet Carolyn Forche and Mary Strine ["Protocols of Power: Performance, Pleasure, and the Textual Economy," *Text and Performance Quarterly* 12 (1992): 61-7]. In this interview, Forche talks about why she dislikes performing her poems, about how she feels angry when people engage in passive clapping in response to her life's work. I understood her anger all too well.

DISAPPEARING

Dianne Rothleder

There are many ways to disappear. We can sneak out in the middle of the night and never be seen again. At least, never be seen again by our familiars. Being seen is appearing; having a face; facing an other. Becoming one with the dark is a disappearing into an alien other; is losing face, and is simultaneously a re-appearing elsewhere—a re(sur)facing. It is hard to remain disappeared. Every disappearance is a re-appearance. There is always a face.

If we choose to live not in the light and dark of visible and changing faces but rather within the words that emanate from faces, then we instead disappear into alien words. We can lose ourselves in alien emanations, in the words of the other. And still there is a re-appearance.

Disappearance can be forced. Force can disappear us. *Desaparecidos*— the disappeared ones—are lost to the night. They are lost in the press of words. Mute and mutant, silenced and alien. They are changed and re-appear in reports. They no longer have words, yet they re-appear in words—in alien words; in international words of amnesty and threat.

The *desaparecidos* lose their faces and voices. They are replaced, re(sur)faced by the words of others. Stories silently told in the faces of others give place to the missing faces. Stories voiced by those who have voice tell us not of each disappeared face, but rather of all the faces that have been and will be disappeared. Faceless faces disappeared.

Mother disappeared into her bloated belly. She was with me. I was unseen but I appeared in my protruding. She was seen but she disappeared in her protruding. We sometimes changed places, entering and exiting from the seen. But this act came later. Though nearly without matter, I mattered. She was large and unmattered. Her only matter was mat(t)ernity.

And now I have joined Mother in motherhood. I have disappeared into my own bloated belly, into an other whose name I know but who has no face yet. Or, who has an unknown face. Is it the same thing?

There are multitudes of words for the comings and goings of appearance, for the loss of beauty, of face, of substance, of presence, for their subsequent arising elsewhere. Every dusk has a dawn, every death gives life. But what is lost is lost. When it is found, it has changed. New days and new lives are new, are different. They do not belong to the old. It is easy to disappear.

Where do we go when we're gone? What are we that we fit into the crevices of cosmic, and commonplace, sponges? Do we feel the upward pull of capillary action? Are we sucked into vacuum bags? What do the tabloids say? There always is a re-appearance. Was there ever an appearance?

In the dialectic, the resolution is always an annihilation. Can there ever have been something that came before? Or do we live in the always already? Does each appearance depend upon an annihilating disappearance? What was the first disappearance? One might say that it was Eve's tempting Adam with an apple. Ignorance disappears into knowledge; Eden disappears into the world; maternity seals the woman's fate of ever disappearing into the newly born(e) other.

> And the movement whereby each opposition is set up to make sense is the movement through which the couple is destroyed. A universal battlefield. Each time, a war is let loose. Death is always at work....
>
> We see that "victory" always comes down to the same thing: things get hierarchical.[1]

Cixous' binary oppositions pit male and female. In the pit, the cock beats the hen. There are no wagerers because the end is certain, certain death. Meaning requires movement; change gives us difference; difference gives us meaning through opposition; but opposition gives us death. Must we die to mean?

Our death is our meaning and hence we are disappeared before we appear; we are lost before we are found. When we are found, we are not we, we are other. We cannot die, cannot be lost, unless we *are* prior to death. Must we mean to die?

The Cheshire Cat is a smile with no cat. And yet, it is the Cheshire Cat. A presence without presence. Lips without a head.

We hope for recovery without scars. We wish to return as we left. We want no substitutes in our place, no scars or wounds on our bodies, no marks of the journey into otherness.

Here again is death.

> ...see whether you think they speak the truth. They say that the human soul is immortal; at times it comes to an end, which they call dying, at times it is reborn, but it is never destroyed....[2]

Here again we cannot die. We can forget and be forgotten. We can, perhaps, recollect. Gather our rosebuds time and time again, each time thinking that we are fresh, new, virginal.

How much better to be in Plato's Cave, or in a living room in front of a flickering screen? To forget and never put the pious back together—to remain unmarked by the previous other. Can we deny life to the other, or do we merely, ourselves, die?

Where are we when we are in language? In Plato's Cave? In front of a television? On a television, inside a script, reduced to the role of reader? If we are readers, whose words do we read? Who are the writers, and are the words written?

> A text is not a text unless it hides from the first comer, from the first glance, the laws of its composition and the rules of its game. A text remains, moreover, forever imperceptible. Its law and its rules are not, however, harbored in the inaccessibility of a secret; it is simply that they can never be booked, in the *present*, into anything that could rigorously be called perception.

> And hence, perpetually and essentially, they run the risk of being
> definitively lost. Who will ever know of such disappearances?[3]

The text, in this case the reader's script, masks its intentions and keeps them from us. We are not to know what the script is telling us for it tells us things for which we have no voice. The script has an apparition-self, a ghostly counterpart that is present without making its presence felt. The faceless script is given the face of its context. The reader's face and the viewer's are together the face of the script. It is all so normal that we cannot question the script itself; and we do not question the usual faces.

A silent script is haunting all the world, the script of capitalism. The script of phallogocapitalcentrism. We speak with the most expensive, and yet efficient phalluses. (Can we write the word "penises"?) Streamlined for deep, quick penetration, today's "penises" are ready for anything. What is the pleasure of the other? The "penis" with its capital says "I".

The microphone engorges the smallest voices. Voice is no longer immediate. The phallomike mediates between the small voices and the large audience. Mass penetration.

> Many women find it tempting to build up credibility in this still-
> masculinized area of political discussion [international relations] by
> lowering their voices an octave, adjusting their body postures and
> demonstrating that they can talk 'boy's talk' as well as their male
> colleagues. One result of women not being able to speak out is that we
> may have an inaccurate understanding of how power relations be-
> tween countries are created and perpetuated. Silence has made us
> dumb.[4]

When there is no phallomike to masculinize our voices, we must adopt other strategies in order to be heard, in order to speak. The phallomike is swallowed, is internalized. We overcome "penis envy" by lowering our voices, by consuming phallomikes. "Penis envy" is the desire to be heard, to speak for ourselves, to stop being dumb.

The phallomikes take our voices from us and use them against us. Our newly alienated voices, which are not our voices at all, speak words which are the words of others. Our voices are made to sell products or calm unruly customers. Our voices lie and are lies. There is no truth in the phallomikes. No truth in the lower octave.

There is, instead, a script. A writing that is other, that is read through the phallomike. But the phallomike is unseen, unremarked.

The reading mouth in this script is "vaginal". "Penises" do not have to speak directly, they mediate by paying others to speak. More subtly, they can ventriloquize from within and from without. The phallomikes are everywhere. Mouths mouth the words placed in them, or with guns (substitutes for "penises") in their backs, mouths mouth the words around them. And we are all convinced that we speak the truth, the unmediated truth.

> In our culture, the notions of "science," "rationality," "Objectivity," and "truth" are bound up with one another. Science is thought of as offering "hard," "objective" truth: truth as correspondence to reality, the only sort of truth worthy of the name.
>
> People in the humanities...either describe themselves as concerned with "value" as opposed to facts, or as developing and inculcating habits of "critical reflection."
>
> Neither sort of rhetoric is very satisfactory.[5]

As Rorty implies, "penises" have tried very hard to keep the world split. Hard "penises" versus "vaginas" and soft "penises". The soft "penises" want to be hard, the softer "vaginas" want it even more. Being good consumers, both "buy into" the hard rhetoric.

Yet all this penetration, all this purchasing, leads us not unto satisfaction; rather it leads to non-orgasmic death. The death of the soft self in the attempt to harden, to be hard and factual, is the precursor to rigor mortis. Only after death can we truly be hard.

In an attempt to save "rational" from rigor mortis, Rorty writes:

> In this sense, the word ["rational"] means something like "sane" or "reasonable" rather than "methodical." It names a set of moral virtues: tolerance, respect for the opinions of those around one, willingness to listen, reliance on persuasionn rather than force. These are the virtues which members of a civilized society must possess if a civilized society is to endure. In this sense of "rational," the word means something more like "civilized" than like "methodical." When so construed, the distinction between the rational and the irrational has nothing in particular to do with the difference between the arts and the sciences. On this construction, to be rational is simply to discuss any topic— religious, literary, or scientific—in a way which eschews dogmatism, defensiveness, and righteous indignation.[6]

The new rationality would require care of the environment, "respect for the opinions of those around one." The penetrators would have to listen to the words of the penetrated. Yet all is not won. "[R]eliance on persuasion rather than force" is not a solution. Persuasion is penetration. Persuaders use their own words, their own phallogi, to convince those who are to be persuaded. To overcome (*vince*) with (*con*). Together, we will find that truth wins out in the end. Both sides come together in the truth. Hard becomes soft for a time during the debate, but regains the firmament through truth. Orgasmic understanding sends us rocketing skyward.

And all the while that the persuaders are persuading, they will be "civilized." They will "discuss any topic—religious, literary, or scientific—in a way which eschews dogmatism...".[7]

If we re-call Derrida's words about hidden and untouchable implications of texts, then perhaps we shall become very much afraid of civilized, normal conversational intercourse.

Much can happen in verbal intercourse. We can be impregnated with alien words whose presence is undetectable but effective. We cannot control this presence within us, we cannot abort it, for we cannot know of its presence.

Any attempt at "birth control," at self-defense, will be taken as antisocial, uncivilized, irrational. In a word, we shall become, once again, hysterical females—women with uteruses that can be impregnated by alien-presences.

To defend ourselves from civilized persuasion, we must silence ourselves, make ourselves dumb. We cannot listen to persuasion; we cannot respond to persuasion.

> We are calling this next position *subjectivism or subjective knowing.* Although this new view of knowledge is a revolutionary step, there are remnants of dichotomous and absolutist thinking in the subjectivists' assumptions about truth. In fact, subjectivism is dualistic in the sense that there is still the conviction that there are right answers; the fountain of truth has simply shifted locale. Truth now resides within the person and can negate answers that the outside world supplies.[8]

If we can make ourselves into gushing fountains of truth, if we can stop up the gushing phallogocapitalcentrists, perhaps we have a new beginning, a way to re-create ourselves, to be our own *arche*. But we must spit out the phallomikes, and we must raise our voices to their highest, shrillest peaks. Still, there is this dueling dualism.

> Both humanists and the public hanker after rationality in the first, stronger sense of the term: a sense which is associated with objective truth, correspondence to reality, and method, and criteria. We should not try to satisfy this hankering, but rather try to eradicate it.[9]

The desire for hard penetration must be "eradicated." In its place we shall situate a desire for persuasion, for soft, unfelt penetration. The sharper the knife, the cleaner the wound and the less the pain. What do we feel when we are in language?

In the language of the other, we feel nothing, nothing of our own. We are not responsible for we have no feelings at all. We have only the script of the phallogocapitalcentrists and their phallomikes.

In *Gender, Identity and the Production of Meaning*, Tamsin Lorraine suggests that perhaps we may not be able to avoid completely the language of the other. Lorraine describes "two poles that represent 'pure' femininity and 'pure' masculinity."[10] Of the feminine pole, she writes:

> The purely and eternally feminine is chaotic flux. It is life in its concrete specificity—so concrete that it escapes all attempts to characterize it via general categories....It is beyond language, beyond all attempts to label, describe, or even point it out....There can be no purely feminine self: Such a self would be completely unable to distinguish itself from the life around it. It would be dissolved into a chaotic flux of life that pulsated along with no beginning, middle, or end.[11]

Of the "masculine pole" Lorraine writes:

> The purely and eternally masculine is changeless, eternal harmonic order. It is a complete, self-sufficient, completely rational map of the universe in which everything and everyone has its unique place plotted out for all time....It is life made perfect, rendered completely intelligible and rational....There can be no purely masculine self: Such a self would be motionless; being perfect, it would not need to change.[12]

Lorraine characterizes the self-strategy of the feminine as "based in connectedness" while that of the masculine "is based on opposition".[13] Neither strategy can be pursued in its pure form just as neither gender pole can exist in its pure form. Yet these are the stories we have inherited, and all power seems to be doled out based on the perceived worth of these apocryphal poles.

Power prefers the hard, the rational, the masculine and it rewards those who remain on the rational side of the continuum. Perhaps the only concession to the feminine that the masculine makes is to be flexible enough to humor the feminine. One can hear in the background an infinity of "yes, dear"s and "whatever you say, dear"s. There is in this response a pretense of flexibility, of agreeableness. And yet it is power that wins out in the end. It is power that holds rationality and truth, and to be removed from these is to be in the realm of falsehood.

Rorty's strategy of persuasion simply tugs those on the feminine side over to the masculine side. Truth will out in the end.

Even to write of the possibility of walking away from the rational is to experience a strong sense of guilt and stupidity. Guilt because to write this way is to betray the truth we worship, and stupidity because truth is obviously true and rationality is obviously rational, and neither can be denied.

This is the language of the other, and I cannot be in my own language. My own language is false even to my ears.

What happens when we have no language of our own? In discussing Blanchot's *Death Sentence*, Derrida writes:

> She is a translator whose mother tongue is a foreign language—a Slavic language—that he doesn't know very well. When, from time to time, he wants to say irresponsible things to her, things that, as he says, do not put him under any obligation—when he wants to have fun or say foolish things to her that are not binding on him—he speaks to her in her language. At that moment he is irresponsible, because it is the other's language. He can say anything at all, since he does not assume responsibility for what he says.[14]

Blanchot's male narrator is softened when he wants to be by speaking her language. He is absolved of responsibility to the truth, to the rational, to the serious, by moving from what is his own into what is alien.[15] Does she ever have her own language? Is she ever responsible for what she says? As a translator, she has no single language. She is ever betwixt and between.

The power to switch languages, to absolve oneself of the duty to truth, of the duty to the other, is his power. He can move from the masculine, rational pole to the other without compromising his masculinity. Power allows for abuse. Impotence allows only for being abused.

> And it is true that I too felt irresponsible in this other language, so unfamiliar to me; and this unreal stammering, of expressions that were more or less invented, and whose meaning flitted past, far away from my mind drew from me things I never would have said, or thought, or even left unsaid in real words....I offered to marry her at least twice, which proved how fictitious my words were, since I had an aversion to marriage...but in her language I married her.[16]

In this alien other language, he can promise without meaning to fufill his promise. He is not to be taken seriously in this other language. He does not know what his half-invented words mean, if they mean anything at all. And when the words mean something, he does not mean the same thing. In this language, he is split, and his self-division gives him power to play. He can still re-join himself and mean what his words mean once again.

This separation of meaning perhaps gives us hope. That he can mean something other than his words suggests that there is escape from the language of the other, but all that Blanchot offers here is an escape from responsibility into the "feminine" irrational babble-speak.

Escape from responsibility is a disappearance, a disappearance into what has never appeared. Responsibility is the ability to respond, to answer, to be trusted to act in turn. In fleeing responsibility, Blanchot's male narrator avoids this duty to follow his words with deeds. He does not know his words, is alien to his words, and hence he cannot act, does not know how to act.

She is always in an alien language. Her words are not hers, not of her making. She merely takes the words of others and changes them while keeping them somewhat the same. She is not given the chance to make her own words in any language. She is never responsible, never needs to respond, never owes, cannot promise. She is not socially present. There is an absence behind her words, an absence that cannot be a disappearance because there never is a presence.

> Woman has no gaze, no discourse for her specific specularization that would allow her to identify with herself (as same)—to return into the self—or break free of the natural specular process that now holds her—to get out of the self....In her case "I" never equals "I," and she is only that individual will that the master takes possession of, that resisting

> remainder of a corporeality to which his passion for sameness is still
> sensitive, or again his double, the lining of his coat....And her work in
> the service of another, of that male Other, ensures the ineffectiveness
> of any desire that is specifically hers.[17]

Hegel's Antigone, for Irigaray, is a wordless absence, a coat lining for a man's coat. She is the inner portion of the coat, the part closest to his body, most molded by his body. She cannot shape herself because she cannot be held responsible, she cannot be stiff, she cannot hold a shape.

The male Other's body shapes her, forces her to serve and protect—his body is protected from the harsh fabric of the coat, and the coat is protected form the abrasions caused by his body. She is the smooth lining between two harshnesses. She is doubly abraded, doubly misshapen. She erodes and can be replaced by another lining.

As a coat lining, she cannot hold her own shape. She is soft and smooth, nurturing, and hidden. She is under the coat, is only glimpsed as he doffs his coat in the entryway. She is hanged in a closet, thrown over the back of a chair, and left to be silent near the doorway. She does not enter the party.

Because she is shaped, because she does not and cannot shape herself, she is not responsible, but is only responsive. She does as she is told, she does not tell. Silent she sits shaped by the male Other.

> [T]he way in which a woman experiences and responds to domestic
> violence will depend on the ways of understanding it to which she has
> access. This will involve her self-image and conceptions of femininity
> and her beliefs about masculinity and family life. If she sees men as
> naturally violent or herself as responsible for provoking violence then
> she is unlikely to see it as an unacceptable exercise of illegitimate power
> which cannot be tolerated.[18]

If her conceptions and beliefs are shaped as a coat lining is shaped, she will bend to his will. She can see herself as responsible for her physical pain and psychic terror, but she cannot see herself as a responsible, capable agent. She cannot carry out tasks, she cannot sign contracts. She is completely manipulable. She is victim and she is held responsible for her victimization and she is irresponsible for all else.

Woman is absent from herself, is absent from her own language. She appears in the language of the male Other, but not as herself. She is other in this other language. Her appearance is distorted in the funhouse mirror of otherness. It is an alien world of eerie shapes, misshapen bodies, distorted images. Is there a true world? A real presence?

Even as she is absent, is not appeared, is not responsible, yet she is still held responsible for her situation. She has been complicit in her victimization, she has tempted, has deceived. She does not follow the rules of logic. She contradicts herself.

She is responsible for her condition; she is not responsible and so cannot be trusted; she is merely responsive as a coat lining; she is frigid.

How can she speak?

There are many ways to disappear. There is no way to disappear. Every disappearance is at the same moment a re-appearance elsewhere. Nothing is entirely lost in the dialectic. Everything changes in the dialectic. Difference is deference. She is different and deferent. He is Other, is not deferent.

Desaparecidos speak. They are disappeared for their words. Their words weigh on their necks as concrete blocks and chains. It's not only the East River in which the disappeared re-appear.

Can woman be disappeared if she has never appeared?

Notes

1. Hélène Cixous, "Sorties," in Hélène Cixous and Catherine Clément, *The Newly Born Woman*, trans. Betty Wing, (Minneapolis: University of Minnesota Press, 1986), p. 64.

2. Plato, "Meno," in *Five Dialogues*, trans. G.M.A. Grube, (Indianapolis: Hackett, 1981), p. 81b.

3. Jacques Derrida, *Dissemination*, trans. Barbara Johnson, (Chicago: The University of Chicago Press, 1981), p. 63.

4. Cynthia Enloe, *Bananas, Beaches and Bases: Making Feminist Sense of International Politics*, (Berkley: University of California Press, 1990), p. 4.

5. Richard Rorty, "Science as Solidarity," in *Objectivity, Relativism and Truth*, (New York: Cambridge University Press), p. 35.

6. Ibid., p. 37.

7. Ibid.

8. Mary Field Belenky, Blythe McVickor Clinchy, Nancy Rule Goldburger, Jill Mattuck Tarule, *Women's Ways of Knowing: The Development of Self, Voice, and Mind*, (New York: Basic Books, 1986), p. 54.

9. Richard Rorty, op. cit., p. 37.

THE EXCESS: AN ADDED REMARK ON SEX, RUBBER, LEATHER AND ETHICS

Sue Golding

[1.1] "Supposing you find these fruits unpalatable? What concern is that of the trees, or of us—the philosophers?"[1]

[1.2] I've always liked the term looking glass instead of mirror, though, for most intents and purposes they name exactly the same thing. But let us offer an imaginary difference, apart from the old slang connecting looking glasses with chamberpots.[2]

Let us say, as one could easily do if in the grand company of an Alice: mirrors reflect what we already know about the surface of ourselves (only backwards), whereas looking

[1.2] So, the room was very dark, save for the small candle flickering quietly by the washroom door. Johnny was wearing her laced leather jeans—tight across the ass, thick cotton shirt, sleeves rolled up, buttons hanging lazily across an open chest. At a certain angle, you could see the harness, and if you smoothed your hand over her sleeve, an arm band with a 'small-bit' attachment could be felt. Next to the belt hung a lovely cat, splayed

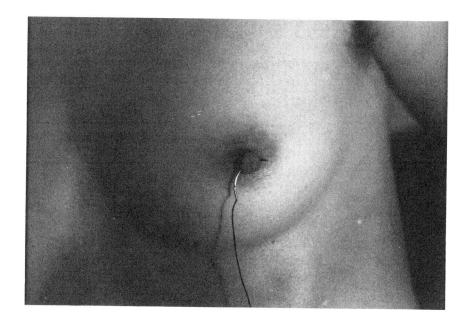

glasses have an ability—if you want to play the game (or, more to the point, if you know *that* there is one)—to pull you right through and into an abyss: the abyss of an/other self or (better put) the abyss of a quasi-self, reflection notwithstanding.

For its pretend surface lets you skim along the edges of a nothing whatsoever, inscribing you within and against a homeland for the not-quite-here/not-quite there[s] of this world.

It's a peculiar place of exile; a kind of distinct arena whose parameters can blur at the edges, bleed over into neighbouring yards, leave an unpleasant stain at the center. Perhaps there's even a smell, though no sure-footed trace of its route seems ready to hand. And as often as not, when it's gone, it's as though it never had been there, nor (just as likely) that it ever could have been any different—seamless nature often being what it is (or, for that matter, what it appears to be); that is, seamless: a vanishing horizon vaporised at the very moment it traverses the past and capitulates, as extant 'trace', into the as-yet-to-be-known future tense.

But what if the looking glass's other side operated in yet a different way, an additional way? What if our exiled wonderland, while

open and mimicking each drawn swagger of her step; a single weave of rope, partially hidden away in a pocket, could just be discerned ...In short, the butch was ready.

At first glance, it was just a group grope—though when she initially entered—to be completely accurate—girls hung together in pairs, not really doing anything—just waiting. Just waiting. 'Waiting for what?', Johnny laughed impatiently, and thought it high time for the party to begin.

In the darkness, she put her hand up to an open face and began to touch the skin ever so lightly. She touched it not unlike the way one might touch a porcelain object in the dark—curiously but not without some intelligence. She ran her fingers around the nose, brows, hair—just 'taking in' the information, so to speak.

Someone grabbed her from behind—suddenly, violently—pulling on her shirt, and through it, grabbing the harness, pulling, pulling. And she probably would have fallen backwards had it not been for the third woman by her leg, fingers tangled in the laces, arms surrounding the leather.

More women came in—this much she saw before she became distracted by the wanderings of a hand that started at her nipple, and con-

precisely 'real', was not precisely 'unreal' either? For we are not talking here of 'fantasy' or 'performance art/theatre' or, even 'make-believe'. Well, not exactly.

We are speaking of 'something' more (and less) than that; we are speaking of a time, a space, a homeland, a-thing, a quasi-location quite a bit stranger than fiction and infinitely more reliable than truth.

We might want to name this bizarre location (long version) 'the-impossible-but-actual-limit-to-the-outside/otherside-of-otherness'. Or we could call it, nodding to its more juicier, distinctly leather variant as simply (short version) 'clit-club'.

For bodies sheathed in leather or in lycra, not to mention pvc or simple lace, all rubbing up against or inside a club so named, become a little like the looking glass itself, slang included. And as with Alice, we go, quite willingly hand-in-hand, with them, through them, breathing them, possessing them, face-to-face confronting them; absolutely borrowing or stealing from them. Taking pleasure seriously or tossing it to the sea, or simply moving to a somewhere quite other than 'the where' we've just been.

In so doing, we pass into a place beyond a natural limit, pulled as it were, 'over there', over into the tinued to pass over her stomach on the way down to the buckle of a thick leather belt. But as this unexpected guest reached a 'no-turning back spot', the fingers felt the top end of the whip, and stopped.

"So pretty boy," a voice attached to the hand whispered, "do you actually use this thing or is it just for show?"

Johnny turned to face her—and as this boy-girl turned round, the other woman, the one whose face she had so deliberately stroked, started to peel off Johnny's shirt and threw it somewhere amidst the other bodies, now swaying to the back beat of the music (barely discernable) outside this little sweat-box of perversion and grace. Johnny's tits stood erect, quite erect now, actually, bound as they were by the harness, and energized by the smells.

The air was getting thicker, and even, I would dare say, 'hot'.

"Well?," she taunted. "Well, pretty boy, what's your answer?"

The cowboy said nothing; just slowly began to pull out the rope. Its perfect whiteness glistened in the flickering light, in stark contrast from her own dark hands and mouth and eyes. Johnny cupped it deep in her left hand, and in one swift move, braced right up against her victim's throat...

elsewhere of sexual mutation, curiosity, and paradoxical decay.

Indeed, the 'we' and the 'them', the 'I' and the 'you', bleed into one another, stain at the center, flicker in the distance without for a moment missing the beat, without for a moment missing the rhythm or the spaces in between this thing we have for so long called the Self. [1.2.1] Gone are the old identities born of either/or distinctions, with their addenda self-referential prophecies of a decidedly discrete Other. For it's a strange kind of spill over, this neither/nor transgression, one which escapes the usual Law of binary divisions like masculine/feminine, black/white, gay/straight, community/individual, public/private, life/death, truth/fiction, etc. and so forth. Simultaneously, it refuses any melted ambiguity between Self and the Other.

Indeed, it entails no (vague) sense of infinite unity, nor for that matter, does it operate off a shameful certainty arising from the (usually) vacuous details of a lack or a castration. It has even less to do with the reflexive relations of an ego/I.

For this exile is both the deep cut, the unrelenting [/], between the 'not' and its 'something', *as well as* their paradoxical and deadly unity. Indeed, it is a wonderland of extravagance in the best sense of

[1.2.1] MARY DRINKS WITH THE FARMBOYS...'Did you come to have fun?' 'That's right,' said Mary. She tried to smile. Her smile seered through her. She took a seat next to the boy, pressed her leg against his and taking his hand put it between her thighs. When the farmhand touched her crack he moaned: 'Gawd!' The others, flushed, fell silent. One of the girls, getting up, pulled back a flap of the coat. 'Get an eyeful of this,' she said, 'she's stark naked.' Mary offered no resistance and emptied her glass. 'She likes her drink,' said the patron. Mary responded with a belch.

...MARY TAKES OUT A DRUNKARD'S COCK...With sadness, Mary said: 'That's right!' Locks of wet black hair stuck to her face. She shook her pretty head, she got up and undid her coat. The empty coat dropped. A lout who was drinking at the back made a rush. He was bawling: 'Naked women for us!' The patron careened

the word: excess and the most reversed sense of the word: denial.

It has more to do with 'sampling': trying something on for size, seeing whether it 'fits' without ever (or only) cancelling out the relative processes of borrowing or digesting or inventing (and in any case as being a part of) the 'that' of life itself, in all its precarious imbalances and delicacies.

Nothing in this game can masquerade, in other words, above and beyond or apart from the real, itself multiple and contingently engaged. Nor is there a proclivity to elevate fiction as its new standard bearer, as its the 'new truth'.

[1.2.2] The claim is much more modest: at best, we are thieves, pure and simple, remaining, fundamentally, in the fractured land of a quasi-negation, the arena of a so-called 'desistance' or double {[de]de}-negation,[3] with all its discretely ironic vaporizations, propertyless ownerships, and run-ins with the Law.

We are the thieves who play with and against that Law, who traverse it (if lucky), who get caught in it (if not). And in so doing, create, disrupt, invent, duplicate, a 'homeland' identity, an 'exiled' identity, precisely at the moment where the past and future meet; an identity, situated somewhere between the

in on him: I'll get you by your snout...' She caught him by his nose and she twisted. 'No, here's where,' said Mary, 'it's better.' She approached the drunkard and unbuttoned him: the cock she took from his pants was floppy. The object provoked much laughter. In a stroke of rage, Mary, red as a mad person, knocked back another glass. The patron slowly opened her eyes up like headlights. She touched between her buttocks. 'Good enough to eat,' she said. Once again Mary filled her glass. She gulped as if dying, and the glass fell from her hands. The crack of her arse lit up the room.[5]

[1.2.2] Did I tell you how your hair floated on the black satin pillow case? It was after you had arched your back so full and wide; it was after the sweat began to pour from your shoulders; it was after you let out the violent gasp, the scream which cut across whatever was left of our gestured civility. I watched you, from behind, I watched your hair begin its weightless adventure; I watched, as it began to crawl, despite its drenched state, over the black satin case. I watched you heave, and moan, and collapse, only to feel wave after wave of cunt muscle close in upon my fist...and I dug up hard against you, feeling you, watching you, feeling you cum.

'that' of techne and the 'not' of its other.

This is a peculiar identity: one that must always bear an excess, the excessiveness of the game itself, the perverse and excessive game of self, of mastery and of submission, all up for negotiation and reformulation, often, though not only, fitted somewhere along the actualities of a sexed pleasure-play.

We have here, in other words, an impossible identity (and indeed, an impossible law): impossible not because it does not exist (or, conversely, that it must exist only at the level of a contingent fiction). Rather, it is impossible because it must (of necessity) exist and not exist, exactly at the same time, creating in its wake a not-space of the other; an impossible, perverse sense of temporal/spatial reality, transacted, in part, at the level of blood and skin and teeth and hair.

[1.3] This fleeting, pulsating arena of excess, pleasurable in the most corrupting sense of the term: erotic, is a re-inscription of the political itself. And as such, it demands not so much that we abandon the question of identities, and with it the problem of law, or the problem of rights, or even, for that matter, the problem of ethics. But rather, that we acknowledge, and indeed, [re]cognize the fundamental para-

Wet and wild, and infinite.

'We finally got past foreplay,' I laughed to myself. Finally got right past it.

Your hair: as if trying to escape in ten different directions at once, with nowhere to go, nowhere to hide; wildly spilling from your head, now slayed in mid-run. Utterly still, as if permanently burned into its now demented state: emitting, if you listened close, a strange tight hum; the kind of hum one cannot hear before it is seen; the kind of humming vision/noise most often associated with the relentless beatings of desert sun, crashing hard against—and sometimes piercing— its target skin. Like a spell. Hot. Bold. Held.

[1.3] So did you know that when you fell back against me, passing in and out of life with that special kind of desperation and utter sense of joy —the kind that mingles best in one's memory as it dances past the eyes; well, did you know that your hair floated once again, though this time, around my cheeks, and nose and lashes, alighting, finally somewhere atop my cap, all leather and sweaty and worn, now pulled down

digm shift an 'impossible-but-actual-limit-to-the-outside/otherside-of-otherness'—that is to say, what a 'clit club'—can imply.[4]

In its most focussed sense, this 'otherside of otherness', this excess, has to do with re/membering the very notion of radical pluralism and the democracy to which it points. For it is one rooted in and expressing the multiplicity of *strategies* necessary to create who we are, and what we can become, in all our fluid—and very real—impossibilities.

Indeed, and more than that, this radical democracy is one whose 'root' no longer fits so neatly under the canopy of a so-called 'community' or 'coalition' politics; rather, the 'root' is itself 'strategy', in the most *profane* and *sweaty* sense of the term plural.

a bit more severe than the occasion required, blocking some of my vision... and yet not so much that I could not see how red and swollen and soft your lips had grown; nor how preciously subtle the hairs on your breasts appeared, still able to reflect whatever light was left in the twilight hours of our romp; nor was the cap so low that I could not see all the vague candle wax drippings flagging the best parts of your thighs, nor the tiny whip bumps reaching over and above the limits of your skin.

Your hair covered me. It swept over me, like your breathing and your sighs and your ejaculations and your pissings and your convulsions and your heat. An intense and fiercely wild heat.

But most of all, it was your hair; it was your hair I remember floating over my mouth. This is what I remember best; this is the last thing I remember as I slid somewhere past the innocent, the corrupt, and the sublime.

[1.4] Or excess: inundated with power; profusely traversing, creating, informing, flailing against, or getting bound up inbetween, the 'that which lies around of us.'

[1.4] "During this agony," Saint Teresa of Avila was known to have murmured, "the soul is inundated with inexpressible delights."

[1.5] Liberty. Freedom. Possibility. Uncertainty. Agony. Curiosity. And a small gesture of appreciation to Blake: "7. In her trembling hand she took the new born terror, howling."[6]

Notes

1. F. Nietzsche, *On the Genealogy of Morals*, translated by Walter Kaufman.

2. Circa 1690-1870. Among many other books noting this connection is the delightful Eric Partridge (ed.), *A Dictionary of Slang and Unconventional English Colloquialisms and Catch Phrases, Fossilised Jokes and Puns, General Nicknames, Vulgarisms and such Americanisms as has been Naturalised*, (London: Routledge and Kegan Paul, 1937/1984).

3. See for example Derrida's introduction to Lacoue-Labarthe, *Typography*, (Harvard University Press: Cambridge, 1989), p. 1, where, in pointing to the 'strangeness' of the verb, desister, he writes: "Perhaps it doesn't mark anything negative. Perhaps the 'de' does not determine the ister, or rather, the ester. Perhaps the de dislodges it radically, in an uprooting that would gradually dislocate the whole series, which seemed merely to be modifying a common stem and assigning complementary attributes to it. A powerful meditation on the root, on the a-radicality of the is, est, ister, ester..."

4. In his *Daybreak: Thoughts on the Prejudices of Morality*, Nietzsche illustrated the implications of that paradigm shift like this: "8. *Transfiguration*: Those that suffer helplessly, those that dream confusedly, those that are entranced by the supernatural—these are the three divisions into which Raphael divided mankind. This is no longer how we see the world—and Raphael would no longer be able to see it as he did: he would behold a new transfiguration." F. Nietzsche, *Daybreak: Thoughts on the Prejudices of Morality*, translated by R.J. Hollingdale, (Cambridge: Cambridge University Press, 1982), p. 10.

5. Excerpt from Georges Bataille, *The Deadman*, in Paul Buck (ed.), *Violent Silence*, (London: The Georges Bataille Event, 1984), p. 13.

6. William Blake, "A Song of Liberty," in the *Complete Prose and Poetry of William Blake*, edited by Geoffrey Keynes (1927), (London: The Nonesuch Press, 1989), p. 192.

WEDDING WOES

Gwen Bartleman

You don't want to go. The thought of hanging out with 60,000 relatives makes you want to heave. These people aren't even your relatives; your family is older and very senile at these functions ("Glenn, isn't it?" "No, Gwen." "You're Glenn!" "No, Gwen." "Aren't you your brother?").

They are someone else's relatives and they are getting married. This is your own private gateway to hell.

But she's your girlfriend, so you seriously consider attending. That lock she has on your clitoris is strong. You find out the dates and check your schedule, hoping and praying that work will provide a way to bow out gracefully.

You're not working. For once, you are more than free to attend.

You rationalize. Maybe it won't be that bad. Maybe it won't be a tacky goyisha wedding with a cash bar and lawn chairs. Finally, the thought that has convinced lesbians throughout history to attend these functions occurs to you: at least it's a free meal.

Free, you soon realize, is a relative term. You borrow a suit from a co-worker (you have men's shoes already, so that's cool). You and your

girlfriend have recently acquired a car, so the whole thing should only cost about 20 bucks in gas money.

Then you discover the breeders' (oops, I mean the happy couple's) preference in wedding gifts. No satin sheets or $50 bills for them. No, no, no. These white suburbanites actually have taste. They want crystal, a wine collection. They're registered at Birks.

You shell out. You cut down on eating at McDonald's for a while. You skip purchasing those new boxer shorts you've been eyeing at Mark's Work Wearhouse. New brakes for your bikes will wait another 30 days. The Bell bill hasn't turned to a warning shake of pink. After all, you do have a five-figure income.

Two days before the wedding, you look into the mirror and you think, "I am playing yahtzee with the devil."

The day of the breed-fest arrives. You're ready; she's ready. Your grey blazer nicely offsets her pale green dress. She's made you a tie, a ridiculous splash of colour in contrast to your funeral suit. Recently you shaved your head, so hairstyle isn't really a concern. You jump into the car, plug *Ramones Live* into the deck and start to roll.

Halfway down the street, you ask her to turn back. "I've forgotten something," you say. She's so grateful you're accompanying her to this horrific display of heterosexuality that she'll do just about anything, no questions asked. You run into your apartment.

You enter through the fire-escape door. You're undercover, a little like Linc from *The Mod Squad*. Your hands are shaking slightly as you reach under the bed for the white oval hat box.

You pull it out and strap it on. Good thing the pants are a little big. You check yourself in the mirror. Perfect. The small seven-and-one-quarter-inch bulge is not too noticeable, not too hidden. The veins are barely discernible.

As you return to the car, your step is a little lighter. Maybe the birds were singing before and you just didn't hear them. And maybe there's no such thing as a free meal, but there won't be one for *them* either. Invite a lesbian to a wedding and you're begging for a gal with a strap-on in her pants.

PERSONAL NEEDS

Linda Dawn Hammond

...IN MASOCH'S LIFE AS WELL AS IN HIS FICTION, LOVE AFFAIRS ARE ALWAYS SET IN MOTION BY ANONYMOUS LETTERS, BY THE USE OF PSEUDO-NYMS OR BY ADVERTISEMENTS IN NEWSPAPERS. THEY MUST BE REGULATED BY CONTRACTS THAT FORMALIZE AND VERBALIZE THE BEHAVIOR OF THE PARTNERS. EVERYTHING MUST BE STATED, PROMISED, ANNOUNCED AND CAREFULLY DE-SCRIBED BEFORE BEING ACCOMPLISHED.

MASOCHISM
Coldness and Cruelty
Gilles Deleuze

discreet. U show me, I show u. NOW BOX 856

New to TO. Long-haired male 23 looks similar to young David Coverdale seeks passionate female, kitten with claws, for possible relationship. Reply to 5468 Dundas St W Suit 930 TO M9B 6E3

Openminded attr col. she sub 26, he 27, lkg for

Dominant plump M39 sks obedient married couple 4his slaves. Photo Box 622 Stn H Mtl H3G 2L5

ELECTRONICALLY YOURS, ETERNALLY ELVIS
Scenes from a history as yet unwritten

Ken Hollings

Without Elvis you're nothing
–Madonna

War Without End

It is day 2037 of Operation Desert Storm, and the allied forces are hopelessly entrenched in a land-based war of attrition against Iraq. The whole campaign has been an absolute disaster from the start.

Responding to a vision he has had in a dream, the President hears the voice of the American people and withdraws the entire U.S. service personnel from the area.

'Despite the image we now have of ourselves,' the President says at a hastily convened press conference to announce his decision, 'the fight for oil has made us an industrial nation once again, and that is something of which we, as a people, can forever be proud.'

He stands against a backdrop of blazing refineries. Thick black smoke drifts across the polluted shoreline on the edge of a radioactive sea. Burning jungles of gasoline lie buried beneath the desert. Memories of a thousand Vietnams have been turned into sand.

A young officer at the final press briefing is asked if napalm has been used in any of the air strikes against the enemy. 'No,' he replies, smiling. 'We've moved on a lot since then.'

And now all you can smell on the wind coming in from the Gulf is burning oil.

Everyone pulls out of the area, leaving behind a scorched terrain surveilled and protected only by satellite-linked electronic defense systems set on constant automatic standby. Officially nothing is happening here anymore. These machines could start a war on their own, if they wanted to.

'This is what our missiles see,' the young officer explains running yet another mission video of exploding bunkers and wrecked supply columns.

One of the departing journalists leaves a hand-written sign tacked to the rear wall of the press room at Desert Storm headquarters. Its large red magic-marker letters state disgustedly: 'TODAY IS THE FIRST DAY OF THE REST OF YOUR MINDS.'

The United States Air Force, meanwhile, has resolved to continue running airborne search and destroy missions over enemy territory.

'Despite the radical redeployment of our forces as of this time,' the young officer confides casually to the remaining members of the press corps, 'our planes are still basically running the same play. Our strategy, gentlemen, remains unchanged: it's business as usual: find 'em, feel 'em, fuck 'em and forget 'em.'

The opposing Iraqi forces have dug themselves down deep into an eternal night of biochemical fumes, hunger, fire storms and dust. Loud rock music is blasted day and night at them through the smoke from booming sound systems installed along the American lines of defense. Originally intended as cover for a new generation of sub-sonic weapons designed to disorientate and confuse the enemy, the songs are now just played for propaganda purposes, and to keep the Iraqis annoyed and deprived of sleep.

The President likes to select the Desert Storm play list himself. It's possible, so some political correspondents claim, to judge the mood on Capitol Hill by the music heard echoing constantly across the blackened dunes.

Out of touch with every reality except his own, the President is lifted up into states of euphoria and ecstasy by his dreams and visions.

'What about Michael Jackson?' he suggests excitedly to his White House aides. 'We're not playing them enough Michael Jackson. He's what we ought to be telling our enemies about. Play them that one of his about how we don't mind if they're black. You know, it really doesn't matter. And push the free food thing too. I think we're finally getting through to them. They've got to weaken some time.'

The President beams at his staff as they all nod together in silent agreement.

'Oh, and find out if he gets royalties for any of this and who pays them, will you?'

Heads bow once more over blank steno pads until the meeting is finally called to a close.

The President knows that Michael Jackson can say more to the enemy than he personally ever could; and in quieter moments, the thought does not reassure him.

'Michael Jackson has become America,' he once confided darkly to his aides. 'He's what everyone wants to be.'

'But, Mr President, he's a Negro,' they reply, trying to forestall the depression they can see beginning to settle in over their leader's shadowy features.

'Only by birth, boys,' the President replies as he sullenly withdraws into his private bathroom. 'Only by birth.'

The Body Electric (With A Weight Problem)

Once upon a time it was Elvis. Embodying the all-around energy of the animal and the machine, Elvis was the Nation's First Atomic Powered Singer. He tamed the electric muse—he made its free-flowing power a part of himself.

On the night Elvis was born, his father, Vernon Presley, stepped outside the little shack in Tupelo, Mississippi which was their home and saw the glowering sky ringed around with blue light.

Elvis always said it was his special colour. It had a spiritual significance for him. In 1956, while the nation dug fall-out shelters in its back yards, Martin Ritchie, a fourteen-year old youth from Chicago Illinois, electrocuted himself while attempting to hang an effigy of Elvis from a powerline.

The President thinks of electricity as being a real fifties thing. It's something that he can relate to at the breakfast table. Solid nostalgic names like Hamilton Beach, McGillicuddy and Westinghouse fill his thoughts with the clicking of meters and the sound of aging hearts in darkened hospital wards.

Electricity, like water, finds its own level and then spreads.

Michael Jackson, as a child in his parents' house, danced to the rhythm of his mother's washing machine even before he was old enough to talk.

Electricity was like a toy in Elvis's hands. He had to play with it before anyone else: from the electronic echo on his voice to the Sony pornographic home videos he made; from eight-track stereo cartridges (who remembers them now?) to the communication satellite anchored in the sky off Hawaii for his concert there in 1972, seen by over one billion of the Earth's inhabitants.

How else could technology ever be real to us unless it had passed through his unreal hands and been blessed by them?

Elvis even had his Los Angeles jewellers transform the horizontal lightning insignia on his Army Tank Corps fatigues (their motto, 'Hell on Wheels' seems to come to us from another age) into his own personal emblem. The jagged bolt of power flanked vertically by the letters TCB stood for the King Taking Care of Business, it connected Heaven with Earth.

Elvis's death left him wide open; a prey to maggots and parasites; a victim of endless misunderstandings. The mythic power invested in the King's body finally came to rest at his home in Graceland. Powerless and bad, betraying us all; the King became a giggling doubled vision of himself: Fat Elvis.

A corpse that turns white in the sun.

Artificial Life

Michael Jackson doesn't like to go out in strong daylight anymore. It's as if he doesn't want the sun to touch him. He looks at the world through dark glasses, or stays indoors watching cartoons all day on TV.

They have their own special darkness about them, one that is quick and lively and cheats death. Michael Jackson is fascinated by them.

'Cartoons are unlimited,' he says. 'And when you're unlimited, it's the ultimate.'

The darkness always has more possibilities hidden within it. There is no end to what it can produce.

'It's like everything's all right,' he says, 'It's like the world is happening now in a faraway city. Everything's fine.'

Michael Jackson loved watching himself transformed into a cartoon character on Saturday morning television. That was quite early on his career, when he was still with his family.

He knows how people can change.

There are drawings of Peter Pan all over the walls of his Neverland Valley bedroom. However, it is difficult to look at the changes in Michael Jackson's appearance over the past few years without thinking that the Disney character he has come most to resemble is Bambi.

Like the rest of us, he is haunted by that moment in animated films when the characters detach themselves from their own world and come alive in an approximation of our own. They step out of the frame and present themselves before us, standing upright upon the photographic reality of the artist's drawing board. They create a bright and graceful chaos all around them, upsetting their creator's pens and inks, demanding that they be re-drawn, transformed into their own fantasies of what they should look like.

Micro-electronic technology and genetic engineering will soon give us the capability of creating new life forms that will exist only in computer-generated space. It is only a matter of time before these artificial organisms start developing their own evolutionary agenda. Computer viruses replicate themselves. Worms, parasites and maggots hide inside micro-processors, infecting entire programmes. Total nuclear destruction can be triggered by the alarm on a Casio wrist watch.

An organism will no longer have to be alive to be alive. It can be a complex adaptive system of information whose dimensions correspond to those of the computer screen. Life forms will then be defined not by their materials, but by their behaviour.

Artificial and without limits, programmed by our dreams and desires, these new creatures will indeed be the ultimate cartoons. Free to pursue their own existence, they will finally take their place as the true inhabitants of cyberspace. Their natural domain will be the vectored electro-magnetic plains of today's Virtual Reality machines which already closely resemble the animator's cell.

Who knows what will step off the workstation screen in the future; and who knows what demands these new life forms will make of their creator?

Michael Jackson draws a picture of himself being menaced by a monster coming out of his TV set.

Fast Money Sex With A Dead President

Deep in the night, the President is having another of his dreams. He rolls about in his own sweat, the soiled blankets sticking to him.

Michael Jackson has just bought the open-topped black Lincoln that Kennedy was assassinated in. Not just a copy, you understand, not even the same model, but the exact same car. The President shivers, his skin prickling.

Only, you see, he's having it cleaned and repaired. The bullet holes are going to be filled in and the glossy black panelwork polished until it shines like new. The upholstery is to be cleansed of its bloody past, and the seat covers sewn back to their original condition.

And then he's going to be driven through Dallas in it. The President lies groaning in the sickening half light of his room. Dripping and feverish, he finally surfaces from his troubled sleep and lies, shaken and quivering, in a bed made safe and heavy by the weight of his wife and the family dog.

'Damn that monkey boy,' he hisses. 'Damn that twitching monkey boy. He'll never get away with it. Not while there's a breath left in my body. That car's a piece of history; and who the hell's going to ride in it with him anyway? Elizabeth Taylor?'

The President sniggers to himself in the darkness at the thought of the stoned and overweight female star struggling to climb out of the slow-moving black limo. He lies back on his damp pillows once more. His wife stirs gently at his side, shifts her position, then drifts back into sleep.

It's always night in the President's bedroom—the dimly lit confines chilled down to zero by the high-intensity whine of the air conditioning which he insists be kept running at all times. Sometimes, when the particle filtration system packs in altogether, along with all the ionizers, the air thickens and grows sluggish around him. Then it's like sleeping at the bottom of the sea, and that's where the President starts to dream his dark dreams.

But the President likes it cold. That's his speed.

Fully awake now and unable to close his eyes, he leans over and picks up the portable tape recorder that stands by his bedside. It's there to keep him company at night and to remind him of the past. That's his speed too. All great men need an echo of themselves.

'Someone has to take care of this,' he whispers into his silently whirring machine. 'Someone has to make it their business. He must be stopped before this whole thing gets out of hand. Damn that monkey boy. Damn him.'

Libidinal Generator

Michael Jackson weeps and runs away. He has made an aesthetic out of disappearing. The paleness of his skin invites the darkness to enclose him. His whole body becomes inhabited by it, making his every gesture, however trivial, however crude, seem real and heroic. And heroes must constantly play hide and seek with their public so that it will continue to believe in them.

Reduced to a pair of staring eyes, the face hidden in shadow, he is the vanishing point of our world.

Only some final sign of cancellation can complete him.

The very nature of his name retreats into hurt anonymity, a receding vortex of fame, glowing darkly.

Michael Jackson, trying to escape from his father in a brightly lit Las Vegas casino lounge, exposed to the blank inquisitive gaze of the crowds, dodging in and out of the games machines, crying like a wounded animal.

Michael Jackson, a fine-boned forest creature of the late twentieth century, hidden in the depths of the trees.

Bambi cowering under the shadow of the hunter's bullet. A timid gaze directed out at us from the black expanse of a record sleeve, calling itself DANGEROUS.

How the names differ from what we actually see.

A spray canned three-letter word stretches itself out across a white tile subway wall: BAD.

Without waiting for his public's answer, Michael Jackson vanishes from the stage, leaving the question 'who's bad?' hanging in the air. Urban graffiti is another sign of one who has gone unseen, its form made up from the traces left behind by a heroic, invisible hand.

It is a mark of disappearance.

Michael learned very early on—his pockets stuffed so full of cash from playing a grim succession of Indiana strip clubs with the rest of his brothers that he could hardly walk—that if you don't get money to help you change, then it can only slow you down.

Elvis used the tremendous flow of the money he generated to keep himself fixed in the same place. On the final life-sapping tours he undertook, he was moved from one identical motel room to another: with their windows covered over with aluminium foil to keep out both the light and the view, each one was specially equipped and prepared to be as much like his Graceland master bedroom as possible. In effect, Elvis Presley toured America without ever leaving his bed.

Standing centre stage, his performances became physically more and more sluggish. Elvis, who in the beginning could not sing without dancing at the same time, decelerated dramatically. It was like watching the slowed down compacting of a car crash—the choreography of a dead body.

The cars, guns and drugs Elvis consumed during his life became the violent transports of a man hell-bent on remaining completely static; growing slower and slower until he finally stopped altogether and became Fat Elvis.

While Michael Jackson's face hollows out and his physical appearance recedes into the unlimited possibilities of change, the massive bulk of Elvis Presley's body swells up, generating clones, imposters, and professional imitators. The air is thick with pictures of the King.

It seems sometimes as if everyone still wants to be Elvis, but the closest they ever get to being him is to turn themselves into his lifeless twin: Fat Elvis without a body.

As a result, the power that once resided in the King's corporeal flesh has been dispersed, the body itself brought to rest at Graceland, beneath a motionless slab of black marble, inscribed with a commemorative poem written by his father.

An eternal flame of remembrance, emblem of the dispersal of matter into energy, burns in the Garden of Meditation; and the TCB lightning bolt hangs down over the grave, pointing towards the ground. Taking Care of Business.

Blown Apart

In a world which has been decomposed and restructured as the coding of images and digital information, death is a mere technical detail. The King suffered nothing more than a momentary break in transmission.

The results of such a lapse, however, were catastrophic. Concealed by memories and desires, the phantom twins of perceived reality, the Presley myth lay hidden deep within the system, an accident waiting to happen.

At a laboratory workstation in a publicly-funded research project into the human immune system, two programmers stare moodily at the gently glowing screen.

'What we got here, basically, is a trunk full of empty,' one of them says. 'I mean, its got the fluid, harmonic kind of motion that you'd expect to find in a real cell, but it's just not operating on the same principles anymore.'

The second programmer keeps on staring into the screen.

'Did it ever?' he asks.

'To begin with, I would have said yes, definitely, but now...'

He shrugs. 'In terms of a basic organism/domain relationship, its showing distinct sociopathic tendencies. It doesn't assimilate, it merely appropriates. All it wants to do is take over.'

The other programmer frowns.

'Response to stimuli?'

'Unpredictable at best: its reactions are almost too random to be considered anything but willful.'

'In other words, the little bugger gets in a snit.'

'There are more technical ways of putting it, but, yes, that's about the picture. If we're not careful this thing will just eat its way out of the screen. The whole programme could be at risk.'

With an impatient gesture, the second programmer turns away from the screen.

'Right, I'm sick of this,' he says. 'Flush the system, debug all the screens and let's start again.

'But...'

'Wipe it. Get it out of my face. I'm sick of the little prick.'

The Corpse Animation Myth Revisited

Every pleasure that a king can gratify through his body can also be inverted or denied to more or less the same effect.

Elvis took pills, getting so whacked out on prescription opiates that he could barely move: Michael Jackson, however, swallows vitamins by the handful.

Elvis gorged: Michael starves himself.

Elvis abused his vital organs, his liver smashed to a pulp by the time of his death: Michael Jackson obsessively takes care of himself and follows a macrobiotic diet.

Both of them, like true kings, have chosen, after their respective fashions, to have their myths reside completely within their own flesh.

If Elvis's money slowed him down to zero, Michael Jackson's millions permit him to change so fast that we can never hope to catch up with him.

Elvis Presley's young body, when it danced, was a conduit for desire. For the eternally youthful Michael Jackson, dance becomes the expression of desire; a slide of images and viscous meanings, contradictory 'moonwalking' illusions of movement, oscillating constantly between backwards and forwards motion.

Elvis, ultimately, could never become anything other than himself, a state of affairs that his legions of fans and imitators maintain even after his death. Michael Jackson turns himself into animals, cars, robots and space machines. He even changes colour, finally disappearing in a puff of pastel-tinted smoke.

Elvis Presley was the king, but only Jacko was ever crowned: in Africa.

'Jacko?' The President rolls over in his sleep muttering and dreaming of monkeys. 'What kind of name it that?'

Worldly power is such a casual thing when seen from the perspective of kings. Elvis was photographed, relaxed and pilled out of his mind, shaking hands with Richard Nixon in the Oval Office. He was carrying a gun at the time. Michael Jackson ran through the White House looking for children, then met Ronald Reagan instead who called him 'our new Dr. J.' What ever did he mean by that? What did President Reagan ever mean by anything he said?

At Michael's Neverland Valley ranch, there is a fully automated robot model of Abraham Lincoln just the like the one installed on Main Street in Disneyland.

But Michael won't drink Pepsi, although he's paid to endorse it, because he doesn't *believe* in it.

And Elvis can't sell it because he's dead.

Fat Elvis sells Nintendo; serenely fingering a Gameboy, his white, wide-bodied guitar slung across his massive, rounded shoulders. Even though you may never have seen it, you know the image is real. It makes sense.

And in return, Nintendo helps sell Fat Elvis to us, its slogans make his bloated white flesh easier to grasp:

'*How much fun can you handle?*'

'*Will you ever reach the end of it?*'

These questions reveal to us the true reality of Fat Elvis without a body: an electronic sprawl without mass or volume. Without organs. A swollen electrical skin with nothing going on beneath it.

Fat Elvis doesn't dance anymore: he floats instead in a coma of dreams.

Twilight of the Living Dead

Vernon Presley's ghost stares out, tired and restless, across the Graceland lawns. Unable to leave, incapable of departing, he broods on the past.

'I allus used to think we was all better off when Elvis was still driving that truck for Crown Electric,' he sighs, watching the world pass by through a ground floor window.

'Just a boy driving a truck,' he says, an ancient and lonely spirit that sits and sits and sits, caught in an empty dust bowl of time, listening to the middle-aged women in blue rinses weeping in the Garden of Meditation where his son lies buried.

'I tried to tell him,' Vernon says. '"You should make up your mind about being an electrician. I never saw a guitar player yet that was worth a damn." My gosh, we sure come a long way since then. But I'll tell you one thing. I was more of a man that Elvis ever was, than Elvis ever could have been. It takes a father to make a son. Elvis made people happy and he made hisself rich, but it was me who made him. I gave birth to a king.'

Vernon Presley sighs again.

'And I guess I paid the price for that.'

There is a fine mist forming in the grounds outside; and a reverent silence hangs over the King's swimming pool.

Vernon watches the lines of people still forming outside the main gates.

'They're letting in anybody these days,' he frets. 'We even got Mexicans and Chicanos now. They let 'em come in and wander around, then they steal all the toilet paper and take it back home with them.'

'We sure have come a long way,' he adds bitterly. 'A long, long way.'

Maniac Android

At the bottom of Elvis Presley Boulevard in Memphis, and a million miles from his home in Graceland, Elvis Presley is hard at work, doing what he does best: his last evening show.

Part mesh-linkage, computerized hydraulics, cloned body parts, grafted facial tissue and liquid crystal projection, a life-sized fully-automated model of the King is coming to the end of his final number.

Better than any imitator, with no one else's dreams or desires struggling to express themselves through him, with no one to be magnified in his presence by his love—in fact with no dreams, no desires, no love in him at all—this Elvis really takes care of business.

He plays guitar, moves around the stage a bit and says things.

Right now he is driving the audience out of their minds.

Men make open display of their grief. Women are screaming. Black mascara smeared down their cheeks, they cry out in delight as Elvis falls face down on the stage, weeping into his microphone.

'We love you, Elvis, we love you,' the audience sobs wildly, blinded by tears and eye make-up.

Elvis moans passionately, crushed beneath his own body weight.

A slave to music and electricity, the first God of the Assembly Line is being worked to death by his owner.

And the fans all flock to see it.

Elvis's new owner is a bummed-out country boy with a smile that's about as wide and as trustworthy as a set of faulty stage lights and a broom in his hands which he uses to beat the King across the head and shoulders with every night.

Sometimes Elvis begs him to stop, and most times he will in the end. But sometimes he just keeps on going.

'After all, it's just a machine,' the country boy tells himself, looking down at the bloated white carcass that kneels, hunched and whimpering, at his feet, 'and like all machines it's only there to fill a gap in people's lives. And when you get mad,' he says taking another swing at the King's prostrate body, 'you hit it. That's what machines are for.'

Every day, three times a day, Elvis does his show and his owner takes his money. In the evenings he has to clean out the toilets and re-stock the concession stands while his owner kicks back in his office behind the stage and laughs.

'I got the king working for me now,' he says, watching Presley, still in his white bejewelled stage costume, struggling to carry his mop and bucket, together with several bulky cans of cleaning fluid, down the aisle of the darkened theatre. 'I'm going to be eating for the rest of my life,' he adds, contentedly ripping the top off another Mountain Dew.

But Elvis begins to swell up under the beatings and abuse—his flesh turns pulpy and soft, as if some secret part of his workings is growing fat on the degrading treatment he receives from the country boy. His stage act becomes a sluggish display of all the hurt, suffering and resentment he has been forced to endure. The fans love it. The sound of his snarling, weeping despair, the sight of his synthetic flesh, bloated and heroic and dripping with sweat, fill them with sorrow. It is as if they have been given one final chance to share in his pain, and they respond with tears and entreaties of such a gripping intensity that the country boy can't bear to watch anymore.

'Just look at you,' he rages at Elvis at the end of his last evening show. 'What do you think you look like? I'll tell you what you look like. You look like shit. The Pillsbury Dough Boy with a set of side burns and an attitude problem, that's what you look like.'

'I'm sorry, sir,' the King mumbles. 'Are you going to beat me again?'

'Naw, you're fat enough already. Just get the fuck out of my sight, OK?'

That night, after the country boy has gone home cursing and grumbling, and the deserted theatre is quiet and still, Elvis pours a can of industrial strength switch cleaner down his throat and waits for the corrosive fluid to have its effect.

They found him next morning, lying curled up in one of the cubicles in the women's toilets, his mop and bucket overturned at his side.

Virtual Reality

After denied pleasures and suppressed cravings have been satisfied, there is nowhere left to go but nowhere; no one else to be but no one. We are following a line that leads to disappearance: to fame as an unseen and omnipresent self-renewing power.

'It's all magic,' Michael Jackson says. He wanted to make a film of himself waking up in his room and saying 'hello to the most gorgeous day ever.' He wanted to be 'moved by the beauty of the sunset.'

'The film must be too good to be true,' Michael specified from the confines of his room, 'like a fairy tale.'

Elvis and Michael both live in such perfect worlds: from Elvis' Graceland Mansion to Michael's Neverland Valley, both have faked the speed of their own destinies. Like fairy tales, they are marvellous for forever staying the same: for always returning to the same point of departure, magical and perfect.

The velocity required for them to stay in that one same place—that is to say, to disappear and, by so doing, be everywhere at once—distorts their external appearance. Every bodily change and transformation they undergo concerns us: Elvis's bloated waist, his receding chin, his glazed over pilled-up eyes, Michael's bouts of plastic surgery, the cleft in *his* chin, his straightened hair and tattooed eyeline: all are perceived as massive virtual shifts in our environment.

To understand how Elvis and Michael responded to the projected velocities of their fame it is necessary to examine how they chose to handle their surrogate selves, the vanishing traces of their own desires, in the form of their pet apes.

Elvis used to get his chimp Scatter stoned and encouraged it to act real nasty, looking up women's skirts and wrestling with a midget stripper in acts of simulated sex—then he abandoned it to die of madness and neglect. Some even say the lonely animal slowly drank itself to death locked in a cage back in Memphis.

Michael turned Bubbles into a star: he dressed him in Osh Kosh dungarees and sat him at his side for a ride through the Tunnel of Love. As soon as Bubbles learns how to sing, he's going to tour Japan on his own.

The whereabouts of Scatter's grave, however, are unknown at this time. Unlike Bubbles, Scatter really understood the price of fame. He really lived it.

Suicide Machine

At radio station WLVS a late night phone-in DJ rambles incoherently, his nerves breaking down under the pressure of calls from the King's grieving fans.

'There will always be those who say that it wasn't an accident, but two words, right? Suicide? Again? I ask you. Assembly line robots in automated car factories have been known to destroy themselves—you know...little isolated examples of mechanical despair, squirting molten plastic into their workings, solvent, ammonia, anything...you just can't predict it.'

Expressions of anguish, grief and despair flood the airways. Anonymous crackling lines of angry, fearful voices are spreading through the night.

'He exploits belief, you know what I'm saying?' one caller states, torn by love and rage. 'A lot of people have spent their hard-earned money to come out and see his show, and the cops are here right now busting heads. Elvis? I wouldn't cross the street to piss on him as a favour.'

Apocalyptic crowd scenes take place outside the Memphis theatre where Elvis lies dead. Hour by hour, the pressing numbers of mourners have grown through the night. The mood turns ugly and resentful.

Swelling lines of people spill out onto the road, blocking traffic. The police can no longer control or contain them. Angry motorists try and push their way through. One driver leans a little too long on his horn and in a second his car is overturned and torched.

Other cars now try to pile their way into the seething mass of angry grief-stricken bodies. More fires are quickly started. Innocent blood runs down the gutters of Elvis Presley Boulevard as cars slam themselves again and again into the lines of mourners.

Vernon Presley gazes out with empty, fleshless eyes through the Music Gates at the rust burst side panels of an old Packard as it ploughs into the crowd.

Across the street from him, women kneel praying by the souvenir stands that have been re-opened for the night while lonely street gangs clash in ill-lit back alleyways where the air reeks of blood and garbage, their chains swinging in the shadows.

Night of the Body Positive

The night Elvis came into the world, radio stations filled the darkness with music, beamed out non-stop from 50,000-watt transmitters all across America.

The sound of it would stay with him for the rest of his life.

The night Elvis came into the world, the first born was already in the house: laid out in a tiny coffin in the front room. Named before birth, Jessie Garon, Elvis Presley's twin brother was taken out the next day and buried in an unmarked grave. Jessie's mother, Gladys Presley, knew that he and Elvis were going to be twins, identical in every way. The only difference was that one of them was dead and the other wasn't: sometimes it would difficult to tell which was which.

Jessie Garon went on to pursue his own destiny at Elvis's side, moving and spreading like radio waves through his brother's life; while Elvis shared the same soil with him, lying lost to the world somewhere in an unknown place.

Elvis vanished into the uncommemorated earth long before he ever reached the black marble tomb beneath the eternal flame and lightning bolt at Graceland.

He disappeared long before he even learned to walk, lost within the shade of his brother's death, a dark outline that fitted him so precisely, matched him so perfectly, move for move, gesture for gesture, that it cancelled out everything he ever did, everything he could ever do.

While an angry mob prepares to hang the country boy in the blazing shadows of Elvis Presley Boulevard, the King struggles to get to his feet. Finally his cold outline slides away, through empty motel rooms and the ghostly hulks of casinos and astrodomes, searching for his true identity; that other self that he knows is out there waiting for him.

Who knows in what junction box, terminal or powerline the dreadful consummation took place: it is enough to say that it happened. The computer-generated rogue cell, driven out of the system by its frustrated programmers, merges with Elvis, taking him back, for the last time, to his point of departure; that sublime moment in Gladys Presley's womb when he was still attached to his twin self.

Elvis Aron was back with Jessie Garon again.

What he felt now was better than drugs, better than the perpetual half-light of the endless succession of motel bedrooms he was forced to sleep in.

The world for him at that moment was transformed.

Moving with an elemental speed, he became a bright discharge of sub-atomic particles: a stream of electrons travelling down wires at lethal velocities.

A new hunger, a new rage burns within the electro-magnetic field he now inhabits. It doesn't take Elvis long to realize that he has reached the one and only, the true and final hit; the one that lasts forever.

And Elvis has to admit that it feels all right.

The Final Call

Michael Jackson is in the throes of his last dance, an assassin's bullet in his brain.

His body can't stop. His limbs whip and flail as he spins about in agony across a Los Angeles soundstage, splattering the set with the scarlet contents of his skull.

'To be honest,' he once said. 'I guess you could say that it hurts to be me.'

Michael Jackson can't cheat death. He has already lived it too often for that.

Transformed into Zombie Jackson, he comes out at night and dances down the empty city streets with the Living Dead. His limbs twitch under his costume, a decomposing second skin of red leather. The zippers on it have snapped, and the teeth have all rusted together, and the press studs are gone. He creates videos made up from, and constructed like, body parts.

'I don't have to bring my own into the world,' he says, staring at the rotten burnt-out shell of the moon. He studies medical books on rare diseases and surgical practices, on how our bodies come apart and breed monsters. Almost his entire family have had nose jobs.

He dresses as a highschool kid and takes a girl out for a moonlit walk through a dark forest. They talk about love, and he turns into a werewolf.

'Michael's Plastic Face is Melting,' a newspaper headline screams, claiming that his elaborate plastic surgery is coming unstitched and untucked.

'I know I'm an imperfect person,' he says. 'I'm not making myself out to be an angel.'

Gulping down oxygen, Zombie Jackson kisses dying children, touches the sick with his white sequined glove.

He bumps and grinds on camera with the computer-animated bones of the Elephant Man.

It could be the last thing any of us ever see: a thin, frantic dancing corpse made up of glad rags and broken limbs.

They couldn't even save his face.

The President reassures himself that it's all just an act. He is amazed at people's abilities still to be amazed. Fame is nothing but a costly misunderstanding.

Anyone prepared to kill for it can own fame.

Michael Jackson took his inspiration from P.T. Barnum and Thomas Edison; they really knew how to put on a show.

Edison even made a short film of the death of Barnum's prize elephant, Jumbo. The grainy silent footage shows the enormous beast being led out and electrocuted, suddenly dropping to the ground when the power hit.

Those few stark seconds contain our entire century within them.

The President has seen that for himself. He knows that it is true. None of us has done anything else but act that same scene out over and over again. There was nothing else we could ever do.

Images of people having sex are more important than people having sex. Wanting to be president makes more sense than being president. Ever since he was a bubble in his father's dick, the President knew what he was going to be. Romance is so heroic. An alien intelligence invades the body of the earth-bound, human politician. He dominates press conferences, flash bulbs popping in his eyes. He says, 'I want to be president,' and everyone applauds. This is no longer fiction. This is no longer even the future.

It has nothing to do with science.

The announcement of Michael Jackson's death was delayed by over three hours while emergency medical teams waited for his corpse to stop dancing. It was 'better than Thriller,' according to one of the camera operators interviewed outside the studio after the shooting took place. 'We haven't seen anything like this since the time his hair caught fire while he was making that Pepsi commercial with his brothers.'

Death was instantaneous: shot in the head by an unknown assassin while filming his new video, 'I'm the Same Sex as You.'

A laboratory technician leans back in his chair as the shattered body is wheeled in by armed paramedics.

'Sounds like a Prince song,' he says dully.

His partner busies himself transferring the singer's remains onto an operating table in the centre of the brightly lit autopsy room.

'Looks like the mesh linkage systems operating in his knees and elbows short circuited and blew out the entire central core. Those beneath-skin implants are always tricky. The bullet must have tripped something inside and, with the brain no longer sending out any signals, there was nothing to control what was happening. No wonder he couldn't stop dancing.'

The first technician switches off the TV and walks over to the table.

'Mesh linkages introduced into the nervous system like that are always unstable.' he says.

'Yeah, right. It's too different. You can never expect it to integrate fully, not with any guarantee of safety. The stuff he's got here is high quality all right, but by the looks of things, he's been put together badly. The whole system's wound up so tight, I'm surprised he didn't start coming apart before. I mean, what you *don't* see is what you get, right?'

His partner picks away under the remains of the smashed skull with a pair of sterilized tweezers.

'We don't have enough to work with here,' he says. 'The cortex is completely scrambled. It would be easier to work with avocado dip.'

'And with about the same effect.'

'Hey, I thought his early stuff was really good.'

'Aw, skip it.'

War Without End (Continued)

There's this fat kid called Gordy and he's never seen the film of Jumbo's death, never even heard of Jumbo in fact, except as a chili dog size. To tell the truth, this boy has arrived so late on the scene that he's really not up on what's happening at all. He carries a pirate software package in the back pocket of his baggy jeans and is hurrying to get back to his room at home. He runs down alleyways of spray-gunned graffiti, listening to the voices of the other kids calling out after him.

'Hey, Elvis. Fat Elvis.'

'Who you calling fat, motherfucker?'

Since the earliest days of biochemical warfare in the Gulf, 'doing an Elvis' meant breathing in at the wrong moment, or being too slow in getting your protective suit on: in other words it meant you were history.

Being called Elvis is worse than having your tag sprayed over, or finding the letters R.I.P. added to it.

Gordy reaches home and makes straight for his bedroom. Then he plugs in the deck of his VR machine, pulls out the software package and settles back to enjoy Black Dildonic Queens Volume IV.

Gordy expects to find himself somewhere else, to be sitting in another room or under an endless sky of electromagnetic screen tone. Instead he sees nothing—not even a colour.

Then a hairline crack appears, which quickly widens into a great gaping hole. Pixels flare up around Gordy's range of vision as the darkness rips itself in half.

Open-mouthed, Gordy watches the whole world collapsing.

Burnt bodies are piled up in the streets, blood oozing from blackened cauterized stumps that have been charred to charcoal. Rotting yellow fluids from long dead corpses wash sluggishly down the parched gutters. Skinned bodies hang in empty towerblocks.

The huddled remains of the city's inhabitants testify to the use of chemical weapons upon the populace. Strangled horses kick against blood-stained walls.

Plague sores open up all over revolutionary Iraq, body lice and malnutrition grow together in the side streets. The blood banks have all been looted and infected. Corpses rise from abattoirs, torture cells, morgues and prisons. Those that refuse to get up and walk are used to create barricades across the filthy back alleys.

And in the centre of it all, stands the King, a radiant smiling creature motioning to the boy.

Gordy opens his mouth to speak, but a ragged scream carries his last words away. A helix of blood and brains twists out of the back of his head as he slumps forward over his deck.

The paramedics find a little starburst made up from parts of Gordy's skull smeared across the back of his chair. And on the TV screen in the front room the same message is being flashed up over and over again:

ELVIS HAS LEFT THE BUILDING. ELVIS HAS LEFT THE BUILD-ING. ELVIS HAS LEFT THE BUILDING.

VENUS IN MICROSOFT:
MALE MAS(S)OCHISM AND CYBERNETICS

Stephen Pfohl

One evening as the moon is waning radon I spy the telematic form of a blonde on blonde goddess at the cinema. Maybe I'm s/he. Her filmic body ablaze to my projective pleasure; her bare legs sex lips ass open to the always only partially visible "ends of Man." For the price of a ticket I get to participate in a dreamy bending of industrial taboos escaping HIStory. I feel at once anxious and numb. This is fascinating. I watch myself watching myself watching my fantasies while watching my fantasies watching myself. This is true. Just look at the statistics.

At the film's climax a stoney cold Goddess dressed in nothing but furs stands transfigured as a blank-faced male double showers her with spurts of white liquid CAPITAL. Maybe I'm s/he. I am transferred into the microsoft: aroused and electric. This is my body—a telematic exchange of faith leaping screen to screen. This is whitemale techno-magic. This is

---

Editors' note: This is the first part of a longer essay to be published by the *Canadian Journal of Political and Social Theory*, Vol. 16, 1993.

obscene. This is fascinating. The next thing I know they're strapping me into a cockpit and blind-folding me with information. "Baghdad's your target," I hear a white man in black face saying. These are my orders. "Jack off as often as you want. Nobody will say; nobody will see; nobody will smell a thing."

As *I was returning from my devotions*, the thought came to mind that no house without a TV is a home (to me). I entered the always open VIDEO PALACE, feeling more sovereign than solid state and more (trans)sexual than ever. Mouth to screen to mouth: I was hungry and wanted what's more than bodies can give. Suddenly I saw a woman's figure glowing electric. As beautiful as celluloid, she was separated from me by a nothing but a cold screen of data; and I was confident I'd access her image. Maybe s/he was I. It seemed as if the PRETTY WOMAN from the screen *had taken pity on me, come alive, and followed me* home in plastic bag. *I was seized by a nameless fear, my heart threatened to burst.*[1]

Theses on the Erotic Geography of HIStory: art in the age of simulation

I

The story is told of an automaton constructed in such a way that it could play a winning game of JEOPARDY, answering each of it opponent's memories with a counter-memory. An orphan in World Beat attire and something unnameable in its mouth sat before the game bored flashing to the home viewing audience. A system of screens created the illusion that this game was transparent from all sides. Actually, a little parasite who was an expert JEOPARDY player sat inside and guided the orphan's maneuvers by remote control. One can imagine a geographical counterpart to this device. The orphan called "Historical materialist geography" is to partially win, just as it loses itself in the timely conjuring of alternative spaces. It can uneasily become a "power-reflexive" match for anybody if it but enlists the services of radical atheology, which today, as we know, is wizened and has to keep out of sight. In mass demonstrations against the U.S. led attack on Iraq all the anarchists wore masks.

II

When something becomes a *structural possibility* it is constituted as positively necessary, factually objective and morally valued or economic. This is what distinguishes a structural possibility from the fleshy contingencies of totemic simulation. Structural possibilities parasite off what (modern) power renders absent. This is no universal law. This is a way of trying to both describe and deconstruct the constitutive violence of white patriarchal CAPITAL.

For better and for worse. Like the soul of a commodity, or the cut up subjectivity of women, slaves and wage laborers, persons tattooed by modern power are cast as tragic actors, whose every thought is scripted by an agency of white letters. This is a way of describing discursive language—representational rites enacted by men whose words one can bank on. Credit-worthy men; men who have much to give to (and thus take away from) the ritual scenes they govern. These are scenes of imperial technology or white magic.

Like all forms of technology (or magic) these white magical scenes operate in the shadows of what appears more originary—the space of sacrifice, elementary religious forms, scientific displacements, or whatever. By contrast, technologies of black magic simulate the disabling powers of sacrifice. In so doing, they return the fantastic surplus that separates them from others. This is what makes black magic technologies so seductive and so healing. Practitioners of white magic technologies, on the other hand, labor to cover over the gaps: securing the losses, extending the boundaries, exacting a fetishized surplus as profit.

Not far from the space in which I'm (w)riting there is a transnational bio-tech firm named NARCISSUS. Its business is both ARTIFICIAL INTELLIGENCE and VIRTUAL REALITY. Its business is the rearrangement of entertaining memories for maximal profit and the forgetting of everything else. Its business is war or the (sacrificial) production of orphans. This business, an extension of sadism, or the masterful male dream of purified enlightenment, involves both more and less than sadism. This business is mas(s)ochistic in the general economic sense of the word. It offers an image of pain or unhappiness as indissolubly BOUND-UP with an image of redemption or liberation—the *ecstasy of communication*. This business blurs the sexualized difference between tragedy (where things appear in the form of their doubles) and farce (where even doubled revolution is premodeled for user friendly markets world wide). The same applies to our view of boundaries, which is the concern of geography. There today appears to be a secret agreement between those (of us) on the outside and those parts of ourselves that are stupidly in the know. This is indistinction, not simply victimization; but on all sides the business of mas(s)ochism parasites off whatever differences remain. These claims cannot be settled cheaply. Historically material geographers are aware of that, even if melancholic about prospects for redemption.

III

A cartographer who maps spaces without distinguishing between major and minor acts in accordance with the following truth: no events should be lost for erotic geography. To be sure, only a partially redeemed (or power reflexive) human/animalkind is given to heterogeneous spatiality—which is to say, its range of self-limiting structural possibilities become (ex)citable as ritual bindings and boundaries spin vertiginous. This is a ruinous awareness. It is stupid to wait for some final Judgment Day when here in the space between us we might be touched by a more poetic form of geography; an erotic geography that plays back upon itself in orphaned waves and (dis)autobiographical musing. But wouldn't such a cursed geography be condemned silence and the chaos of dark laughter? Perhaps that's just the point (at which such a wicked form of geography begins again and again and again).

IV

Seek for signs of food and clothing first, then the Symbolic Order shall be added onto you, if at the same time subtracted from your bodies.

—Black Madonna Durkheim, 1991

The class struggle, which is always partially present to an erotic geographer influenced by Marx, is a fight for the material and imaginary spaces of memory. "Nevertheless, it is not in the form of the spoils which fall to the victor that the latter make their presence felt in the class struggle. They manifest themselves in this struggle as courage, humor, cunning, and fortitude. They have a retroactive force and will constantly call in question every victory, past and present, of the rulers."[2] An erotic geographer must be aware of this most inconspicuous of transformations—the contradictory accessing of spaces in excess of a given order of things in time.

At eight o'clock on June 23, 1787 in the heat of revolutionary CAPITALIST expansion (of the "Rights of Man" over "Nature"), the Marquis de Sade began composing a new novel. A preliminary note reads:

> Two [orphaned] sisters, one, extremely dissipated (Juliette), has a happy, rich and successful life; the other (Justine), extremely strait-laced, falls into a thousand traps, which end by causing her ruin.[3]

Justine's story was completed first. It appeared in 1791, the year in which the new French Penal Code announced mathematically precise punishments for each and every infraction of the law. This was also the year of the Voodoo-inspired revolt of Africans enslaved by the French in Haiti. It is tempting to read Sade's pornographic enclosure of Justine's orphaned body as a monstrous allegory of a New World Order of economic restrictions. The libertines who assault Justine inscribe their truths upon her skin, penetrating her with rational logic and the promise of control. Justine resists being incorporated into this narrative of western (male) desire, but her resistance brings nothing but tragedy. She is tortured and raped, and although she tries to escape, there is no escape. Unlike her Haitian counterparts, Justine is on her own. She is denied what African slaves kept secretly alive—ritual access to spaces less vulnerable to the narcissistic terrors and death-defying promises of a CAPITALized selfhood. Her hopes for better futures LIE (nostalgically) in what's past. She is slain by the electricity of this novel moment in HIStory.

Justine's death is tragic. This is not the case with her sister. Juliette is an orphan who mutates in accordance with the structural possibilities of an unprecedented space of modern subjectivity. Hers is a story of the farcical pleasures offered (even, if in contradictory ways, to women) by giving oneself over to the cynical demands of life within the disciplinary thickness of one's own skin. Juliette's story appears in 1797. Unlike Justine, she prostitutes herself, becoming a "grand thief" and property owner. This is HIStory. Juliette is well paid for her sacrifices. At the end of her novel existence she dies at peace, well defended from those she parasites.

Between the (w)ritings of one orphan sister and anOther the world has changed. Justine could not be rationally persuaded, but her sister is seduced into a new form of sadistic training. She has been converted to the ways of modern "men" by a corrupt abbess in charge of the orphans' education. She joins in the educative process, or so it appears in the (w)ritings of sadism. As Foucault remarks, between Justine's text and Juliette's, a new form of power has entered the world; a new form of parasitism. It feeds ruinously upon all that remains outside the narcissistic confines the normalized ego.

The disciplinary hollowing out of interior psychic space has begun. In this, "violence, life and death, desire and sexuality will extend, below the level of representation, an immense expanse of shade that we are now attempting to regain, as far as we can, in our discourse, in our freedom, in our thought. But our thought is so brief, our freedom so enslaved, our discourse so repetitive, that we must face the fact that that expanse of shade below is really a bottomless sea. The prosperities of *Juliette* are still more solitary—and endless."[4]

<h2 style="text-align:center">V</h2>

The true picture of erotic spaces barred from what is structurally possible flits by. Such spaces are recognizable only as images which flash in an instant; fleeting gaps that defy words, left-overs from some unacknowledged sacrificial meal. These uncanny spaces involve the ghostly reappearance of what's been made to disappear; seeing what's been rendered as unseeable; hearing what's been silenced; tasting what's forbidden; touched by the smell of rotting fruit.

During the first half of the nineteenth century such useless spaces were by no means forgotten (or fully repressed) by those most sacrificed for the sadistic expansion of CAPITAL. Whole classes fought back, only to be defeated by superior military and industrial force. In 1848, while CAPITAL spread westward across the U.S., deploying wholesale genocide and slavery, in Europe resistance disrupted the geography of the market nearly everywhere. But not for long. The revolutions of 1848 were met with excessive state violence. The brutal subordination of Czech proletarians in Prague was a case in point. One of the bloodiest restorations of CAPITALIst power, the suppression of the popular uprising in Prague was also a scene of sacrifice witnessed by a ten year old boy, Leopold von Sacher-Masoch. His father was the Chief of Police.

Two years earlier, the young Masoch had been exposed to similar stories of violence in Galicia, a district forming the northeast corner of the Austrian Empire. During a revolt of Polish landlords, that turned into a three-party war involving nationalistic aristocrats, Polish peasants and the Austrian army, fantastic scenarios of revolt were met by even greater counter-revolutionary violence. Tales of indiscriminate massacres—mass hangings, burnings, torture and burials alive—passed into the ears of the Police Chief's son. Masoch's memories of such revolutionary defeats did more than fuel a passion for repeating such ill-fated dramas in the spectacles he staged with tin soldiers and puppets. They also provided a material context for the imaginative form of (w)riting with which his name has come to be associated, and for the paradoxical pleasures and pains such (w)ritings elicits in HIStory. From the nineteenth century to the present, Mas(s)ochism signifies a contradictory erotic flight-path from the disciplinary confines of sadistic CAPITAList expansion.

In both his immediate family situation, where Leopold found himself enamored by the seductive charms of his scandalous paternal aunt, the Countess Zenobia, and in his memories of the HIStorical scenery of defeated revolutions, the role of powerful Slavic women loomed large. Indeed, within the cultural geographies of Galicia and Prague there circulated many stories of the public actions of brave and powerful women. One curious aspect of the 1846 Polish rebellion in Galicia involved women in "a fantastic plan for the strangling of their Austrian dancing partners at a great military ball in Lemberg. Wires were to be fitted to the necks of the officers as an incident in a sort of allegorical masque, then applied in grim earnest."[5] Although a death in the Hapsburg family led to the cancellation of officers' plans to attend the ball, thus derailing this cunning act of rebellion, Leopold himself forever related stories about the bravery of women during the bloody events in Prague. He "used to tell his friends...that he had been out on the barricades, as a boy of twelve, with a girl cousin named Miroslava, some years older than himself. She wore a beautiful fur jacket, he would say, and carried pistols in her belt. She ordered him about, shouted commands, he hastened to obey. Amid these scenes of death and destruction he conceived a passionate adoration of her."[6]

Mythic in appearance, these images of women's power were translated by Masoch into allegories of men giving themselves as consenting slaves to cruel female tyrants. This represents a fantastic (if also fantastically distorted) mode of keeping alive certain images of resistance to the sadistic male demands of profit driven CAPITAL. This is to read subversive, if contradictory, male pleasures in Masoch's tales and the mas(s)ochistic rites for which they are culturally emblematic.

A century later, Barbara Erhenreich would locate a related space of contradictory subversion in the pornographic rituals of middle class U.S. men. In *The Hearts of Men*, Ehrenreich theorizes that—if only in fantasy—these men were able to partially escape CAPITAL boredom by giving themselves in masturbatory pleasure—not to fleshy women—but to glossy *Playboy* centerfolds.[7] Without condoning pornography's distorted representations of women, Erhenreich argues that the contradictory pleasures of having fantasized sex with glossy magazine images may have engendered spaces not fully integrated into the disciplined patriarchal circuitry of post World War II CAPITAL. Within the historical geography of the moment, these perverse spaces—although susceptible to further colonization—made visible contradictions that might, otherwise, have remain disguised. For indeed, "every image ... that is not in some way recognized by the present as one of its own concerns threatens to disappear entirely."[8]

VI

To articulate spaces of contradictory erotic possibility does not mean to recognize the totality of all geographical relations at a given point of time. It means, instead, to attend to the form of a particular fantasy as it flashes up at a moment of danger. Erotic geography wishes to reflex upon that image of space which unexpectedly appears in a terrain fraught with bodily and/or psychic danger. For the critical geographer is vigilant in the awareness that in order to spark hope in the realizability of less hierarchical spaces, one must be "firmly convinced that even the dead will not be safe from the enemy if he wins. And this enemy has not ceased to be victorious."[9]

As a professor of HIStory, Leopold von Sacher-Masoch believed this as well. Masoch suffered passions which he read as symptomatic of a diseased culture—a society haunted by the failure of revolutions to stem the sadistic spread of CAPITAL. Masoch's published texts are typically read as pornographic tales of excessive male submission to the cold tyranny of cruel women masters, among them various figurations of "Mother Nature." These stories are better understood as elements of Masoch's life-long project of allegorical social commentary. Indeed, *Venus in Furs*, the classic text of mas(s)ochistic male literature, was itself part of a series of six stories which were to figure as but one of six larger cycles comprising *The Heritage of Cain*.[10] Masoch selected this title to suggest "the burden of crime and suffering" that had become the cursed heritage of modern "men," for whom nature was nothing but an icy cold Mother. As Gilles Deleuze points out, "the coldness of the stern mother is in reality a transmutation from which the new man [of CAPITAList modernity] emerges."[11]

Venus in Furs, along with *The Wanderer*, *The Man of Surrenders*, *Moonlight Night*, *Plato's Love* and *Marzella*, constituted the first phase of this cycle. Published under the title *Love*, these controversial texts provocatively mirror and excessively articulate the sickening impossibilities of enacting free and generous forms of erotic exchange in a society governed by self-serving economic contracts. By "'desexualizing' love and at the same time sexualizing the entirety HIStory of humanity," Masoch's (w)ritings cross his own biographical desires with the parasitic economic exigencies of CAPITAL.[12]

The texts comprising *Love* were completed in 1870. The following year, international CAPITAL violently closed-in upon the heterogeneous, nonauthoritarian, and "vernacular" erotic geographies defended to death by the Paris Commune. Before being massacred, the Commune conjured into existence a form of space conceived "not as a static reality but as active, generative ...[and] created by interaction, as something that our bodies reactivate, and...in turn modifies and transforms us."[13] The spatial erotics engendered by the commune, like the remaining cycles of Masoch's *The Heritage of Cain*, would remain forever fragmentary and incomplete. Indeed, the proposed names for the remaining cycles in *The Heritage of Cain* are suggestive of ritual enclosures dominating the western imagination of erotic life during the late nineteenth century—*Property*, *The State*, *War*, *Work* and *Death*.

Masoch's life ended in fragments as well. Blocked by personal, HIStorical, and geographic circumstances from forming more reciprocal alliances with others, Masoch—like Sade before him—retreated into the imaginary pleasures of male fantasy. Until the fantasies imploded and left

Masoch striking-out in mad rage at the woman he called his wife. But by then, Masoch was old and his prestigious literary reputation slipping. On March 9, 1895, Masoch, an author compared to the greatest of his European contemporaries, was committed to an insane asylum in Mannheim.

During his lifetime, Masoch's literary and personal fantasies were already (mis)diagnosed by the psychiatrist Kraft-Ebbing as passive counterparts to Sade's. A more careful reading of Masoch's texts suggests something more contradictory. Masoch's (w)ritings engendered ambivalent spaces of erotic fantasy in excess of the dominant discourses of his time. In this, Masoch's allegorical narratives, with their ambivalent displays of fantastic male submission, foreshadowed aspects of the erotic geography of the emerging industrial "masses." Like Masoch's male protagonists, the *masses* may have ritually absorbed, rather than identified with, CAPITAL's most virulent economic restrictions. This is not to suggest that perverse spaces of erotic resistance are ever free of the violence of CAPITAL. Nor are they timeless. Indeed, less than a half century after Masoch's death in 1905, the mas(s)ochistic spaces prefigured in texts such as *Venus in Furs* would play host to a new and more flexible form of CAPITAL. But even here the enclosures are not fully sealed. Unlike the demonstrative negations of law embodied in Sade's criminal irony, Mas(s)ochistic (w)ritings float suspended in dense and imaginative layers of aestheticized disavowal.[14]

More allusive than frontal in their artful plays of resistance, and more seductive than declarative in their deployment of signs, Masoch's texts—like the hyper-conformity of the "masses" imagined by Baudrillard—threaten to disappear into the cool enclosures of an imaginary that is void of interpretive reference. This poses a challenging dilemma to the culture of CAPITAL. How might the secrets informing such popular and literary practices be recuperatively mastered? How, in other words, might such perverse bodies of (w)riting be made to work for a system that demands their incorporation? Certainly not by force alone. Virtually nobody is forcing anybody to watch television, and yet masses of people keep their eyes/"I"s on the screen. Why? Is it because somebodies are manipulating everybody else? Or, do the mas(s)ochistic pleasures of watching life fade to screens of premodeled information give magical access to spaces of erotic uncertainty, repressed by the sadistic demands of modern CAPITAL?

Is this what makes mas(s)ochism today so attractive—its promise of pleasurable spaces in excess of discipline? This is hinted at in the (w)ritings of both Masoch and Jean Baudrillard. But so is the danger that, in response to such ritual perversions of discipline, CAPITAL will arm itself with new technologies of image management, supplementing the rigidities of "normalization" with the more flexible seduction of consent. This is a danger of contemporary geography: the threat that mas(s)ochism, like MTV, may become a magical tool of the ruling classes.

VII

> Consider the cold blankness of the screen glowing. It is within this space of almost electric transference that one today rediscovers mystery.
>
> —Jack O. Lantern, Threepenny Soap-Opera

To geographers who wish to replot space in time, Reno Heimlich recommends ignorance of everything that LIES outside the borders of everyday life. There is no better way of characterizing the method with which critical erotic geography must break. For without exception, "the cultural treasures" the geographer works with have a sacrificial origin which cannot be acknowledged without horror. For, in truth, "there is no document of civilization that is not at the same time [and space] a document of barbarism. And just as such a document is not free of barbarism, barbarism taints also the manner in which it was transmitted from one owner to another."[15] The erotic geographer, therefore, reflexively doubles back upon one's complicity with barbarism, re-mirroring the sacrifices that recurrently give birth to culture itself.

Mirrorings, replicas and copies of mirrored images are also present throughout Masoch's texts. In the opening sequences of *Venus in Furs*, the narrator encounters a strange Goddess with "stony, lifeless eyes" and "marble body." Complaining of the coldness of men from northern regions—"you children of reason"—this "sublime" figure, draped in the fur of a sable, informs the narrator that she is an advocate of more archaic pleasures. Desire, she says, is weaker than pleasure. "It is man who desires, woman who is desired. This is woman's only advantage, but it is a decisive one. By making man so vulnerable to passion, nature has placed him at women's mercy."[16]

The cold marble woman's voice rings true to the narrator. But before he can act upon this truth he is awoken from his dream. The narrator, it appears, has fallen asleep reading Hegel, only to find himself captivated by an image of "a beautiful woman, naked beneath her dark furs." This image—a "large oil painting done in the powerful colors of the Flemish School"—hangs in the study of his friend Severin.[17] This, the narrator now believes, must be the erotic origin of his dream. But after informing Severin of this fact, the narrator's eyes are redirected to yet another image. "It was a remarkably good copy of Titan's famous Venus with the Mirror," itself but another copy of a model. And so the story unfolds—one seemingly true copy fading as but a screen for others. Mirror image to mirror image; one fantastically screened memory after another.

In *The Eighteenth Brumaire of Louis Bonaparte*, Marx analyzes the failure of the 1848 revolution in France and the "ghostly" restoration of monarchy. Central to Marx's discussion is the way in which bourgeois social movements may "hide from themselves the limited ... content of their struggles." This, they accomplish, by "masking" contemporary social forms in the cultural iconography of past triumphs, such that "men and things seem set in sparkling diamond and each day's spirit is ecstatic."[18] Thus, the "gladiators" of French bourgeois struggles replicate "the ideals, art forms and self-deceptions" in order "to maintain their enthusiasm at the high level appropriate to great historical tragedy. A century earlier, Cromwell and the English ... had borrowed for their bourgeois revolution the language, passions and illusions of the Old Testament."[19]

Worse, yet, were the "restoration years" 1848 to 1851, when parasitic images of bygone glories were used to mask the defeat of revolutionary actions by the resurrection of their ghosts. Depicting the crowning of Napoleon's nephew as monarch as a parodic flight from the reality of present contradictions, Marx concludes that, "an entire people ... suddenly found itself plunged back into [the costumed drama of] an already dead epoch."[20] This led Marx to re(w)rite Hegel's observation that "all the great events and characters of world history occur, so to speak twice," adding, "the first time as tragedy, the second as farce."[21]

But what if such doubled appearances return a third time? And this time, not as a farcical copy of a tragic original, but as a copy of nothing but that which is modeled on a copy? Laughter rolls from the mouths of the studio audience. I am (w)riting about a form of eroticism that is characteristic of mas(s)ochistic texts and the "masses." I am (w)riting about simulation.

VIII

"The tradition of the oppressed teaches us that the 'state of emergency' in which we live is not the exception but the rule."[22] In order to embody this teaching, critical geographers must articulate a method that is in keeping with this insight. This may entail considerable unlearning. Rather than normalizing our scientific procedures we must seek to remobilize boundaries that have separated our knowledge from others. This will improve our position in the ongoing struggle against fascism: to retheorize the geography of simulation as *aboriginally conjured* in resistance to the sickening violence of disciplinary cultural enclosures. Given the terrorism of contemporary forms of cybernetic simulation, this may seem like a strange conceptual reversal. Nevertheless, in articulating a genealogy of resistance, it is important to remember that simulation is first called into existence as a defensive manoeuvre on the part of the oppressed.

Simulation resists the believability of a given symbolic order. To simulate is to pretend to possess what one doesn't possess—imaginary control over a world where things appear as naturally given. But things are never naturally given without other (possible) things being taken away. This, simulators recognize, if secretly. The pretense of simulation feeds off the fetishized reality of representational power. Representational power, on the other hand, is rooted in dissimulation, or the promise that signs might ever equal the things they signify. But they never will. Signifiers never equal what they reference. Words never equal the things they order. Money never equals the body. Simulators know all this but act as if they don't. This is simulation's challenge to an existing social order. Simulation threatens to deconstruct the hegemonic character of all binding representations, of all hierarchy. This is its magic—a strategic prize for all players in any game of power.

Notes

1. Leopold Von Sacher-Masoch, *Venus in Furs*, trans. Uwe Moeller and Laura Lindgren, (New York: Blast Books, 1989), p. 66.

2. Walter Benjamin, "Theses on the Philosophy of History," in *Illuminations*, trans. Harry Zohn, (New York Schocken Books, 1969), pp. 254-55.

3. Marquis de Sade, as quoted in James Cleugh, *The Marquis and the Chevalier: A Study in the Psychology of Sex as Illustrated by the Lives and Personalities of The Marquis de Sade (1740-1814) and the Chevalier von Sacher-Masoch (1836-1905)*, (New York: Duell, Sloan and Pearce, 1951), p. 107.

4. Michel Foucault, *The Order of Things*, trans. Alan Sheridan, (New York: Vintage Books, 1970), pp.210-11.

5. James Cleugh, *The Marquis and the Chevalier*, p. 154.

6. Ibid, p. 155.

7. Barbara Ehrenreich, *The Hearts of Men: American Dreams and the Flight from Commitment*, (Garden City, N.Y.: Anchor, 1983).

8. Walter Benjamin, "Theses on the Philosophy of History," p. 255.

9. Ibid.

10. Leopold von Sacher-Masoch, *Venus in Furs*, trans. Jean McNeil, in *Masochism* (New York: Zone Books, 1989).

11. Gilles Deleuze, *Coldness and Cruelty*, trans. Jean Mc Neil, in *Masochism*, (New York Zone Books, 1989), p. 12.

12. Ibid.

13. Kristen Ross, *The Emergence of Social Space: Rimbaud and the Paris Commune*, (Minneapolis: University of Minnesota Press, 1988), p. 35.

14. For a more detailed discussion of these themes in Masoch see Gilles Deleuze, *Coldness and Cruelty*.

15. Ibid., p. 256

16. Sacher-Masoch, *Venus in Furs*, p. 146.

17. Ibid., p. 148.

18. Karl Marx, "The Eighteenth Brumaire of Louis Bonaparte, trans. Ben Fowkes in *Surveys from Exile*, David Fernbach (ed.), New York: Vintage Books, 1973), p. 150.

19. Ibid., p. 148.

20. Ibid.

21. Ibid., p. 146.

22. Walter Benjamin, "Theses on the Philosophy of History," p. 257.

FROM FALSE CONSCIOUSNESS TO VIRAL CONSCIOUSNESS[1]

Dianne Rothleder

My father wants nothing more for me than that I acquire a good job, and a good husband, and that I make a few children who will be very good grandchildren. My maternal grandfather wanted the gender-appropriate version for his daughter—a good job was not in my mother's profile.

When we reproduce, we want confirmation of our own worth. We also want to make amends for our own failures. These two goals are contradictory in that our worth is compromised by our failures. This contradiction makes us want both to reproduce ourselves as clones and to produce not ourselves, but something other, something monstrously other.

The reproduction of ourselves as clones falls under the broad rubric of economy and its concomitant circling and return to the origin. If the figure of economy is the circle, as Derrida suggests, then to want our children to return to us what we have presented to them as a gift is to annul the gift.[2] In truth, we give nothing to our children, rather we sell them and we sell things to them. We always want a return for our effort.[3] And since the desire for return precedes the "gift of life", there is in essence no gift, and perhaps there is no life. "Life", here, as freedom to choose (how) to live.

The child of reproduction is born to indentured servitude, is enslaved by parental desire and by the economic debt of return. This debt can only be repaid through the return to the same, through the subsequent recycling of history.

My father wants nothing more for me than that I acquire a good job, and a good husband, and that I make a few children who will be very good grandchildren.

To see the production of children as a function of capital is to see the extent to which capital has invaded our bodies and our being. Capital penetrates to the very DNA which allows us to replicate and makes us reproducers—makers of the same. We make children who will have good jobs and good spouses and who will make good children who will have good jobs...

Jobs always figure prominently in this economic scheme. We are producers of producers, machines who are makers of machines. Capital replicates itself indirectly through the creation of progeny who act as job-seekers and job-holders. The value of the replicators is predicated on the job-worthiness of their progeny, and so the replicators will always strive to replicate, to reproduce more of the same.

Capital, then, as akin to viruses. Both capital and viruses are non-living yet highly effective agents. Both latch onto living beings, penetrate them, and colonize them. Both capital and viruses multiply indirectly through the beings they colonize, and both cause genetic replication which serves them as masters and does harm to the slaves. Just as capital circulates, so there is always a virus "going around."

We can go so far as to call capital a kind of virus, but it is a special kind. When capital invades a person and causes that person to reproduce, the person reproduces him- or herself as a maker of capital; whereas when a virus invades a cell, the virus co-opts the cell's DNA or RNA and forces the cell to produce new viruses. The cell loses its ability to reproduce itself and becomes instead a producer of the monstrously other.

In discussing Derrida's views of phallocentrism, Gayatri Spivak writes:

> By virtue of the father's name the son refers to the father. The irreducible importance of the name and the law in this situation makes it quite clear that the question is not merely one of psycho-socio-sexual behavior but of the production and consolidation of reference and meaning. The desire to make one's progeny represent his presence is akin to the desire to make one's words represent the full meaning of one's intention.[4]

Derrida, via Spivak, here suggests that   to reproduce one-self phallocentrically is to make oneself the font of meaning, to place oneself at the center of value, and to create like value in one's progeny.

What we see here is a reversal of valuation from what we discussed above. The two versions, again, are first that we reproduce children who will become valued members of the economy so that we can then confirm our own value as makers of things which have marketable value, and second that we reproduce so that we can see ourselves as the source of all that is valuable. We make our children take our names and our values in an effort to confirm the worth of our name and our values.

In both cases, we reproduce ourselves. That is, we have children so that we can see ourselves once again—ourselves either as valued for having made valuable children, or ourselves as valuable for being the source of all value.

An economy of capital production and accumulation is based upon reproduction—that is, upon the production of the same. Our children must have our values, and our value, if capital is to continue its rule and aggrandizement. Seen from the point of view of the family, we have children as a way of proving our worth in a noble, moral sense, but under the logic of capital, we have children to demonstrate our economic worth.

Each of these selves, the family self and the capital self, is at work at the same time. The family self is the self of Marxian ideology, or false consciousness. In discussing the overlapping of ideology and false consciousness, Engels writes: "the real motives impelling [the agent] remain unknown to him, otherwise it would not be an ideological process at all. Hence he imagines false or apparent motives."[5] Terry Eagleton adds, "Ideology is here in effect rationalization—a kind of double motiva-tion, in which the surface meaning serves to block from consciousness the subject's true purpose."[6]

An ideological attachment to children as proof of one's moral worth is a fiction designed to cover up the truth of the underlying economic exigencies of reproduction.

The contrast between the Derridean phallocentric reading and the Marxian economic reading is a sharp one. For Derrida, as we noted above, phallocentric reproduction of the same arises in response to the desire to be the font of value. That is, re-production is entirely self-serving when it is seen in its true light. For Marx, on the other hand, re-producers of a capitalist economy cannot, on this reading, be truly phallocentric because they are not really reproducing themselves so much as they are making capital.

The level at which we might see the phallocentric is rather that of capital. Capital is phallocentric in that it reproduces itself and gathers itself solely for its own greatness. Capital desires to be the sole value, the sole measure of value, and the sole source of value.

Capital takes over the reproductive capacity of its victim, alters the victim's reproductive functions, and causes its victims to reproduce beings who will reproduce capital. In this way, capital acts as a virus potent enough to overcome the potentially deep-felt desire either to reproduce phallocentrically, or the desire to produce rather than to reproduce. ("Production," once again, is taken to mean creation of what is monstrously other.)

✳ ✳ ✳ ✳ ✳

It will be helpful here to pause to steep ourselves in biology for a few paragraphs. "Biology" is to be taken loosely because biologists do not think of viruses as living beings, and biology is the study of life processes.

For a virus to invade a cell, the cell must have a receptor site which complements a binding site on the virus. That is, virus and cell must be compatible in a specific way before there can be an invasion. The cell "recognizes" the virus' binding site, and the virus "recognizes" the cell's receptor site.

The virus attaches itself to the cell, breaks through the cell wall, inserts its genetic coding, either DNA or RNA but never both, into the genetic material of the cell, and, just like that, the virus has control of the cell's reproductive functions. Viral reproduction occurs by the cell's producing viral particles which then escape from the parent cell in search of their own cells to occupy. This escape can either be a painless passing through a cell wall, or a sudden bursting of the cell wall as the internal pressure of many viral particles increases to the breaking point. With this latter event, the cell explodes from the pressure and the viral particles are scattered.[7]

Viruses cannot multiply without helper cells, and these helper cells must be compatible with the virus even as the virus must be compatible with some kind of cell. That is, viruses cannot do what they do without some kind of community within which they simultaneously recognize and are recognized. Mere exposure to a virus, then, is a necessary though not sufficient condition for infection.[8]

Two kinds of viral infections suggest themselves here—computer viruses and AIDS. We know that computer viruses spread when two computers are linked by wires, telephones, or shared disks. The viral program travels across the linking medium, attaches itself to a new victim, and forces the new victim to replicate the virus. Computer viruses are not living beings, but rather have some kind of mediated existence.

Computer viruses cannot be transmitted between computers that are not somehow compatible. The computer that adjusts my car's fuel consumption does not recognize my IBM PC. And since my PC has no modem, it can recognize other computers only through floppy disk insertion. If I use only pure disks in my computer, it will remain mute, isolated, and virus-free.

Recognition equally plays a role in the transmission of AIDS—especially in the media coverage of the disease. In the beginning, somewhere around 1982, AIDS was a Haitian disease, a gay men's disease, an intravenous drug user's disease, and an African disease. Somehow, AIDS only travelled within these communities of mutually recognized people. Haitians had, perhaps, some genetic or national susceptibility to the disease. "We" did not recognize "them," and so "we" were not at risk. (Parenthetically, we still do not seem to recognize the plight of Haitians.)

Each of the groups that was reported to have widespread AIDS infection was just that—a group—them, not us. As long as we did not recognize any of these groups, we were safe from infection.

But just as my computer could in principle recognize nearly any 5¼" floppy disk inserted into its A or B drive, so could nearly any body recognize the insertion of AIDS-infected bodily fluids, and since people have more than two drives, AIDS spreads rather handily. Still, we try to protect ourselves through declarations of non-recognition, as if mere language could protect us from the sense of community that viral transmission requires.

This denial of commonality allows us to talk about mutually exclusive groups: the gay community, IV drug users, promiscuous people, and "us". As we learn that these boundaries, far from being fixed, are actually fluid and flowing, we have two choices. The first is to admit our community with these communities. The media did not do this. The second is to place large barriers around all susceptible orifices as if to say, "we may be somewhat intertwined temporarily, but really we are not open to each other, we are separate and have nothing in common." Thus, dentists wear rubber gloves, paramedics wear face masks, lovers wear condoms. George Bush "wears" rhetorical garb which says that Haitians are fleeing economic misery and not political misery—as if these two could possibly be separated. The United States "wears" laws that bar people with AIDS from penetrating the nation's borders. Ronald Reagan wore "silence." In defiance of Reagan's cloak, people with AIDS wear buttons that say "Silence = Death," and indeed, they are right.

This death comes about both literally—through ignorance and through absurd bureaucratic delay, and figuratively through the refusal to recognize in the Hegelian sense of recognition. Self-consciousness dies without recognition of the other. By refusing to recognize these others then, we not only destroy them, but we also destroy ourselves. What silence cannot do, however, is destroy the virus. Nor can it destroy what "we" share in common with "them."

The "bio" statement for Arthur Kroker in the *Panic Encyclopedia* says, "*Arthur Kroker* is the Canadian virus. His aim is to invade the postmodern mind, replicate its master genetic code and, in this clonal disguise, endlessly proliferate critical thinking."[9] Kroker wants to be a good virus, a virus for the good. Perhaps this means that he cannot be the American virus, for American invasion is necessarily imperial, while Canadian invasion sounds merely impotent. We should wonder as well whether or not Arthur Kroker is critical thinking, for as a virus, he would be causing postmodern minds to replicate Arthur Kroker in all of us, at least insofar as we recognize one another.

The two traditionally recognized ways of subverting capital are first, the Marxian returning to producers the right to what follows from their production, and second, emphasizing the non-productive. The second way—emphasizing non-production—comes from Adorno and Horkheimer's critiques of Marx's insistence on production as the sole medium through which human beings realize their essence. The second way, then, is a critique of the first way. Martin Jay's characterization of this second position follows Arendt and Adorno. Jay writes, "Implicit in the reduction of man to *animal laborans*...was the reification of nature as a field for human exploitation. If Marx had his way, the entire world would be turned into a 'giant workhouse.'"[10]

The violence implicit in the phrase "The world is my oyster" is the self-same violence of conquest and exploitation. It is the violence of production and workhouses. We need merely crack open oyster shell after oyster shell after oyster shell in search of the perfect pearl. If millions of oysters die in the process, that matters little when compared to the dis-covery of a pearl. Even if the opener of the oyster gets to keep the profits from the pearl, still there has been violence. It is worth noting that although the pearl is a thing of beauty and value for humans, it is a sign of disease for oysters.[11]

The fruit of the sea, the fruit of the land, and of the air are all there to be used, to be re-made, to be the source of human profit-making. Not only is all of this available to us, we must make use of it all if we are to become fully human. Under this logic, to become self-realized, we must deny the value of all that is other, we must dominate all that could conceivably exist independently of us.

To demonstrate our own liberty, we must enslave otherness and bring it into the circulation of the money economy. This is the logic of capital, of the phallocentric reproduction of the same. The circle emerges as the perfect figure, as the infinite repetition of itself, as the endless return *to* the same, and as the endless return *of* the same. The circle is the figure of the cosmos.

The phallocentric reproduction of the same is mediated reproduction. That is, it demands otherness recognized as otherness as a mediator. More concretely, males require females for the making of more males; the Lacanian Symbolic requires the Imaginary; Hegelian self-consciousness requires the awareness of the other. The other, then, is a fundamental category for possibility of reproduction of the same.

Because otherness becomes a reified category in this scheme, essential-ist gynocentric glorification of the other merely serves to uphold the status quo in the same way that Marx's emphasis on production serves to uphold a capitalist framework. Gynocentrism may attempt to overthrow the yoke of mediation, and hence to be subversive, but because the basis of gynocentrism is still otherness, it cannot be a completely radical strategy anymore than production can radically subvert capital.

With this argument in place, we can see the attraction of non-production for those who wish to subvert, and we can see the reason that capital fears the non-productive.

Any threat to production is met with stern disapproval. Hence, the popular dismay with drugs that alter consciousness (e.g. LSD); the popular support for those which enhance production (e.g. caffeine); the traditional loathing of both homosexual relations and birth control which turn sex into non-productive recreational activity; and the general commodification of all human activities so that no matter what we are doing, we are still in the production/consumption scheme.

We have gone, then, from Hegelian "being" to Marxian "doing." Non-production is an attempt to return to being-as-non-doing. Hegelian being, though, is not a stable state, and Marxian doing and the reification of otherness seem to be logical followers to being. For Hegel, the opposition between being and non-being is resolved through becoming. Becoming is both the flow of time and the ever-circling movement towards self-realization. Becoming is the enabling condition of doing, and hence also of self-realization. Neither being nor non-being is stable, whereas doing maintains a kind of dynamic stability. Thus, we are perpetually trapped in the Hegelian circle of doing. Given a Marxist spin, this doing becomes producing, and producing means exploiting.

If we are to subvert capital and the exploitative nature of production, we must find a way to break out of the Hegelian circle of doing. Here, we can begin to see the possibility for subversive viral production.

Viral production of the other is different in kind from phallocentric reproduction of the same. Where phallocentric reproduction requires a mediating other to make the same, viral production requires a mediating same to make the other. In this way, the terms of production are, as it were, stood on their heads. There is still making, but it is the making of the other rather than the making of the same.

It is this other that breaks out of the circle, that is launched not into orbit, but on to some unpredictable tangent. There is, here, a sharing of origin and hence the figure of the tangent. Tangential relations are communal to a point, but then they diverge in unpredictable, even monstrous, ways.[12]

If we re-think Marx's emphasis on production and see not production so much as control of what is produced, then we can see even more space for subversion. That is, when the same and the other are reified, when relations of production are fixed, the results are purely pre-dictable, "pre-dictable" in the sense of "saying before" and creating a self-fulfilling prophesy. If the other is a mediator rather than a product, a catalyst or reagent instead of a chemically imbalanced substance, then the result of the reaction is precisely reactionary and not revolutionary.

Viral production of the other is uncontrolled and uncontrollable. It is monstrous in the sense of always leading to unpredictable results. It is not safe. But then we should consider what safety and predictability mean within the status quo.

AIDS, guns, poverty, pollution, and war are predictable in their results, and profitable for their phallocratic makers. Death is a *safe* bet, but the stability that leads to such good odds is not perhaps the stability that we should desire.

Viral production of the monstrously other is prima facie risky and fearsome, but when compared to the sacrifices made in the name of the phallocentric reproduction of the same, perhaps the risk is less than it seems.

The question remains, can there be a good virus? A productive virus?

One possibility that viral replication opens up to us is that of genetic production as opposed to genetic reproduction. Instead of remaking ourselves over and over again, as we do under the logic of capital, we can produce something new.

Viral consciousness, then, can be seen as mutant consciousness. It is an escape from the capitalist and phallocentric logic of the same. The virus is the other that recognizes and is recognized; it is the other that will allow us to produce otherness, rather than to reproduce ourselves.

Viral consciousness is thinking the production of the monstrously other—the other we cannot predict, the other whose beauty may well be unrecognizable because it is originary. Even with the originary nature of the product of viral production, still there will be recognition—recognition not of the same, but of a community of tangentially related differences.

Viral production invades us, occupies the reproductive organs of capital and of the phallocentric order, and fundamentally alters the process of reproduction. Or even, altogether ends the logic of reproduction. There is now only production.

My father wants nothing more for me than that I acquire a good job, and a good husband, and that I make a few children who will also be good grandchildren.

I want nothing less for my daughter than that she...

Notes

1. An earlier draft of this paper was presented at the Popular Culture Assocation annual meeting in March 1992 in Louisville, Kentucky. I am grateful to the Adjunct Advisory Council of Indiana University at South Bend for a grant to support the presentation of this paper.

2. Jacques Derrida, "Given Time: The Time of the King", in *Critical Inquiry*, Vol. 18, #2, (Winter 1992), pp 161-187.

3. "And because the first instruction of Children, dependeth on the care of their Parents; it is necessary that they should be obedient to them, whilest they are under their tuition; and not onely so, but that also afterwards (as gratitude requireth,) they acknowledge the benefit of their education, by external signes of honour....nor would theire be any reason, why any man should desire to have children, or take the care to nourish, and instruct them, if they were afterwards to have no other benefit from them, than from other men." Thomas Hobbes, *Leviathan*, (New York: Penguin Books, 1985), p. 382.

   "Yet this freedom exempts not a Son from that *honour* which he ought, by the Law of God and Nature, *to pay his parents*. God having made the Parents Instruments in his great design of continuing the Race of Mankind, and the occasions of Life to their Children, as he hath laid on them an obligation to nourish, preserve, and bring-up their Off-spring; so he has laid on the Children a perpetual Obligation of *honoring their Parents*....From this Obligation no State, no Freedom, can absolve Children." John Locke, *Second Treatise*, in *Two Treatises of Government*, (New York: Cambridge University Press, 1960), p. 354.

   Hobbes and Locke clearly demonstrate in these passages that the creation of life is the creation of debt, and is not at all a gift.

4. Gayatri Spivak, "Displacement and the Discourse of Woman," in *Displacement: Derrida and After*, ed. Mark Krupnick, (Bloomington: Indiana University Press, 1987), p. 169.

5. Quoted in Terry Eagleton, *Ideology: An Introduction*, (New York: Verso, 1991), p. 89.

6. Ibid.

7. Much could be said about parallels between viral re-production and family structure.

8. I am grateful to Tom Platt, Professor of Biology at Saint Mary's College, Notre Dame, Indiana for information on the nature of viruses.

9. Arthur Kroker, Marilouise Kroker, and David Cook, *Panic Encyclopedia: The Definitive Guide to the Postmodern Scene*, (New York: St. Martin's Press, 1989), p. 265.

10. Martin Jay, *The Dialectical Imagination: A History of the Frankfurt School and the Institute of Social Research, 1923-1956*, (Boston: Little, Brown and Company, 1973), p. 259.

11. A pearl of wisdom is equally a sign of distress, for wisdom seems to arise mostly from pain.

12. The pain inherent in getting off on a tangent is visible in the faces of students who want concise notes from concise lectures so that they can predict their grades. Lectures that yield either bizarre notebook figurations, or worse, no notes at all, cause endless pain.

ELECTRONIC DISTURBANCES
TELECRITICAL PERFORMANCE

Critical Art Ensemble

Where are the resources for performance research? For some, they seem to rest in organic interiors such as reconstituted memory or a socially framed imagination. Autoperformance claims to have made these territories visible. For others, the interior of the unconscious and the latent routes of desire have been designated the primary resource for performance, which in turn often manifests itself in ritual performance. For the less introspective, the empirical resource of the perception of the other, which is then reprocessed and represented in character bits, monologues, and "multicultural" pastiche performances, has acted recently as the dominant resource for performance. Both options have provided spectacles of interest over the years, and yet as the postmodern critique continues its drift, these models have become increasingly questionable. They are constructed on the assumption that there is an inspirational originary act that is traceable by backtracking the linear chain of representation. Consequently, in a time of imploding borders, there is an expanding process of separation between performance and performance theory, as the latter continues to reject the notion of the originary act. With convincing arguments that have ranged from Irving Goffman's dramaturgical model of everyday life to Judith Butler's notion of gender as performance (gender as an endless cycle of imitation without an original or essential quality), it has become increasingly difficult to find a stable resource to act as a foundation for any performance model. Part of the problem is the prejudice for stability, as well as a refusal to believe that the location of performance resources could be beyond the organic body, which acts as the master link in performance models of representation. In the age of electronic media, it seems inappropriate to argue that performance exhausts itself under the sign of the organic. Herein it will be suggested that the virtual world of the organic moves at parallel speed to the interior virtual world of the electronic in an infinite mirrored exchange, dispossessed of the original. In particular the organic body is mirrored by its doppelgänger, the electronic body, separated only by the microfracture of the screen. It is the examination and mapping of this interaction and intersection between the electronic and the organic that could redefine performance and performance research. After all, the electronic body always performs *in absentia*, regardless of the performance model. It is time to remove the camouflage.

The term "electronic body" is somewhat of a problem since its connotation, when amplified, carries quite a resonance. Springing to mind is the notion that it is the body of political and economic institutions with capital flowing in its veins and information speeding through its neural system, objectifying itself in the appearance of the commodity. The body's presence is forever felt in its panoptic gaze which blankets society. Or perhaps what comes to mind is the notion that the electronic world, both visible and imagined, constitutes a new body—a receptacle for the mind—which allows some to shed their useless organic appendages as unfit for continued survival due to their rigid physical boundaries and a speed that lags too far behind the rapid imaginings of the mind. To be sure, such notions are key elements in the general understanding of the electronic body, but within the context of performance, it should be conceived of as in its most urgent phase—appearance self-contained in screenal space. In such a context, the electronic body as macro institution, or as future body, is of lesser importance. It is the interaction between the appearing organic and electronic bodies themselves—one constituting the other as re-presentation in a conflict of imposed meaning—that is key. Both bodies are similar in appearance, both lay claim to being the "natural" body, generating crash identity in gender, ethnicity, sexuality, health, etc. Crash performance. The body collapses.

Virtual reality is already here and yet it is always one step ahead. It seems that virtual reality is always about to arrive with the next technological breakthrough. It is that curious feeling that we are currently in a real environment that leads to the conclusion that virtual reality is located in the near future, in science fiction, in the technology that is still being developed. Perhaps it is because we are already enveloped by the virtual that makes it so unrecognizable, for since the development of the "first window," a door that separated the interior and the exterior, the virtual world began to displace the natural world. At the development of the second window, one through which a person could simply look, the virtual took control. The exterior world made its appearance as image. Dürer went virtual with simple painting technologies by copying the window image and re-presenting it as aesthetic object. From the elite form of high culture, the window as image spilled into the democratic form of the suburban picture window. In industrial culture the window became nomadic, conquering space and reframing culture within the parameters of the windshield. Finally in electronic culture the third window appeared—the cathode—and virtual reality took a huge leap in restructuring its own appearance. The window no longer moved only the image contained in it. Transportation technology, with the interruption of travel time, and with its focus on space, became an anachronism. The image could now take the viewer anywhere instantly. Virtual travel and virtual facts for a virtual culture.

The desire for the freedom of the electronic body, roaming the world free of physical limitations, inverted the window. People no longer look to the outside through the window, but to the inside of screenal space. Utopia at last? The painting, the windshield, and the picture window are not enough. We need to jack-in, but it is not yet possible. Virtual reality goggles are but a glorified game of Pong. Virtual reality again seems to be elsewhere. The electronic Dasein is still elsewhere.

We must return to the question indicated by Virilio: How does the image present itself to me? This is the core of performance research. The organic body's performance at the intersection with the video or screenal performance is the mystery, the unknown, the confusion. It is not necessary to jack-in. Do not look to the future, the present is still unknown.

There is every reason to desire the electronic body, and every reason to despise it. This pathological blend occurs on viewing the electronic body, when feelings of sympathy (Husserl) and envy (Benjamin) implode in a schizophrenic moment. As Baudrillard states: "In spite of himself the schizophrenic is open to everything and lives in the most extreme confusion. The schizophrenic is not, as generally claimed, characterized by his loss of touch with reality, but by the absolute proximity to and total instantaneousness with things, this overexposure to the transparency of the world." In the ruins of intersubjectivity, the organic and the electronic face each other. The electronic body looks so real. It moves around, it gazes back, it communicates. Its appearance is our appearance. Identity appears and is reinforced, as subjectivity is extracted/imposed by the electronic other. How can such a perception not conjure a sympathetic response? Yet in that same instant of unity comes the burning feeling of separation that is born of envy. The identity of the electronic body is not our own. Consumption is required; it is the only way to make our appearance more like its appearance. The desire for greater access to the signs of beauty, health, and intelligence through the never fully attainable accumulation of cultural artifacts brutally remind us that the perfect excess of the electronic body is not our own. The limitations of the organic abound, and what is achieved seems vulgar and unnecessary at the point of achievement. All that remains is the unbearable moment of enriched privation. Sympathy and envy are forever spliced together in the form of a hideous Siamese twin. This is the performance of everyday life, so near, so instantaneous, eternally recurring, and yet unnamed. The time has come to liberate this secret from the modernist anxiety closet of the absurd.

Artaud's only misjudgment was in believing that the body without organs still needed to be created. The electronic body is the body without organs. It already dominates performance, and has recentered the theater around empty identity and empty desire. The body without organs is the perfect body—forever reproducible. No reduction to biology now. Two hundred Elvis clones appear on the screen. Separate them: Turn the channel; play the tape. Each performance is on an eternal loop. These clones are not made in a test-tube; they reproduce of their own accord, each as precise and as perfect as the last. No fluids, no plagues, no interruptions. The orifices of the body without organs are sewn tightly shut. No consumption, no excretion, no interruptions. Such freedom: Safely screened off from the virtual catastrophes of war, capital, gender, or any other manifestation teetering at the brink of a crash, the body without organs is free to drift in the electronic rhizome. The theater of the street and its associate cultural debris collapses. Civilization has been washed clean—progress is complete—dirt, trash, rot, and rubble have been screened off and erased from the perfect world of the electronic body. The electronic body, free of the flesh, free of the economy of desire, has escaped the pain of becoming.

Imitation is stacked on imitation, which in more sentimental moments seems to be traceable back to a bedrock that consists of individual units containing an essential or definitive quality. In this utopian moment, the body without organs is refilled, as it surrenders its generic appeal to a specific identity type known as the celebrity. Under such conditions, the counterfeit passes as authentic, and once more there is proof that an individual can be identified. The electronic body can appear in the flesh—a flesh that can be touched. It is truly a Hobbesian magical moment when the screen is lifted, and a "live" fantasy enters perception. The flesh becomes the referent of the electronic sign. The celebrity is not a body without organs, s/he is for real. Is it any wonder that the body without organs' first colony, the United States, despises ensemble and character actors; after all, the flesh is missing. Such actors are counterfeits. But celebrities like George Bush or Julia Roberts, they are "real." They pass as the same identity with or without the screen. Who can deny it?

For those unable to empty themselves and turn their flesh to image (Elvis), an equally unpleasant fate awaits. Forever caught in the economy of desire, the organic body fruitlessly searches for the products with which screenal space may be constructed around it. Erroneously believing screenal space to be a result of blockage, the organic body inverts its desire, spewing forth an endless performance of excreting labor and vomiting money, followed by a vain attempt to hide behind the accumulated piles of excess. Cosmetics and plastic surgery only serve to continue the performance, as these commodities can only temporarily hide the signs of the organic. The anxiety produced by the thought of the organic bursting forth in an unsightly public display is a constant companion to the organic body fully entangled in the eternal recurrence of consumption/excretion. This anxiety manifests itself in a constant performance and metaperformance. Perhaps one more product would soothe the twisting stomach. Rather than just patching the flesh, for some, a more militarized answer is in order. Surround the body with armor. Hide the flesh and its social infidelities. Extend the flesh by inserting it into the "safe" virtual environments of car and home. Let the window and the windshield become the screen. Such disappointment arises when a head gasket explodes, or a transmission drops spraying unnatural fluids all over the highway. And what if a sewer line breaks leaving a cesspool in public view? The mechanical has organs too; it is a fortress that is easily penetrated.

Descartes may have introduced the problem of the flesh when he suggested the separation of mind and body, but it was the electronic body that necessitated the understanding that the organic body is just a slab of meat. It was the electronic body that took us from panic to horror. Organs do, of course, appear in screenal space; however, whether the appearance is presented as fiction or nonfiction, it still rests under the sign of horror. The endless stream of greasy kid stuff films in which terror revolves around the appearance of the body's interior, and the connection of all manner of evil with excretory fluids, act only as an exaggerated form of the fears of the organic body. The appearance of bodily organs or fluids is the transgression. The moral is: If you do not want to perceive your own body as the meat that it is, identify with the perfect body without organs. The good and the heroic always maintain their status as a body without organs. The United States' war with Iraq was good and heroic because the body never presented its organs. It was a war without blood—only statistics (body counts). The Viet Nam War was anti-heroic—guts were spilled and blood was let. The secret was revealed: The soldiers were meat. The United States can take pride in its troops, for again there is an army of bodies without organs.

Why such a dreary parade of sucked-dry, catatonicized, vitrified, sewn-up bodies, when the BwO is also full of gaiety, ecstasy, and dance? Artaud's theater is here, and with it has come a decentering in history of theater. Schechner's formula for the centering of visionary performance is in need of an addendum. According to Schechner, the playwright was the first universal link in theater. It was the vision of the author that set in motion the meaning of performance. This power base was eventually usurped by the director, who acted as the hinge between the actor and playwright. Finally, the theatrical division of labor was collapsed, becoming encapsulated in the body of the performer. In autoperformance (Grey, Lecompte), the power of the center dissolved, boundaries collapsed, and performance drifted desperately searching for the self amongst the entwinement of personal and social histories. The world became a potentially solipsistic performance-text. This latter model of reintegration, drift, power dissolve, and performance as everyday life was a penetrating analytical step; however, it stopped right at the point where it most needed to continue. To add to Schechner's formula, a fourth stage has appeared, one which was the underpinning for the third. The performer, whether on stage or in the street, is entwined with its electronic counterpart. In fact, this notion might be an anachronism. The theater, as distributor of meaningful cultural image, has left both architecture and the street. For a performance to have meaning, it must be re-presented in the nomadic electronic theater. The performance of the organic body can only have meaning (however unstable) in relation to the electronic body. It can only be hoped that the denial stage of performance is over, and that electronic media will become present, and explicitly researched, rather than letting it continue as a silent partner.

In the realm of critical and counter cultural production, the body without organs has managed to keep much of its influence hidden by using the contradictions of such endeavors as camouflage. In the case of traditional media, such as painting, sculpture, and photography, critical efforts have been severely limited to particularized architectural spaces. The critical artists of the 80s were successful at subverting the space of the gallery, museum, and to a lesser extent, the university, through the use of the cynical joke in combination with a theoretical underpinning derived from the postmodern critique of culture. Originality, creativity, essentialism, and other myths were pushed into the vacuum of scepticism, causing a sense of doubt to surround the sacred relics of high culture. Duchamp's project was completed to the extent that the museum and other centers of cultural worship have these objects of doubt hanging on the walls, thumbing their noses at their predecessors. To be sure, this was a masterful accomplishment, and yet the dissemination of the critique into other social and cultural sectors still left much to be desired. In spite of the movements' exceptional use of conceptual structure, it failed to embrace parallel decentralizing media. Its model of production was a renaissance model (or at best a 19th century model in the case of photography), and hence had no means by which to pass beyond the chosen spatial limits. The critical movement eventually became a victim of its own cynicism, not just because of its inability to decentralize, but also due to its inability to introduce a democratic mode of inventive thinking into the cultural arena. From Marshall McLuhan to Gregory Ulmer, it has been argued that one of the more significant utopian aspects of contemporary cultural (electronic) production is not just its decentralizing speed and reproducibility, but also its democratization of the role of the cultural producer. Free from the need for the genius, the computer and video offer the multi-track speed and the memory to overlap semantic networks, typically thought to be exclusive of one another, in a way that creates a space for accidents—the space where invention occurs. In such a space, there is a possibility that a strategy could be discovered which at best could lacerate the body without organs, or at the least, more clearly map the organic interaction with it in a way meaningful outside of the museum and the university.

Performance art (metaperformance) has been resistant to explicitly introducing electronic performers into the sphere of activity. The critical metaperformers do not seem naive to the probability that the body without organs is at the heart of their work, in that it is the very target of their critical negation. In the work of metaperformers such as Karen Finley, Holly Hughes, or Tim Miller, there is a clear attempt to reinstate the integrity of the organic body, by separating it from the electronic mirror that controls its appearance and acceptability by whatever spectacle is necessary. Although the body without organs is consistently absent, there is always a failure to break with it no matter how radicalized the action might be, since on reflection, the viewer cannot help but to think of the body without organs from which they are trying to escape. Foucault's paradox is forever attached to the work. This strategy has been effective in the arts and the activist communities, as well as provoking mainstream power sectors into confronting the organic secret. In fact, it seems to be much more successful than the work of many electronic cultural producers who seem to be content spinning their wheels in the production of endless documentaries on marginalized subcultures, guerrilla wars, and street protests, as if such work is more real or more true than Hollywood cinema or the evening news. In spite of the sophistication of critical metaperformance, its provocative elements seem to reinforce the consumption of the organic body under the sign of horror. Its effectiveness could be increased by crash juxtapositioning of the organic body with the electronic body, thus potentially revealing the secrets of both without losing the successes of the purely organic metaperformances.

Overcoming the electronic body seems like such a lost cause. The linkage between it and the organic body presents itself as indestructible. The great homogenizer, the body without organs and its techno-foundation, already with fifty years of capital-saturated research behind it, is a central link in social organization. The subversive performance then consists of reopening the orifices of the body without organs, by cracking its screen and injecting it with the infection of the organic. Computer hackers and video pirates may be the avant-garde of performance. They introduce interruption into the electronic world. Under such conditions, the role of the metaperformer becomes more than just injecting scepticism into the common perception of the electronic body. There is also the need to seduce the technocratic class into joining the synthetic underground and the resistant cyber-performance. After all, what class knows better that there is no recapturing the flesh.

Forgive our textual infidelities.

Body without Organs

I

BwO NOW.
BwO NOW.
BwO NOW.

Imperfect flesh is the foundation of screenal economy. The frenzy of the screenal sign oscillates between perfection and excess, production and counter-production, panic and hysteria. Screenal space inscribes the flesh as the abject. The screenal space seduces the flesh into the abyss of the surface. The electronic body is the perfect body. The electronic body is the body without organs positioned in its screenal space. It is both self and mirrored self. The electronic body is the complete body. The body without organs does not decay. The electronic body does not need the plastic surgeon's scalpel, liposuction, make-up, or deodorant. It is a body without organs which cannot suffer, not physiologically, not psychologically, not sociologically; it is not conscious of separation. The electronic body seduces those who see it into the bliss of counter-production by offering the hope of a bodily unity that transcends consumption. But the poor, pathetic, organic body is always in a state of becoming. If it consumed just one more product, perhaps it might become whole, perhaps it too could become a body without organs existing in electronic space.

The electronic body oscillates between panic perfection and hysterical aphanisis. The electronic body inscribes the flesh as the abject. At any moment the organic body could fracture and its surface could decay with sickness, ooze and squirt anti-social fluids. The electronic body has shown *ad nauseam* that the spilling of guts, the projecting of vomit, the splitting of skin, the eruption of pus, or any sign of the organic in screenal space exists there only to instill fear, contempt, and embarrassment.

BwO dreams of a body that never existed.
BwO dreams of a body that never existed.
BwO dreams of a body that never existed.

BwO NOW.

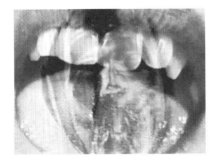

II

The mouth fragments the body. What remains? A narrow constipation, a violent meaning that makes vomit reason. The grotesque colonization of the oral cavity chews on the silenced body and spits out a bestiality of signs. What remains? Spasms.

The screenal tongue floats freely from its pillars. A sliding surrealistic appendage.

The eye spasms before the virtual tongue, blinding the dominant need for appropriation. What remains after the system digests everything? A nomadic tongue riding the waves of its digital secretions. A post-biological cannibalism that reborders the body. What remains?

The nipple is the matrix of a lost cause, a nostalgia of a network plurality in which one is too few and two is only one possibility. What remains? As screenal tongues cleave and suck the pacifier of unreal ideologies and unreal referents, the cancer of the techno-democracy reveals itself. The nipples mandate the electronic passion of diachronic doubles that blur desire and labor.

Cyber saliva slides in little jerks punctuating farts and knuckle cracks.

The spasm of digital bytes legitimizes the violence of information. Both the left and right hand are driven by the ritual of representation and sacrifice before the keyboard of dromographic speed? What remains? Hyper-real hands, sociologically unconscious desiring machines, always already possessed. What remains?

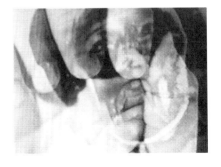

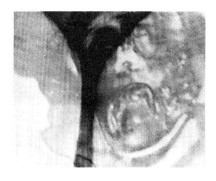

The sex speaks of a language based on lubricants, a different kind of saliva.

The virtual tongue fuses with the hot and cold units of pleasure. Unlike things join, tugging sensory hair and a cannibalism is turned inward. Diseased rumors float back and forth between nano peckers and macro cunts. What remains? A discharge of blind desire moving in and out of virtually gossiping genitals.

Would the virtual tongue multiply and separate toes or simply lick between them?

The big toe is the horror of a base materialism that spasms beyond suitable discourse. Toes lead an ignoble life. Seducing the data base with corns, blocking electronic interface with calluses and resisting the drift of information with dirty bunions. What remains after the system digests everything? The ecstatic deformity of pure labor, laughing before the solar anus, flicking mud at the virtual body above it. What remains? The brutal seduction of abandonment more acute in movement.

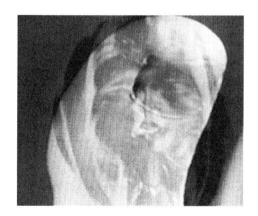

The spasm of the digital body breaks open the orifice of profound physical impulses.

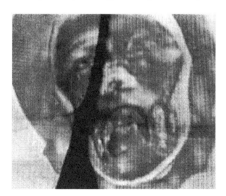

The anal night calls the virtual tongue to leave the mouth and enter it, red and obscene. An eruptive force of luminous thirst that demands indecent rupture and debauched hacking. What remains? An ontology of farts, of breathless lacerations that reborder the body and begin to speak. A revolutionary breakthrough of a post-biological sound. What remains after the system digests everything? Virtual gas.

DOMINATING PETER GREENAWAY

Carel Rowe

"There is no obligation for the author of a film to believe in, or to sympathize with, the moral behaviour of his characters. Nor is he necessarily to be accredited with the same opinions as his characters. Nor is it necessary or obligatory for him to believe in the tenet of his construction—all of which is a disclaimer to the notion that the author of *Drowning by Numbers* believes that all men are weak, enfeebled, loutish, generally inadequate and incompetent as partners for women. But it's a thought."

Peter Greenaway, *Fear of Drowning by Numbers*

During the first press screening for *The Draughtsman's Contract* (1982) that I attended the projectionist had mistakenly switched the last two reels. Nobody was aware of it at the time and this confusion seemed to have had little effect on the attending critics; going down the elevator at 1600 Broadway, the press was unusually vociferous about the "intriguing story." Nobody admitted they did not understand it and they dispersed to write generally favorable reviews. The visuals had so foregrounded the narrative, that understanding the film became a secondary consideration.

I returned to view the film again. With the reels projected in the proper order, the film provided the unexpected pleasure of narrative closure. But I began to see how Peter Greenaway's narratives were tales that could be run backwards without significant loss of narrative tension. My second viewing experience was also enhanced because this time the entire mise-en-scène played a delicious counterpoint to the plot; I say "played" because, regardless of the moribund subject matter, Greenaway's films are intellectually and pleasurably playful, the very act of watching his films compels audience-involvement: to watch is to actively participate. It is necessary to collaborate with him to remain amused because he requires a quality of attention from his audience that most filmmakers would never dare to ask for. Greenaway films are meant for multiple viewings and readings. They don't wear out. Instead, they encourage a curious wish to return to that filmic space in order to understand the game more completely, but this return is illusory, an impossible task, for the audience is actually played "with" as much as "to."

His painting and filmmaking always involve naming and counting, and incorporate elaborate calculations based on arbitrary factors and yielding haphazard results which he always justifies. He explains, "Just as *The Draughtsman's Contract* was based on twelve drawings, and *A Zed and Two Noughts* on the eight Darwinian stages of evolution, *The Belly of an Architect* is based on the figure seven for the seven hills of Rome." *Drowning by Numbers* is, itself a numbers game, a countdown in reverse, "until it reaches 100 and you know that your number is up." All very evocative, all equally disorienting, all visually and intellectually seductive.

Peter Greenaway is one of very few directors doing anything innovative or interesting in feature filmmaking today. Although he has made six internationally distributed features over the last decade relatively little film scholarship on his work has appeared in this country. Recently, several books, which are mainly collections of his own published scripts, synopses, paintings and production materials, have been published by *Dis Voir* and others in Europe. This isn't surprising, given the ground his talents cover: painting, directing experimental films and television documentaries in Britain, in addition to playwriting and aesthetic theorizing. Like Jean-Luc Godard, he is one of a rare breed: the artist/intellectual, *par excellence* and, like Godard, he exercises an unusual degree of artistic control over his productions, from script-to-screen.

Following the American premiere of *Prospero's Books* (1991) in New York, his storyboard collages for the film were on exhibit at the Klagsbrun Gallery. These incorporated texts, photographs and drawings of the allegorical creatures who might populate Prospero's Island: Caliban, Ariel, the Minotaur, etc., as well as those from his own mythological pantheon: The Architect, The Midwife, The Cook, The Coroner etc., "all to appear in a hypothetical sequel to *Prospero.*" Simultaneously, coffee-table book versions of his early paintings and drawings and of his painterly visualizations for *Prospero's Books* appeared; his work is linked together into one long, extended afterthought and he is continually recycling his art; nothing is wasted, including unrealized ideas. This habit adversely influences his interviews, most of which engender recycled answers to various questions. Audiences either love or hate his work (at worst it seems infuriatingly pretentious) and even some journalists who love his work end up hating him for his elusive arrogance. Obviously, Greenaway is not interested in currying favor with the press or audiences, but his egoism has not detracted from his success with backers and funding for planned projects spanning the next five years (which include, in addition to directing several films, curating a show for The Louvre and writing, producing and directing an opera *(The Death of Webern)* in Milan.

Greenaway's first decade of feature-filmmaking has produced six difficult, intriguing works: *Draughtsman's Contract* (1982), *A Zed and Two Noughts* (1986) *The Belly of an Architect* (1987), *The Cook, The Thief, His Wife and Her Lover* (1989), *Drowning By Numbers* (1990), and *Prospero's Books* (1991). The first five, which are Greenaway's original screenplays, are unique in narrative and mise-en-scène. While *Prospero* is a technical triumph of adaptation, a virtual tempest of visual wizardry, he admits he had "a splendid scenario writer in Shakespeare" and was strongly influenced by John Guilgud as Prospero. Therefore, it is only the first five films which concern us here, in particular: *A Zed and Two Noughts, The Belly of an Architect* and *Drowning by Numbers.*

It is my thesis that Peter Greenaway creates unprecedentedly powerful cinematic heroines (not since Von Sternberg has a male director fabricated such willful and ingenious women); however, he has a blind spot when it comes to power-relations between the sexes. It is not useful to try to categorize Greenaway as a feminist or anti-feminist, but rather to examine the images and the contexts he designs for these comparatively liberated women and to ask how these characters fail to extend to their unique potential beyond a phallic perspective. Greenaway's elegant females are fetishistically feminine, exhibitionistic, seductive and exert a potentially lethal power over men but are too vulnerable to be called simply "femmes fatales." While "phallic" women embody traits of both stereotypes: maternal saints and "femmes fatales," these "virile" heroines initially appear to be gender-benders of a new sort. But this is contradictory; the transgressive parts they play are often in service of an old ideology and Greenaway finally sabotages his own re-coding of sexual difference. While these women are erotic and determinative subjects (masquerading as objects) the males are passive/reactive and/or hysterical. Therefore, despite their originality and intellectual sophistication, these texts too often retell the same old story about power relations, with the players ideologically cross-dressed. This time the sheep are in wolves' clothing; the phallus wears skirts; Greenaway is still working out the old but potent themes of male repression: a male masochism, a female sadism, played out as a female supremacy over narcissistic males who are punished. The male protagonists in *Zed, Belly,* and *Drowning* exhibit gender-envy in response to female fecundity and, in many instances, it is evident that being a woman is now preferable to being a man. This gender-envy encompasses everything from reproduction to destruction and Greenaway's male protagonists embody what Mary Ann Doane has identified as the classic cinema's entire pathology of the feminine: "masochism, narcissism, hysteria." I do not want to imply that he *consciously* sets out in films to sabotage his male characters; as with any ideology, it just seems to happen that way.

Greenaway's well-worn proclamation that, "The Cinema is too important an art to be left for the storytellers," is deceptive. No matter how abstract his narratives may seem, they are loosely linear stories about initially empowered men who become pitiful losers, and sympathetic women who cannily conspire to survive the odds and become winners. A thumbnail sketch of these stories points up this theme:

In *The Draughtsman's Contract*, Mr. Neville is coerced by two women who use him for their own ends; he becomes a victim who is blackmailed, framed and finally murdered. But not before providing his killers with an heir.

In *A Zed and Two Noughts*, a woman who loses both legs to amputation successfully manipulates twin brothers into serving her sexual and maternal needs before they commit suicide.

In *The Belly of an Architect*, the hero, a victim of paranoid delusions and stomach cancer, loses his wife, his work and his child to a younger man before virtually giving birth to his own death, which takes place at the instant his wife gives birth.

In *The Cook, The Thief, His Wife and Her Lover*, an emotionally and physically abused wife successfully revenges herself and her murdered lover by orchestrating the consummate humiliation and murder of her tyrannical spouse.

In *Drowning by Numbers*, three women successfully murder their husbands and, after using the local coroner as collaborator, murder him as well. Liberated, they live happily ever after.

These female characters acquire narrative empowerment which works positively to place them in the subject's position. Even when the stories are *about* men, it is the women who ultimately engineer the narrative to serve their own needs and to suit their own ends. Here, power flees its base in sexuality, generally, and in male subjectivity, specifically, as the males abuse or relinquish their positions, until they are left with only a power which speaks in the previously transgressive language of feminism: absence, rupture, and the trace.[1]

Reproduction/Production

Reproduction is a consistent theme with Greenaway, both serially, with the repetitious reproductions of visual images, and biologically, with pregnancy. In *Draughtsman*, *Belly*, *Zed* and (in the case of the youngest wife) in *Drowning*, pregnancy becomes a sort of McGuffin, motivating the seemingly inevitable succession of events which lead to the males' downfall. Pregnancy always produces patriarchal dilemmas involving heirs, legacy and adultery. More importantly, being capable of reproducing also gives the women a phallic power which is impossible for the men to achieve.

This subject of reproduction also takes the form of male gender envy. The architect, Stourly Kracklite, has his own "female trouble" and his abdominal cramps are not psychosomatic, as originally diagnosed. His physical pain and his misgivings about the patrimony of his unborn child result in his obsessive xeroxing of photographs of male bellies.[2] This relentless reproduction solves nothing, and only results in enlarged reproductions of reproductions. xeroxing illustrates Kracklite's creative infertility, the emptiness of all his obsessive preparations for his commemorative about the French architect, Etienne-Louis Boullée.

Early in *Belly* we learn that, during their seven years of marriage, the Kracklites have wanted a child but Louisa has only had numerous miscarriages. She says, "You could say I'm a lot like Stourly, I've never been capable of bringing a project fully to completion either." When she discovers that she is pregnant once more, a strange competition is set up between the couple, each gestating creative projects for the next nine months. While his ends in ruin and death, hers results in success and birth. In possibly the cruellest line of all of Greenaway's bitchy dialogues, Louisa's lover, Caspasian, admitting he has been sleeping with his wife, assures Kracklite of patrimony by adding, "Your unborn child makes the most perfect contraceptive."

Most clearly, this theme of pregnancy/patriarchy/paranoia infiltrates the narrative in Greenaway's most eccentric feature, *A Zed and Two Noughts*. Alba Bewick (her name suggests Goya's ample mistress and the early nineteenth-century nature painter Thomas Bewick, as well as the car), the lusty heroine of *Zed*, is prototypical. Alba, (the "Zed") who was pregnant at the time of her car accident, loses her baby as well as her left leg. She subsequently becomes pregnant by the Deuce brothers, Oliver and Oswald, (The "Noughts"), without knowing which one is the father (when they protest she asks,"What's a little spermatozoa between brothers?"). Nevertheless, after giving birth to their twin sons she takes away even their shared patrimony and bestows it on her new lover, Phillip Arc-en Ciel, an aristocratic double amputee. Like the draughtsman and the architect, the noughts become disenfranchised surrogate fathers. They end up jobless, homeless and wifeless as Alba replaces them with a more "suitable" father figure; this final betrayal leaves them childless and, ultimately, lifeless. Even though Alba's physical and sexual power is punished by double amputation and she ends up as a legless, helpless "phallus", she is still a phallus who gives birth and insures her children's future within patriarchal society.

Impotence/Castration

These themes of production/reproduction are counterweighted by their darker "twins": the themes of impotence/castration. Greenaway's films are filled with instances of sexual paraphilia (in *Zed* alone, sado-masochism, necrophilia, fetishism and zoophilia are woven into the thick tapestry of the text), but it is the spectre of castration that hovers, to some degree, over all of his work. This takes symbolic and physical forms, as the major male characters loose their powers. There is often vivid graphic evidence of this: in the nightmarish murder scene at the conclusion of *Draughtsman* all the draughtsman's work is set on fire and his eyes are burnt out. In one of many horrific scenes in *Cook*, the angelic kitchen boy (whose *a capella* singing haunts the score and is reminiscent of a *castrati*) is tortured by the thief and his henchmen, who eviscerate his navel. (Greenaway explains this as a way "to cut him off from childhood forever.")

In *Belly*, the architect becomes impotent and loses everything to his wife's lover, and in *Drowning*, the coroner's prepubescent son, Smut, performs a bloody circumcision on himself in order to impress The Skipping Girl (described by Greenaway as..."an innocent, but she mocks sexuality...All the time she wields a rope that will eventually hang her child-lover..."). Pointing up the castration theme in *Drowning*, Greenaway explains,

> ...Samson is the conventional demonstration of man's vulnerability to woman... emasculation with the snip of a pair of scissors. Circumcision is an act of licensed symbolic castration—an act of emasculation lightly disguised under a range of justifications...masochism and self-mutilation—it was, after all, that Samson, through lechery aided, of course by the perfidy of women, brought about his own downfall...he voluntarily assists in his own emasculation.[3]

The plot of *Drowning* is very simple: three generations of wives (all with the name Cissy Colepits) kill their husbands for the following reasons: Cissy One (Joan Plowright) drowns hers in the bath because, "he was unfaithful, because he stopped washing his feet, because he wouldn't cut his hair...because he had a hairy backside." Cissy Two (Juliette Stephenson) submerges hers in the ocean during a massive heart attack ("..he drowns bellowing like a bull seal,") because he is fat and boring and impotent (his idea of sexually satisfying her is to use a frozen popsicle as a dildo—the act of a "frigid man"); and Cissy Three (Joely Richardson) does away with her childish spouse in a swimming pool, once he has served the purpose of impregnating her. According to the director, "It is an affectionate, ironic tale of male impotency...in the face of female solidarity... The subject is about comradery and conspiracy between women, which can't exist between men, who are driven by competitiveness."

> *Drowning by Numbers* is all about impotency and potency; it certainly may be about the development of enfranchisement towards feminism. The males try to readdress problems about potency. There is a way in which circumcision is related to castration, the child is following the attitudes and aspirations of the father...it is a gesture which focuses the whole film on ideas of male impotency.[4]

Drowning does not simply explore mythologies of male potency and powers of feminine solidarity; it is about a conspiracy theory in which strong, dissatisfied women are unbeatable, invincible goddesses and that their brand of feminism is deadly for men. As in all five films, women are dangerous enemies and the men are out-maneuvered, outplayed, out-lived. Masculinity is repeatedly nullified and turned into a big zero.[5]

Symbolic female castration is described when Alba tells a prophetic fable about a legless whore in Marseille, at the beginning of *Zed*:

> She'd had both her legs amputated at the groin. Imagine that, gentlemen, no limbs to hinder entry...some admirers thought she might like to be buried in a short coffin...others thought that the empty space should be filled with flowers. In the end, of course, her family turned up—and they had the corpse fitted with artificial legs...Imagine that, gentlemen, the body in all its delicious detail fading away—leaving a skeleton with iron legs.[6]

This is a synopsis of what is about to become her own story. Alba's mutilation is physical as well as symbolic; she loses both legs, yet she lacks far less than the noughts; she tries to heal the widowed brothers with her compassion (and passion) but the noughts, irrevocably crippled by grief, can only continue to mourn their losses and conduct their self-destructive experiments.

Alba is a female subject given privileged male access to the spectacle of male lack. This can have a correlation with the narrative of the Hollywood post-war film, *The Best Years of Our Lives* (1946), in which the wives of the mutilated, crippled servicemen are also sympathetic witnesses to the males' various lacks. However, no effort is made in either film to align male subjectivity with phallic values. In her essay, "Historical Trauma and Male Subjectivity," Kaja Silverman describes this situation as it appears in *The Best Years of Our Lives*:

> Far from obliging the female subject to display her lack to the gaze of her sexual other, it repeatedly calls upon her to look acceptingly at this lack—to acknowledge and embrace male castration... Instead of classical cinema's organization of the viewers' desires around the masochism of women and the magnamimity of men, it reorders organization of the viewer's desires around the masochism of men and the magnanimity of women. [7]

In *Lives* it is the healthy wives who compassionately heal their husbands' intolerable absence or loss, while in *Zed* we have a mutilated woman who tries to heal two biologically sound men who are undergoing emotional absence and loss. The message here is that even "half a woman" without legs lacks less than these two men who are physically whole.

While Alba's physical helplessness situates her in the position usually reserved for the female subject within the medical discourse of classical cinema (in everything from *Dark Victory* to *Camille Claudel*), she never disavows her condition or willingly succumbs to it, nor has she lost her power to be sexually aggressive; in the guise of sympathy she seduces both twins, each time using her missing leg as an added erotic attraction. In her symmetrical, Beardsleyesque boudoir, her missing limb(s) hidden by the sheets, her white face framed by wild, flaming red hair, her heavy French accent (actress Andrea Ferreol, who did not speak English, had to memorize her lines, by rote) and bawdy sexual innuendos all testify to her lust for life, in spite of her handicap. Alba resists the image of medicalized femininity, just as she resists her surgeon's fiendish attempts to transform her into a specular object. Instead, it is the narcissistic Deuce brothers who are helplessly on display, "The brothers play the two zeros of the film's title—put together to make a spectacle of themselves." [8] When her affairs are in order and she prepares to commit suicide, Alba promises the brothers they can use her body for their post-mortem photographic experiments but even then her legless corpse is threatened with being turned into a fractured spectacle. When asked why they want to record her decay although her body is only half there, Oswald replies, "Then you'll fit better into the film frame." Her reply is "...A fine epitaph: 'here lies a body cut down to fit the picture.'"

Suture

If we define suture as a symbolic sense of seeing the world in terms of presence or absence ("lack") and the obliteration of that difference, we may recognize the term, with all of its splicing, surgical and sartorial metaphors in tow, as a castration subtext in *Zed*.

> Trauma, according to Freud, is "the rupture of a biological or symbolic order which aspires to closure and systemic equilibrium by a force directed toward disruption and disintegration....The dominant fiction thus isolates the sensory organs both from excessive amounts and unsuitable kinds of stimuli. It does this in part by negotiating defensive mechanisms such as projection, disavowal and fetishism."[9]

This healing of traumatic rupture is precisely what Oswald and Oliver seek in their obsessive quest for the "meaning" of life and/or death. At the conclusion of the film we learn that the brothers were Siamese twins who underwent a symbolic castration when their bodies were separated at birth. Their subsequent lack of desire for the "other" is displaced by their marriages to similar women (both die in Alba's accident). In other ways their relationships with their wives are non-existent; while grief remains a theoretical obsession with them, the brothers do not have actual memories of their spouses. They tell Alba that their wives did not know that they were twins; in this case, the dead women cannot even have known how old their husbands were. The Deuces deflect their interest exclusively onto the decay of their wives' bodies instead of the persons themselves who are decomposing and in this situation loss of the object effectively displaces the object itself.

When their wives are killed the brothers suffer a return to the repressed, the original separation from one another. Attempting to heal their bereavement, they make a zoological study of the natural world which will naturalize tragedy as part of the inevitable order of things. The twins embark on their elaborate quest for the dominant fiction but the sutures do not hold. In their search for signification they intermittently project films on Darwinian evolution, only to discover "it's all such a dreary fiction." Concurrently, in a cavernous laboratory, they film time-lapse segments of vegetable and animal decay. These images violently break into the film with strobe light flashes of decomposition, synchronized with Michael Nyman's manic score, which seems written expressly for the choreography of bacteria and maggots. If the stroke separating the signified from the signifier is the stroke of castration, then, instead of suturing/healing their original wounds, these flashes of death-at-work exacerbate the brothers' trauma. Like the "birth of life" sequences from the Darwinian documentary, these images break randomly into the text of the film, providing both "excessive amounts and unsuitable kinds of stimuli," instead of projecting "biological or symbolic order and equilibrium." Images of life and death become forces "directed toward disruption and disintegration" instead of closure. These sequences work to rupture the narrative and visual chain of signification for the viewer as well, serving as intrusive reminders of mortality.

Forced to abandon their quest for significance the brothers seek to become reunited in death, as they were at birth. They insist that Van Meegeren, the surgeon who originally separated them, re-stitch them together into their original state. Their devolution is made even more obvious by their physical similarity which increases as the film progresses, until they are once more "identical" and have themselves sewn together quite literally into their "Siamese suit." They then orchestrate one final experiment: filming their double suicide and decay, but this also fails when a few hours after they die their time-lapse camera is short-circuited by swarms of snails. Greenaway concludes his script: "The final experiment requiring the brothers' personal self-sacrifice comes to nought."

Fetishism

Greenaway claims that his script for *Zed* was inspired by three items: a photo of a legless gorilla, a time-lapse film of a decaying zebra, and a snapshot of the British filmmakers, the twin brothers Quay, flanking a "smiling, assured woman". Later, we will see how this photo evolves into Alba's image as an idealized fetish, a legless dominatrix with slavish male devotees. Her conditions specifically link her to two male fantasies: with one leg, to masochistic fetishism and later, legless, to the rapacious male fantasy of the absence of sexual resistance.

> Fetishism, the ability to balance knowledge and belief and hence to maintain a distance from the lure of the image—is also inaccessible to the woman, who has no need of the fetish as a defense against a castration which has always already taken place. [10]

Greenaway cleverly illustrates this idea when Alba describes her tormentor, the evil surgeon Van Meegeren (named after the forger who actually painted fake Vermeers), as a fetishist possessed by Vermeer women:

> "Van Meegeren says I look like the 'Lady Standing at the Virginal'. I suspect it's because you never see her legs—she's not standing really—she's strapped and stitched to her music stool. Van Meegeren has a great reputation for stitching....suturing—sewing up wounds—operations. He's made a beautiful job on me. Look." (She lifts up the sheet for him to see.)[11]

In a pivotal scene Van Meegeren orchestrates tableaux vivants as simulacra of Vermeer's paintings 'The Concert' and 'The Music Lesson'; he has her sewn into a replica of the costume worn by Madame Van Ees in these two paintings and, delighted with the result, remarks, "…We now nearly have the entire wardrobe seen in Vermeer's paintings." Alba is then pinned and tacked into a rigid position onto the piano stool. Horrified, she demands the Deuce brothers help her escape because she is becoming, "an excuse for medical experiments and art theory…stiched and sewn to the music stool. Look, I'm imprisoned." She has been sutured into a fetish for a disempowered subject. Van Meegeren punishes Alba's resistance by removing her other leg, in order to restore symmetry and accuracy, because, "You never see a female leg in a Vermeer."

The photograph of the filmmaker-twins, the Brothers Quay, flanking a smiling, assured woman, which inspired the characters for *A Zed and Two Noughts*, can provide the missing link between Greenaway and his heroines via the artist Bruno Schultz. Schultz wrote the original tale for the Quay's animated film, *Street of Crocodiles*. This unique, experimental film is one which Greenaway deeply admired and he wrote an illuminating article about it when it first appeared.[12] In reading this article, I was struck by the way in which Greenaway's descriptions of other artists' works so insightfully describe his own work. He identifies the Quay twins as scholars of the little-known aesthetics of Bruno Schultz. Schultz, a sort of Polish Kafka, was a draughtsman and writer whose drawings and descriptions of his hometown of Drobycz, Poland: *Street of Crocodiles* and *Sanitarium Under the Sign of the Hourglass*, brilliantly evoke a cynical, corrupt world of phantasmagoria. Greenaway also aligns Schultz's style with Italo Calvino's descriptions of Venice in *Invisible Cities*. He writes,"both authors (Schultz and Calvino) could hardly be said to have written short stories with a narrative, more like descriptions with some narrative content..." Describing the Quay's narrative strategy in creating their film of *Street of Crocodiles*, he continues: "It is an analogous method to Schultz himself, who takes a single fact or proposition and extends and elaborates it, building a complex system of metaphors without strain which takes you far from the original starting point". This is precisely the method Greenaway uses to evolve his own narratives, based on two or three unrelated ideas with which he builds "a complex system of metaphors." Greenaway assembles single images and facts which take us far from the original starting point and, in the process, he actually visualizes the narrative content. After all, what relationship *does* a one-legged gorilla have to a woman flanked by twin brothers and a time-lapse study of a putrifying zebra? Is it Surrealism or is it Memorex? By transposing the Quays onto the Noughts and the smiling woman onto the Zed, Greenaway's sign-slide between the images shifts "a Zed and Two Noughts" into the same visual arena with Schulz's drawings.

What is curious and intriguing in Greenaway's praises of Schultz's methodology and aesthetics, is the absence of any description of the highly erotic content of most of Schultz's drawings. Schultz's contemporaries describe them:

> ...The greater part of this work consisted of pen and pencil sketches, of which the chief motif was male sexual enslavement to the beautiful contours of the female body: the women finely drawn,...wearing either nothing or black stockings and small slippers...invariably holding a little whip in their tiny hands; the men in poses of servility, the fear in their eyes set off by glints of desire...The entire compositional impulse and conception of this artist was dominated by the tyranny of the female body over the slavish sexuality of man...This is the general territory of Schulz's imagination; his special area within it is female sadism, linked to male masochism.[13]

Schultz drove the expression of both these psychic couplings to almost monstrous pathos. To him, the instrument of oppression of men by women was often the leg (and the foot). According to Polish dramatist Stanislaw Ignacy Witkiewicz,

> ...that most formidable part...of the female body...It is with their legs that Schultz's women tease, trample, drive to sullen, helpless madness his dwarfish men-freaks, cowed as they are by erotic torture, degraded and finding supreme painful relish in their degradation.[14]

The process by which an invented symbol acquires the weight of familiarity and tradition is fetishism. A woman's leg or foot, separate from her body, becomes a fetish for the phallic power of her sexuality. As everyone knows, male masochists, terrified by the idea of castration, abject themselves before the leg, grateful that, "thank God, there's (at least) a leg (phallus) there!" Schultz's dominatrix are sisters to Greenaway's heroines: they join together at the cultural crossroads where the sexual revolution transforms itself into sinister seduction.

The voyeuristic surgeon, Van Meegeren, in *Zed*, with his Vermeer fetish, is re-enacting the old male fantasy of creating the representation of the idealized woman, to repress and replace the real one. Greenaway's own preoccupation with re-creating 'Old Masters' paintings, as scenes in his films, here becomes his Vermeer fetish (his admitted intent to slavishly reproduce Vermeer lighting and angles wherever possible in *Zed*) and it is one of several methods he uses to maintain a distance from the lure of the image, to suppress the erotic, to replace desired objects with simulacra, people with things (or reproductions of things). His heroes are characteristically repressive: the draughtsman, who obtains sex "on demand" from two beautiful women, making fetishistically precise drawings from which every shred of human evidence must be removed, or the architect who alienates his wife and ignores his unborn child in favor of creating an exposition for a dead French architect, the brothers Deuce, preoccupied with their wives' corpses instead of remembering their wives, or even with the strategy of elaborate game-playing that forgrounds the murders in *Drowning*.[15] By setting up these situations Greenaway gives us a glimpse into his own obsessions which lead him to create fetish and ordering systems as strategies to subvert the emotional and highly erotic content of his films.

Actors

In the conclusion to his article on *Street of Crocodiles*, Greenaway suggests that the next logical step for the Quays is to work with live human beings. He advises the animators to "scale up their world and bring in their dramatic lighting, their use of colour, their creation of atmosphere." He tells the animators that "their talents could be yoked to the use of actors and free them from the drudgery of the time-lapse animation camera." This is the way in which Greenaway himself uses characters as human "ciphers" in his conceptual dramas, and for which he is often criticized by reviewers who find his work "cold." Regardless of their avowed passions, most of his characters are psychologically arid. In addition, there is a lack of human empathy, a missed connection in his direction of actors and this presents an unforseen drawback, another limitation on the portrayal of believable sexual power relations; this lack is compounded by his scripts about the intriguing and complex, unequal battles of the sexes which are ultimately resolved by simply shifting the power.

Greenaway intends that his characters carry the weight of allegorical significance and though he is "not really interested if their grandmother was called Grace and had a dog called Fido," [16] something important is missing. Allegory is not always enough to carry a feature film and the dangers inherent in allegory, obscurity, and obviousness can inhibit the meaning of metaphorical narratives.

Jean-Luc Godard also relied on allegorical methods and with his antipathy toward narrative, his films are often a series of tableaux with much less plot than the dramatic situations we find in Greenaway. But Godard's characters reveal certain vulnerabilities, a certain, compelling *tendress*.

> Godard is generally considered as a cold and intellectual filmmaker who likes to remain aloof from the public, so that they adopt a reflective attitude towards his films. However this attitude allows him to induce emotions which do not call on the latent sentimentality of the spectators.[17]

While Godard's films are consummately theoretical and intellectual, his characters are not concepts "yoked to the use of actors." Instead, his philosophy and politics are investigated, lived out, through his actors' performances. (Even when self-reflexively portraying themselves as actors, Godard's direction allows them to reveal their personal, human complexities.) With Greenaway, we get very little of this critical role-playing. The language Greenaway uses to speak of himself through his characters does not translate emotionally through his direction of actors. Although Greenaway insists *The Belly of an Architect* is his most autobiographical creation (he even refers to it as "The Belly of the Filmmaker"), we come away with almost no understanding of the intended "central argument between public and private life." Nor does the architect's story "really examine this question of 'Can art make you immortal?'"

Godard's film, *Contempt (Le Mepris,* 1963) shares a common love story with Greenaway's *The Belly of an Architect.* Both narratives are built from an initial misunderstanding between a married couple, foreigners in Italy, and from this mistrust emerges the inexorable mechanism of tragedy. The story for Godard's script originally came from Moravia's novel, *Voyage to Italy,* but Godard has admitted, "The same story could take place in virtually any other set of circumstances (Adam and Eve)." Between the two films, *Contempt* and *Belly,* similar circumstances are too numerous to ignore: From the beginning, both men have already lost their wives' respect; the lovers prove attractive to the wives only to the extent that the husbands relinquish their hold and fail as alternatives. *Contempt* is based on the Ulysses myth of The Odyssey and on the spectacle of foreigners making a modern movie (producing a creative project) about the myth of Ulysses in Italy. The protagonists in both films seek self-awareness within the historical reference of Roman antiquity and both measure themselves against ideal artists of the past who act as their superegos; in *Contempt,* it is Fritz Lang, in *Belly* it is Etienne Boulée. But instead of complimentary levels of meanings between the classic and the modern, which we get in *Contempt,* to explore questions about art and immortality, in *Belly* we get a story of panic and decay, an epic of male menopause. Yet we empathize with the tortured portrayal of Stourly Kracklite by Brian Dennehy, an actor who, Greenaway admits, was allowed to "direct himself" and, as a brilliant professional, Dennehy brings the film to life. A review by William Parente describes the actor as "enormous, sweating, soaking, irredeemable human, he supplies the heart that Greenaway's films have lacked." And Nigel Andrews: "Dennehy creates a figure of monstrous egotism and despair; a tragicomic Falstaff, pregnant with his own death."

Point of View

As William Van Wert has pointed out, Greenaway provides "a very rare experience for the spectator, that of no point of view"; and describes "Greenaway's avowed refusal of character identification...as the uninhabitable point of view."[18] In fact, point of view is intentionally denied, continually contradicted in order to confuse us, to keep us involved in the play of unexpected narrative games.

These stories are told by the camera, playing a deceptively neutral but untrustworthy character, one who reveals either more or less than we need to know. Instead of following a story we must follow the lead the camera takes as it accentuates events in the narrative and provides a metonymic function. "What it shows and swallows up in contiguity, is to complete in overall filmic terms what the incomplete and arrested characters and surface narrative cannot complete." [19] The viewer is being forced, or seduced, into assuming responsibility for creating meanings and perspectives to psychologically complete these characters.

Longshot-longtake cinema with infrequent close-ups and langorous editing do not simplify this process. Actors pose or move about uncomfortably in the landscapes and architecture like two-dimensional characters struggling to come to life in three-dimensional paintings. Sometimes they are missing from the frame but overheard on the soundtrack; often they are lost or dwarfed by architecture or overwhelmed by elements of mise-en-scène like art direction and musical score. Foregrounded, they must be searched out. This narrative hide-and-seek is played within obsessively-compulsively well ordered frames, each with its own exquisite balance, remote and artificial, where loss of symmetry is death (like the cold geometry of *Invisible Cities*). In that regard, Van Meegeren points out, "...animals, are designed with a view to symmetry...one of decay's first characteristics is to spoil that symmetry...",(remember the one-legged gorilla?) so he insists on performing double amputations for reasons of symmetry. This is a place where a woman is "cut down to fit the frame" but is buried in a long coffin, according to form.

Another result of these visual strategies is that we are constantly expected to participate in interpretations of events which seem to have little or no relationship to each other. This postmodern world, so overcrowded with subjects, objects and concepts, is one, Greenaway

implies, where everything is connected, if only surrealistically, by whim-
sey or coincidence, and we must "connect the dots"; linking up events,
concepts and characters with one another and ourselves. We are kept so
busy searching for significant clues it is easy to lose track. Whose point of
view is it anyway?

This opens a critical Pandora's Box about where the "ungendered gaze"
comes from or where it goes when liberated from narrative drudgery and
characters' viewpoints. Instead of the privileged gaze of the male hero/
camera angle toward the heroine as object of the gaze, we now get both
genders in voyeuristic abstraction by a camera which takes on a life of its
own. Here the female subject's trajectory of the gaze is not obvious, nor
does it appear at issue. It is invisible. A tyrannical male gaze dominates the
draughtsman's (and our) perspective of events but does not help him
survive; it deceives him instead as his highly regulated point of view
becomes increasingly untrustworthy until, as the film nears conclusion,
"We see that reality itself, e.g. Neville's world of neutral objects, is the
product over which neither Neville nor we have any control."[20] We do not
see Mrs. Herbert's or Mrs. Talmann's points of view until, too late, we
become aware of their crucial omission, as invisible but structuring
absences. The sexual conqueror is turned into the sexual slave, used like
a praying mantis, to impregnate his destroyer.

Like the draughtsman, the architect's point of view is dominant but
fatally impotent. Kracklite's perspective, at the keyhole, as he passively
watches his wife's sexual cavortings with Caspasian (hilariously using
Kracklite's model of Boulée's tower as a giant phallas) destroys him
emotionally, just as the proctoscopic images of the fiber-optic camera will
reveal the cancer in his bowels. In both cases, his worst fears are realized
and here the male gaze becomes the belly button meditation of the
architect, who, turning his gaze inward, finally implodes.

These obsessively "accurate" viewpoints are fatal to their male bearers
and in *Belly* the viewer must continually be on alert for a woman's covert,
yet tell-tale point of view. Flavia, the sinister sister of Caspasian, the wife's
lover, surreptitiously takes photos which document Stourley's illness and
failures. Her appearance with her camera in scenes is arbitrary and often
hers is an almost impossible point of view, recording the most intimate
moments in his life, as well as public ones. She documents the architect,
his wife and her lover, from the first day the Americans arrive in Rome.
In a scene near the end of the film (which may have influenced

denouments in two subsequent films: Paul Schrader's *The Comfort of Strangers* (1990) and Jocelyn Moorhouse's *Proof* (1992), with their similar photomontages of the desired male subjects secretly shot and diplayed by villainous women-as-desiring-subjects), she forces him to confront these reproductions as decisive evidence of his professional and sexual impotence and his wife's adultery. Unlike the architect's xeroxes, Flavia's photos are virile, potent images. They prove Kracklite has become incapable of continuing to produce the retrospective (unreliable both physically and psychologically) and that production of the exhibition must be turned over to her brother, his rival, Caspasian.

Conclusion

While Greenaway's writing and direction leave little sympathy for anyone in his films, his texts behave most sadistically toward his male characters. Although females suffer physical and psychological humiliation, they learn more, develop more and, ultimately, prevail. The most exhilarating progress appears to be made by Georgina, the long-abused wife in *The Cook, The Thief, His Wife and Her Lover*; while she does not so much defeat the power of her dominator, she takes over this power metaphorically, "in drag", to "turn the tables" on him. Like the wives in *Drowning by Numbers* and the victim-heroines of American slasher films, she "takes up the phallus herself, as weapon rather than instrument of pleasure—to join them in order to beat them, as it were".[21] *Cook*, despite its bloody, theatrical vision, worthy of Artaud or Bataille, only reinscribes the Symbolic. The result is that both male and female viewers identify superficially with the females in *Zed*, *Cook* and *Numbers*, but do so for different reasons: the women because of anger with familiar images of exploitive men and the men because the women are "wearing the balls" and it is unlikely that men *consciously* identify with exhibitions of male impotency and hysteria.

Greenaway's chauvenizing of men is as simplisic as Hollywood's bimboizing of women. *Thelma and Louise*, a film which breaks the taboo on portraying real, even violent, sexual power relations, includes among its contemptuous and predatory male characters, (even if gratuitously) a supportive lover and sympathetic detective who try to understand the females' transgressions. In *Draughtsman*, *Zed*, *Belly*, and *Numbers* there are no admirable male characters at all and the Lover and the Cook are the only consistantly sympathetic males in all five films.

Greenaway's creation of uniquely empowered women is wasted, undermined in the context of plots where men are so inferior they are simply no match for the women. The different genders often do not even seem to resemble the same biological species and sexual "difference" loses all relevance, is suppressed, if not entirely eradicated, in lop-sided stories about sexual warfare if the Other is not another in the same domain. When men are *that* inferior, female superiority itself is hardly remarkable. As Alba Bewick says, "In the land of the legless, even the one-legged woman is queen".

Notes

1. See Arthur and Marilouise Kroker, *The Hysterical Male: New Feminist Theory*, (New York: St. Martin's Press, 1990)

2. About the architect's xeroxing Greenaway says, "There is a concern for immortality, positing the idea of fecundity. The female can directly reproduce by production of babies, and then there are 'babies' from the male's position: all the forms of creativity by which he tries so hard to organize immortality for himself, his own 'babies', his own projects and works of art...The copying machine is a cloning mechanism, rather like the reproductive organs of the female...there is a sensation that bellies are coming out of bellies..." (personal interview with the filmmaker, September, 1991).

3. Peter Greenaway, *Fear of Drowning by Numbers*, (Paris: Dis Voir, 1988), p 117.

4. Ibid, p. 119.

5. "All the men are written as slobs and wimps," said Juliette Stephenson, in a press interview, "The men are unfit, nonswimmers. The women are practical, funny and strong...Peter gave us almost no direction because he found himself, just slightly awed by the solidarity among the trio of actresses he hired to impersonate that solidarity." Some of that solidarity was, undoubtedly, the result of the director's physical demands on location. The scenario was set in mid-summer but shot in fall, during the brutal hurricane season of 1987; this meant flooding the Suffolk landscape with artificial light, filling barren trees with artificial leaves and instructing the actresses to "act warm" while swimming and appearing in summer clothes. Remarkably, they did.

6. Peter Greenaway, *A Zed and Two Noughts* (London: Faber and Faber, 1986), p. 26.

7. *Psychoanalysis and Cinema*, ed. by E. Ann Kaplan, (New York: Routledge, 1990), pp. 119-120.

8. *A Zed and Two Noughts*, p 15.

9. Kaplan, p. 117.

10. Mary Ann Doane, *The Desire to Desire* (Bloomington: Indiana University Press, 1987) pp. 12-13.

11. *A Zed and Two Noughts*, p 46.

12. Peter Greenaway, "Street of Crocodiles," *Sight and Sound* 55 (June/July 1986): pp 182-183.

13. *Letters and Drawings of Bruno Schultz*, ed. by Jerzy Ficowski, (New York: Harper and Row, 1988) p 108.

14. Ibid., p 109. See also: Linda Williams, *Hard Core*, (Berkeley: University of California Press, 1989), p. 105.

    ...fetishization involves the construction of a substitute object to evade the complex reality of social or psychic relations. Fetishes are thus short-term, short-sighted solutions to more fundamental problems of power and pleasure in social relations.

15. The subtext of *Drowning* is an orgy of gamesplaying—most often dangerous games linking sex and death, like "Bees in the Trees," a version of musical chairs played to funeral music, "Hangman's Cricket" where Smut's body is inscribed with injuries, or "Deadman's Catch" in which the losers (all males) are wrapped in a shroud, in the order which they will succumb to violent deaths and "The Great Death Game" or the "Endgame" (Smut's suicide which he describes as "the best game of all because the winner is also the loser and the judge's decision is always final").

16. Marlene Rodgers, "Prospero's Books —Word and Spectacle" *Film Quarterly*, 45, (Spring 1992): p. 14.

17. *The Films of Jean-Luc Godard*, Ian Cameron, ed. (New York: Praeger, 1969), p. 54.

18. William Van Wert, "Review: The Cook, The Thief, His Wife and Her Lover," *Film Quarterly* 44, (Winter 1991): p. 44.

19. Ibid.

20. S. Malcomson, "Review of The Draughtsman's Contract," *Film Quarterly*, (Winter 1983-84): p.37.

21. Williams, p. 209.

POST–COMMUNIST SEX

Marika Pruska-Carroll

At every second newsstand, one can see a shapely female butt staring at passersby from the cover of the new men's magazine, "Andrei." Next to it, pamphlets like "Marxist Theory of Ownership" and "A Short History of the Communist Party of the Soviet Union" are becoming even redder from the outrage. They still have not been swept away by the winds of history or by the hands of careful sellers. They will go soon. Obviously, the Communist Revolution is behind. There is a new Revolution brewing ahead—a Sexual Revolution.

When, in 1988 in Moscow and soon afterward on screens around the globe, the film *Little Vera* appeared, there were insider rumors that it owed its release to the influence of the then Politburo Member, Alexander Yakovlev. During a special showing for the top Party brass, the believers in the communist norms that guide male-female relationships left the screening room after the leading actress, Natalia Negoda, assumed a top position over her partner—covering the details with her skirt. Only Yakovlev remained in his seat. When the show was over, he gave his permission for the film's distribution to movie houses, without any cuts.

After that break with the ranks, events started moving faster and faster. Soviet art began to shed its puritanical girdle; close encounters of the sexual kind began to be a natural ingredient in artistic creations.

After art, as it happens sometimes, life has followed. Sex, that had functioned earlier on the margins of a world led by Communists ideology, has become a public matter. The secret Russian soul is showing the world that it also has a body and that it has nothing against making it public for the right price.

Communist Classics in the Bedroom

Lenin, an experienced hand in conspiracy matters, could not be proven to have had extramarital sex with Inessa Armand despite many tales to the contrary. True, he addressed her by the intimate Russian form of "you" in some of the letters he wrote to her. But then, perhaps he just got excited by the topic he was discussing—The International Women's Movement.

Lenin's followers were less careful, or it may be that they were simply bolder in enjoying their life of privilege and unlimited power. Stalin was known to prefer simple sex with his close comrades' wives, lots of vodka and Georgian wine. With time, however, following the suicide of his wife (one version of this accident says that she shot herself after discovering that Stalin was with one of his mistresses), he is said to have spent more time in masculine company. After such manly gatherings, he suffered from bad hangovers for which mankind paid dearly.

The ultimate example of the dissipation of morals and the exploitation of power under Stalin was the case of Lavrenti Beria, the head of the NKVD, what was later to become the KGB. When he was arrested in 1953 after Stalin's death, the investigators informed his wife that 760 NKVD female employees admitted to having intimate relations with the boss. She did not believe it. "Lavrenti worked days and nights; he would not have time to spend with these women," she told the press shortly before she died in 1990.

Contrary to his wife's protestations, a remarkable sexual appetite and an enormous ruthlessness in fulfilling it were clearly Beria's characteristic features. This plain, fat man with the placid face of a kind uncle was in the habit of watching through binoculars the women in the audience of the

Bolshoi Theatre in Moscow. Young females that attracted his fancy were known to disappear without a trace.

Beria's other known practice was to follow young school girls in his black Zil limousine when going from his Lubyanka office, NKVD headquarters, to his mansion on Alexsei Tolstoy Street to have lunch. One move of his hand was sufficient: his ever-ready infamous Colonel Sarkisyan would pull a selected teen into Beria's Zil—never to be seen again.

This was Beria's personal side. As a head of the NKVD, Beria was so concerned about the Soviet purity of morals that he became notorious in his relentless persecution of prostitutes and homosexuals.

The intimate preferences of subsequent Soviet leaders and ideologists did not become the subject of conversation because they removed themselves far from the bedroom. The *idée fixe* of Nikita Khrushchev was of growing corn on the North Pole and battling the pornography that he was able to "see" in the paintings of abstractionists.

Leonid Brezhnev, besides medals, collected limos and sports cars. As long as he was able to, he got his kicks flooring the gas pedal. After his death, along with the buckets of medals, they found in his garages some forty cars, including a totalled Rolls Royce.

As for the wives of the Communist leaders, with the notable exception of Raisa Gorbachev, they were never seen by ordinary citizens except dressed in black at their husbands' televised funerals.

But for The Cause

When Bulat Okudzhava, the Russian bard and poet, sang for the first time about a woman as a woman and not as a Comsomol member or a heroic worker, he was accused of being petty and of the middle-class banal. The positive figures of Soviet art were giant kolkhoz workers, giving their best and the most to the motherland.

The Soviet superman gallery was also dominated by socio-political giants rather than biological ones. These were the busy middle-level party workers whose wives were there to warm up their dinners rather than their beds. Or, they were single engineers who needed only fifteen minutes to pack their lives and belongings to go to the ends of the Communist earth to build another hydro-power station. Somehow, nobody talked about the heroes of the nuclear power stations in places like Chernobyl.

"At all times, the Soviet superman thought only of work, work and work. Even during the war, there was work and work, and all ups and downs were related to work," wrote Russian author Vasili Shukshin in the 1960s. He was an honest writer, but was the reality as he saw it? Or, was it only a part of it?

It appears that already in the sixties, Soviet citizens wanted to live the way other people lived elsewhere in the world. They were trying to furnish their humble apartments with furniture from Finland, they were trying to become car owners, they were dreaming about country houses, they were going to work on contract to friendly countries (including some in Africa), and they went on vacations to Bulgaria while dreaming of France and Hawaii.

Gradually the West ceased to be associated with revisionism, racism, and homeless people living under bridges. Instead, it began to be thought of as lands with luxurious stores, populated by people that smelled good and who enjoyed freedom to speak, write, and live as they wished— including the freedom to participate in a sexual life that suited one's wishes and preferences. The lifting of the Iron Curtain led to the realization that all human instincts not controlled by the State were dangerous for a totalitarian system. And this was why a bare breast was attacked no less ardently than a political heresy under the Soviet regime.

You Can Do Anything, But Do It Cautiously

The crisis of faith in ruling Soviet ideology was getting deeper. At the beginning of a new era in 1917, it was declared that "a sexual selection ought to be made on the basis of class compatibility. In sexual contacts, elements such as flirtation, conquest, and other sexual games are not proper" (Zalkind, "Revolution and Youth"). Within this context, until recently it was sufficient to accuse one's partner of class incompatibility to receive a divorce in a matter of hours, without the agreement or even presence of the other side.

Yet, flirtation and other sexual games were not weeded out, and repeated attempts to forbid people everything that is human brought results contrary to those intended. Soviet intellectuals, finding themselves in the West, made their first stops at porno movies and striptease shows. For entire decades on all steps of the social ladder, the principle ruled: "You can do anything but do it cautiously."

Double moral standards and double thinking became the chief principles operating within a world structured by restrictions and rules. Breaking rules became unavoidable. It was perhaps within the sphere of one's sexual life where feverish attempts to lose oneself in someone's arms compensated for the lack of other pleasures or self-fulfilment.

To get a bigger, better apartment, a higher position, a trip abroad—these goals were mostly impossible to achieve by the average citizen. The simplest way of changing something in one's life was to change one's partner. Thus, there was a very high divorce rate in the Soviet Union.

Student dorms were guarded by mean old women, and Moscow University was guarded by Militia. One could not visit the rooms of the opposite sex. Walking the grounds surrounding the University was treacherous, however—one was in danger of tripping over the countless couples making love all over the place.

Conditions are Bare and Happy

The disintegration of the Soviet Empire caused the State to have more pressing concerns than censoring cinematic scenes of passion, confiscating pornographic magazines, or jailing homosexuals.

Whoever visits the Commonwealth of Independent States today, for the first few days, has difficulty believing his own eyes. In the book stores, on the streets, in the underground passes, on the newsstands, at train stations—there is suddenly plenty of colour and nudity. Imported calendars full of bare-breasted beauties compete for attention with the locally produced ones. The free market has already shown its claws in the printed world. To survive, even traditionally very respectable publications are trying new ways of selling themselves.

The weekly magazine "Ogonyok" prints, next to the confession of Alexander Murzin which describes how he wrote the books for which Brezhnev received the Lenin Prize, photos of the largest breasts imaginable. "Moskievski Komsomoletz," the biggest Moscow daily, specializes in sensational trash and contains as much nudity as it can or cannot justify.

Magazines that do not even pretend to do anything other than sell nudity (published for some reason mostly in Latvia but sold in Russia), have names such as "Intimate Club," "Maximum," "Red Hood," "Sex-Hit," "Erotic Gazette," or simply "The Butt." Their prices range from three to thirty rubles, and they differ in quality of print and colour. The magazine "Andrei," for thirty rubles aspires to become the Russian "Playboy." Its paper and photography are of a fairly high quality. The three-ruble "The Butt," is printed on such a poor quality paper that it is not quite clear what part of the body is being shown and whether it belongs to a male or female.

The written content of these magazines ranges from tasteless infantilism to honest attempts at concrete assessments of sex-related problems in Russia. Judging by the letters and questions from the readers, there are enormous problems with sex in Russia indeed! Russian sexology has taken only the very first steps. Therefore, readers are directed to translated books about sex. Poland has become the most treasured source of knowledge and information about "civilized" sex.

Among the most popular sex periodicals is one called "The Subject." It began to appear illegally a few years ago, circulated as illegal photocopies by readers, and distributed from person to person. Today, it is the official magazine of sexual minorities.

Homosexuals, or as they are called in Russia "the blues," used to meet in front of the Bolshoi Theatre in Moscow, only to be dispersed by police when they gathered there. They are today united through clubs, and the telephone numbers of their leaders—gay Roman Kalinin, President of the Sexual Minority League, and Zhenya Debryanska, the leader of lesbians—are publicized in numerous newspapers. Activists of the movements willingly give interviews, they fight for the recognition of their rights, they promote safe sex, and they distribute free condoms on the streets. This last activity, more than anything else, makes them very popular.

As a result, the meetings of the minority attract many and take place without unpleasant incidents. Last year, the League organised its first national gathering with invited foreign participants. Pictures of the same sex couples kissing passionately under the monument of Moscow's founder, Yuri Dolgoruki, appeared in many papers without creating any particular stir. It is astounding how many sensitive and dramatic issues ceased to be so virtually overnight.

I Am All Yours—For Hard Currency

Reading the classified ads, one cannot resist the impression that the main concern of young people (and not just the young), of both sexes, is the best possible sale of their bodily charms—preferably abroad and definitely for hard currency: "Sixteen year old real blonde wishes a German sponsor"; "A charming, curvy beauty under 30 looks for an American—for keeps"; "Young and intelligent with a big temperament will make any women—18 to 50, very happy, for a reasonable fee, preferably in dollars." The latter professes to specialize in "oral arts."

Such declarations have replaced proverbial statements of love from the era of Socialist Realism, when a young man spoke of his love for his girl and his tractor.

Among the ads about the sale of purebred dogs or family heirlooms, there is an ad of a photographer who is ready "to capture forever the most intimate moments of your love life." "The sperm-donor, healthy and educated" will visit your apartment at a convenient time. A young couple wishes "to enrich their experiences in contacts with other couples". A club for group sex is advertised in Rostov, and the Post Office Box number is given. A "blue" from Briansk has an idea for "the perming of pubic hair."

Besides individual activities, service agencies are mushrooming. They will arrange for foreign wives, husbands, and for roles in porno movies, or pictures in international catalogues of "models," and for lessons in erotic dances, with assurances of finding jobs in the West for students.

A bared breast and butt appears to be the cheapest ticket to a "better" world, and not only because the prices of tickets went up so high recently. Thus, courses in striptease are being organized, even in Siberian towns. The normal price for a six-week course is 1,500 rubles (an average monthly salary).

To enter the first sex shop in Moscow costs 5 rubles. All merchandise sells for hard currency. If one subscribes to the "Red Hood" magazine, however, one can buy one item for rubles.

When in 1986, at the beginning of Perestroika, a young Russian woman was asked by an American TV reporter, "How is sex in the Soviet Union?" she answered without a moment of hesitation, "There is no sex in the Soviet Union." Six years later, there is plenty of sex, but there is no Soviet Union.

Contributors

Arthur and Marilouise Kroker are editors of the CultureTexts Series and of the electronic review, the *Canadian Journal of Political and Social Theory* (ctheory@vax2.concordia.ca). Arthur is author of *Spasm* and *The Possessed Individual* and co-author of *The Postmodern Scene*. Together, Arthur and Marilouise edited two other volumes in feminist theory: *Body Invaders* and *The Hysterical Male*.

Kathy Acker is a leading American writer. Among others, her books include *Empire of the Senseless, Don Quixote* and *Blood and Guts in High School.* Her most recent book is entitled *My Mother: Demonology.*

Dianne Chisholm is Assistant Professor of English at the University of Alberta. She is author of *H.D. Freudian Poetics: Psychoanalysis in Transistion* (Cornell UP, 1992) and advisory editor of *Feminism and Psychoanalysis: A Critical Dictionary*, edited by Elizabeth Wright (Blackwell, 1992). When not practicing a wholly libidinal lesbianism, she is at work on three new books, including *Avant-Garde Sexualities: Eroticism in an Age of Barbarism.*

Rhonda Hallquist, Audrey Joy, Jamie Lantz, Kim Lowry, Cynthia Meier, and *Lori Scheer* are performing artists living in Tucson, Arizona, and are the originators of Bloodhut Productions, a feminist theatre company.

Shannon Bell is a pastiche feminist philosopher. She teaches classical political theory, feminist theory and workshops on female sexual pleasure for both women and men. Her book *Reading, Writing and Rewriting the Prostitute Body* is forthcoming with Indiana University Press, 1993.

Toni Denise (aka Lisa Alden) is an information specialist at the Leon County Library, Talahassee, Florida. She performs regularly at Club Park Avenue.

Shar Rednour is assistant editor of *On Our Back* magazine and lives by Annie Sprinkle's 'creed:' "Let there be pleasure on earth and let it begin with me." Den thanks to the boys and thank you to Randi.

Kate Bornstein is a Buddhist M-to-F transsexual performance artist and gender educator. Kate has been both male and female and now is not one nor the other, but both-and-neither, as indicated in the title of her play *The Opposite Sex ... is Neither.*

Frederick C. Corey, an assistant professor at Arizona State University, teaches performance studies in the Department of Communication and coordinates the HIV Studies Network in the College of Public Programs.

Dianne Rothleder is a doctoral candidate in political science at the University of Chicago. She is writing on the relationship between Richard Rorty's epistemology and his politics. Her non-dissertation research is currently concerned with theorizing the family. She is an instructor in philosophy at St. Mary's University in Notre Dame, Indiana.

Sue Golding is a senior research fellow at the Centre for Theoretical Studies, Essex University (U.K.). She is currently working on her next book, *The Cunning of Democracy*, which plays with (and against) the ethics of sexual pleasures, democratic rights, and the importance of the urban city-scape, in the context of a kind of space-time (as well as other multi-dimensional) quanta.

Gwen Bartleman is a twenty nine year old lesbian who works in theatre. She has been a drag-dyke since the age of five, when she first stole her brother's clothes. She spends her spare time gazing into a perfect, sculptural pair of Mona Lisa's eyes.

Linda Dawn Hammond, photographer and shapeshifter currently residing in Montréal, seeks accomplice in her quest to subvert the planet in her own image.

Ken Hollings is a London-based writer and editor whose work has appeared in many international journals and magazines. 'Electronically Yours...' is from a work in progress dealing with the Gulf War and its hysterical media fall-out.

Stephen Pfohl is author of the CultureTexts book, *Death at the Parasite Café*. A video-maker and performing artist, he is Professor of Sociology at Boston College.

Critical Art Ensemble (CAE) is a collective of six artists of different specializations committed to the production of a new genre art that explores the intersections among critical theory, art, and technology.

Carel Rowe is a filmmaker/videographer whose work includes *Grand Delusion*, *Panic USA* and *Baudrillard in the Mountains*. She is currently preparing a project on Suriname.

Marika Pruska-Carroll received her PhD in Russian and East European Studies at New York University. She taught at University of Illinois in Chicago and now teaches at Concordia University in Montreal. She is currently working on a book tentatively titled: *New & Old in Russia—Political Generation Gap*.

Louise McKissick is a Canadian visual artist presently studying at the Art Institute of Chicago.